NEW THEORIES IN GROWTH AND DEVELOPMENT

New Theories in Growth and Development

Edited by

Fabrizio Coricelli
Dipartimento di Economia Politica
Università di Siena

Massimo di Matteo
Dipartimento di Economia Politica
Università di Siena

and

Frank Hahn
Emeritus Professor of Economics
University of Cambridge
and
Dipartimento di Economia Politica
Università di Siena

First published in Great Britain 1998 by
MACMILLAN PRESS LTD
Houndmills, Basingstoke, Hampshire RG21 6XS and London
Companies and representatives throughout the world

A catalogue record for this book is available from the British Library.

ISBN 0–333–68229–7

First published in the United States of America 1998 by
ST. MARTIN'S PRESS, INC.,
Scholarly and Reference Division,
175 Fifth Avenue, New York, N.Y. 10010

ISBN 0–312–17621–X

Library of Congress Cataloging-in-Publication Data
New theories in growth and development / edited by Fabrizio Coricelli,
Massimo di Matteo and Frank Hahn.
p.   cm.
Includes bibliographical references and index.
ISBN 0–312–17621–X
1. Economic development.   I. Coricelli, Fabrizio.   II. Di Matteo,
Massimo.   III. Hahn, Frank.
HD75.N49 1997
338.9—DC21   97–8583
                                                      CIP

This book is printed on paper suitable for recycling and made from fully managed and
sustained forest sources.
10   9   8   7   6   5   4   3   2   1
07   06   05   04   03   02   01   00   99   98

Printed in Great Britain by
The Ipswich Book Company Ltd
Ipswich, Suffolk

Contents

PART III ECONOMIC POLICIES, THE ROLE OF THE
STATE, AND GROWTH

List of Contributors

Philippe Aghion   University College London and European Bank for Reconstruction and Development

Mario Amendola   University of Rome 'La Sopienza'

Pranab Bardhan   University of California, Berkeley

Guillermo A. Calvo   University of Maryland, College Park

Fabrizio Coricelli   University of Siena

William Easterly   The World Bank, Washington, DC

Jean Luc Gaffard   University of Nice Sophia-Antipolis

Frank Hahn   University of Cambridge and University of Siena

Peter Howitt   University of Western Ontario

Heinz D. Kurz   University of Graz

Massimo di Matteo   University of Siena

Neri Salvadori   University of Pisa

Andrés Solimano   The World Bank, Washington, DC

T. N. Srinivasan   Yale University

Moshe Syrquin   The World Bank, Washington, DC

Lance Taylor   New School for Social Research, New York

1 Introduction

Fabrizio Coricelli, Massimo di Matteo and
Frank Hahn

After a decade of almost complete neglect, the 1980s and 1990s witnessed a revival of attention for economic growth, with an abundant
production of literature on endogenous growth. It is fair to say that –
given the importance of the topic – it is harder to explain the causes
of the lack of attention to growth during the 1970s and beginning of
the 1980s, than the causes of the more recent boom. For instance, in
an often-quoted passage, Robert Lucas asked: 'Is there some action a
government of India could take that would lead the Indian economy to
grow like Indonesia's or Egypt's? If so, what exactly? If not, what is
about the "nature of India" that makes it so? The consequences for
human welfare involved in questions like these are simply staggering:
Once one starts to think about them, it is hard to think about anything
else' (Lucas, 1993).

Although the renewed interest on growth should be welcome, even
the recent literature on endogenous growth touched only tangentially
some of the key issues in development economics. The novelty of this
book – and of the workshop from which it originated (the International
Summer School of the Department of Economics, University of Siena,
and CNR, held at the Certosa di Pontignano, Siena in July 1994.) – is
in its attempt to stimulate intersections between the two strands of
economic literature, growth and development theories. As noted by
Moshe Syrquin (Chapter 6), the time is ripe for a fruitful communication between development and growth theories.

Such a communication is crucial as it is understood increasingly
that growth hinges upon institutional and policy aspects that are generally neglected in the stylised models of growth, but highly relevant
for development. However, one needs simple formalisations to walk
through the complexity of real economies. It has been noted that the
construction of an 'endogenous theory of economic history' is unlikely
to be a fruitful and attractive project (Frank Hahn, 1993)).

Mancur Olson has recently emphasised the role of institutions and
policies in explaining divergent growth paths (Mancur Olson, 1996).
He provided extensive evidence suggesting that what matters is how

resources are used rather than how large they are. Thus government policies and institution design become central to the explanation of divergent growth paths.

To development economists this hardly sounds new, as Hirschman stated as early as in 1958 that 'development depends not so much on finding optimal combination for given resources and factors of production as on calling forth and enlisting for development purposes resources and abilities that are hidden, scattered or badly utilized' (quoted by T.N. Srinivasan, in Chapter 5 of this volume).

Although it is still unclear how these aspects can all be incorporated into a simple analytical framework, progress can be made in developing models that incorporate some of them. As stated in several chapters of this book, effort should be directed towards strengthening the microeconomic foundations of growth and development theories. The recent experience of transition from planned to market economies has brought to the forefront of economics the role of property rights for the performance of economies and, more generally, the complex process that leads to the creation of markets. Liberalising prices and letting economic actors make their own decisions freely is not enough to create an efficient market economy. Indeed, dysfunctional arrangements emerged at the outset of market-orientated reforms, such as a barter economy, or the dominant role of the Mafia. Thus economists are faced with some fundamental questions.

Why do dysfunctional institutions arise and persist, affecting the long-run growth of a country? What roles do economic policies have in determining different growth paths? Very few economists would object to the statement that policies do have some effect on economic activity, at least in the short run. By cumulating small effects, say a fraction of a percentage point per year over a long horizon, one can have enormous effects on the income and wealth of a country.

Decades of failed stabilisations and cycles of hyperinflation are bound to have had significant effects on the dismal performance of many Latin-American countries. However, the recent experience of the Mexican crisis indicates that in a world of highly volatile financial markets, real economic activity can suffer even when domestic economic policy is apparently on track.

The book tries to put together different theories and empirical evidence that may offer important insights, especially if seen as complementary, in the analysis of growth and development issues. As was the intention of the organisers of the Siena International Summer School, the book contains a profitable debate between different schools of thought.

Indeed, the broad spectrum of views makes this book rather different from other recent books on growth and development.

The book is divided into three parts. The first part emphasises the theoretical debate. In Chapter 2, Philippe Aghion and Peter Howitt give an insightful up-to-date model of the Schumpeterian approach to endogenous growth. In contrast with the most elementary Schumpeterian models, they show that competition and growth are positively correlated in a modified Schumpeterian framework. The result is achieved by focusing on the innovation process and not only on the appropriability of the returns of innovations, as it was done in the elementary Schumpeterian models. The revised Schumpeterian approach, focusing on the role of innovation and R&D as the engine of growth, has several interesting implications, such as the non-linear relation between unemployment and growth, and the relationship between financial-sector development and growth.

While the chapter by Aghion and Howitt illustrates the important results that can be reached by using a Schumpeterian version of optimising equilibrium dynamic models, the other two chapters that make up Part I present a somewhat sceptical view of the capabilities of optimising equilibrium models to address the economics of growth.

In Chapter 3, Mario Amendola and Jean Luc Gaffard provide an 'Austrian' model that attempts to go beyond endogenous growth. They develop a sequential out-of-equilibrium model that generates different growth trajectories. They offer an analytical framework that can accommodate specific working rules, different original shocks to the system, and as a result produce different dynamic paths, through numerical simulations. The main thrust of the contribution, defined by the authors as 'illustrative', is to think about growth as a dynamic process out-of-equilibrium that takes place in chronological time. The authors claim that this approach can account for empirical facts on growth.

Heinz D. Kurz and Neri Salvadori, in Chapter 4, offer a review of the main models of the new endogenous growth theories. They find that most results of the new theories were anticipated in earlier work on growth. Thus they speak of the new theories as 'old wine in new goatskins'. Moreover, although they acknowledge some of the merits of the new theories, Kurz and Salvadori argue that the new theories 'preserved several of the disquieting features of the neoclassical growth theory of the 1950s and 1960s', such as the homogeneity of goods, capital goods, and homogeneity of behaviour. They feel that the 'classical' approach offers a fruitful alternative to old and new growth theories.

Part II contains contributions dealing with the connection, or lack of it, between growth theories and development issues. In Chapter 5, Pranab Bardhan discusses the possible contributions of the 'new' growth theory to the understanding of development issues. First, he notes that, contrary to what is often stated in the 'new' growth theory, in the 'old' growth theory there were several attempts to make technological change endogenous. He then argues that the so-called convergence literature that occupies a large space in the 'new' growth theory has little to offer to a development economist. More promising seems to be the contribution of the 'new' growth theory in formalising endogenous technical progress within a tractable imperfect-competition framework. Moreover, the 'new' theory made important progress in the area of dynamic economies of scale associated with learning by doing. Other important areas explored in the 'new' growth theory are co-ordination failures in models with multiple equilibria, and the endogenous determination of agglomeration economies in models applicable to economic geography. Despite these contributions, Bardhan concludes that 'notwithstanding popular impressions to the contrary, the advances made so far in the new literature on growth theory . . . have barely scratched the surface, and let us hope that the new interest in necessary model-building in this area does not divert us from the tough organizational, institutional and historical issues of underdevelopment which are less amenable to neat formalization'.

T. N. Srinivasan, in Chapter 6, gives a thorough review of the new growth theory within the perspective of development theory. He shows that in contrast to the old growth theory, the new approach embodies several processes that were central to the early development economists: accumulation of physical and human capital; technical change, foreign trade, and investment.

Interestingly, a key aspect of the endogenous growth theory, namely the fact that per capita output can grow indefinitely, can in fact be derived in the Solow model if one simply assumes that the marginal product of capital is bounded away from zero as the capital–labour ratio grows indefinitely. Similarly to Bardhan, Srinivasan is very sceptical about the value of the empirical literature on convergence based on cross-country regressions, and concludes that the endogenous growth literature provides an important justification for government policy. However, the theory is still very stylised, and the empirical analysis inconclusive.

Moshe Syrquin, in Chapter 7, complements the analyses of Bardhan and Srinivasan, by focusing on the role of structural change in the growth process. After a thorough review of both theories and empirical evidence, Syrquin concludes that endogenous growth theory and its empirical implementation could become highly relevant for development economics. However, this potential remains largely unexploited, as the bulk of the work on endogenous growth has not tackled some of the key empirically-established stylised facts of the process of development.

In the final chapter in Part II, Lance Taylor reconstructs a map of growth theories, their building blocks and the connections between different theories. He observes that the 'new' growth theory builds upon a very limited set of issues tackled in the literature. Similarly, the mainstream approach to policy intervention (the 'market friendly' strategies) has a very limited perspective. His chapter critically reviews these mainstream discourses, and tries to show ways to widen their narrow focus. Taylor argues that the fundamental aspects of development are largely neglected in the new growth theories. Central to development are political economy issues and the role of state intervention. The 'classical' approach devotes more attention to these aspects than does the neoclassical approach underlying new growth theories.

Part III discusses the relationship between economic policies and growth, focusing on empirical evidence, the possibility of co-ordination failures and the effects of different development strategies in Latin America. In Chapter 9, William Easterly evaluates the relative importance of initial conditions, random shocks and policy changes in affecting long-run growth. He first discusses the importance of these different factors in the old and new theories of growth. New growth theories emphasise the role of random shocks, as the presence of thresholds and multiple equilibria implies that a random shock can shift the economy from a low to a high growth path, or vice versa. Empirical evidence seems to support the importance of random shocks for long-run growth. For example, this is illustrated by the fact that growth rates are highly unstable. However, the empirical analysis carried out by Easterly shows that policy matters as well as favourable exogenous shocks ('luck'). Among policies that seems to play a key role, he finds financial sector reform, investment in infrastructure, low budget deficits and low inflation.

Guillermo A. Calvo, in Chapter 10, discusses recent experiences of major reform attempts, both in former centrally-planned economies and in Latin America. He presents a simple model which illustrates the possibility that the economy gets trapped in low-output equilibria as a result of the transformation process itself, and not because of policy mistakes. The model considers countries starting from a high stock of foreign debt (Latin America), or countries that suffer large fiscal deficits because of the transformation process (former centrally-planned economies). The model displays multiple equilibria associated with different levels of initial debt. Under perfect capital mobility, the economy can get stuck in low-output equilibria. Economic actors may expect high rates of distortionary taxation in the future and thus move capital abroad. Their expectations will be validated because capital flight will imply high rates of taxation and low growth. In this context, controls on capital mobility may have a positive effect on growth and welfare. However, the same model can yield cases in which welfare declines with capital controls. The recent experience of Mexico points out to the relevance of the topic discussed by Calvo, and of the key role that 'international' economic policy (co-ordinated policies and the activity of international institutions) can exert on growth.

In Chapter 11, Andrés Solimano concludes the book with the analysis of alternative development strategies followed in Latin America from the 1940s to the 1990s. He compares the experience of the 1940s and 1950s, characterised by state dirigisme and import substitution, with the recent phase of market liberalisation. Solimano concludes that the high rates of growth displayed during the 1940s and 1950s were achieved at the cost of large inefficiencies that contributed to the low growth rates experienced since the 1960s. The recent phase of market liberalisation in some way reversed the process. It raised the efficiency of the system, paving the way for sustained growth in the future. However, such strategy involved high transition costs. A key issue is to determine whether these costs were inevitable for increasing the future growth potential.

To sum up, the contributions in the book point out the importance of searching for a middle ground between extremely stylised models à la Solow, and excessively descriptive analysis of various experiences. Overall, it emerged that the main empirical issues raised in the development literature should serve as the starting point for analytical models. Moreover, the role of policies and institutional design should become more relevant than simple and *ad hoc* assumptions about technology and technological externalities.

References

Hahn, Frank (1993) 'On Growth Theory', mimeo., University of Siena.
Lucas, Robert (1993) 'Making a Miracle', *Econometrica*.
Olson, Mancur (1996) 'Big Bills Left on the Sidewalk: Why Are Some Nations Rich, and Others Poor?', *Journal of Economic Perspectives* (Spring).

Part I

Theories

2 A Schumpeterian Perspective on Growth and Competition

Philippe Aghion and Peter Howitt

The revival of growth theory in the 1980s was originally stimulated by 'technical progress within economics' – by the development of new tools for handling old ideas. The neoclassical models of the 1960s had already shown that growth in per capita income was sustainable only through the continual growth of technological knowledge. Also, it had long been understood that technological knowledge, like capital, grows only because people find it profitable to make it grow; research, development, study, experimentation and learning by doing all employ resources with alternative uses. The neoclassical model of Solow and Swan ignored these activities and treated technological growth as exogenous, not on grounds of realism but because there were no available techniques for incorporating them into standard economic analysis.

The main difficulty arose from increasing returns. Developing a technology requires a lumpy setup cost, which does not have to be incurred again as the technology is implemented. Dealing with this in a dynamic general equilibrium framework required the gradual accumulation of knowledge in various subdisciplines of economics, especially international trade theory and industrial organisation theory. Macroeconomists have taken these techniques and adapted them to the study of economic growth. As a result, we now have an array of relatively simple models with which to study the economic determinants of economic growth.

Some of the more aggregative models in the endogenous growth literature deal with knowledge-generating activities in an abstract way and treat knowledge as little more than another capital good. By contrast, the Schumpeterian models[1] that focus on R&D as the engine of growth treat technological change more directly and explicitly by positing particular forms in which new knowledge is created and used; they show how innovations impinge on individual markets, and work out the consequences of the gains and losses generated by Schumpeter's process of creative destruction.

9

Schumpeterian models allow one to study detailed structural aspects of the growth process, making use of the particularities of technological change. One can see in some detail how regulation, taxation, intellectual property regimes, and various non-economic factors affect the incentive to perform the innovative activities driving growth. One can also examine the role of strategic interactions between innovative firms in the growth process, and see how the intensity of competition affects the rate of growth. Organisational aspects of R&D can be introduced, and interaction between different sorts of innovation and different sources of technological knowledge can be studied.

These models have now taken endogenous growth theory beyond the point of pure technique, and are shedding new light on several structural aspects of the growth process. For example, the interaction between fundamental and secondary research (research versus development, basic versus applied research and so on) and the implications of this interaction for growth are being explored by various authors, often with surprising results. Jovanovic and Nyarko (1994) show that if people have developed an existing fundamental technology beyond a certain point they may rationally choose not to adopt newer technologies, and hence the economy will not grow, even though under other initial conditions positive growth would be sustained in the long run. Aghion and Howitt (1996) find that this distinction alters the usual Schumpeterian tradeoff between competition and growth, as illustrated below.

A second structural aspect being explored in the literature is the two-way relationship between business cycles and economic growth. Stadler (1990) shows how recessions can have permanent hysteretic effects on the long-run growth path because they retard R&D and learning by doing. Stiglitz (1993) points out another effect in the same direction that arises because cyclical downturns threaten the survival of the small new firms that tend to introduce radically new technologies, but that are rationed relatively tightly in credit markets during recessions. On the other hand, Galí and Hammour (1991) show how recessions can stimulate growth by their 'cleansing effect'; that is, during downturns the opportunity cost of switching technologies is reduced, as is the ability of weak, non-adaptive firms to survive. As for effects of growth on cycles, many Schumpeterian models have the property that innovations underlying long-run growth tend to come in cycles, because of technology spillovers or network externalities of various sorts (Shleifer, 1986) or because there are multiple dynamic equilibria (Aghion and Howitt, 1992).

A related structural aspect of growth is introduced by considering what Bresnahan and Trachtenberg (1995) call 'General Purpose Technologies', such as steam power, electric motors or computers, which affect the whole economy. The analyses of Atkeson and Kehoe (1993), and Helpman and Trachtenberg (1994), show that the introduction of radical technological change will typically proceed not smoothly but through an irregular wave of innovations. Unlike the productivity shocks of real business-cycle analysis, however, the initial effect of such a wave will not be to raise the levels of output and employment but to reduce them, as people take time to learn the new technology, and as they must devote resources to developing secondary innovations and components in order to make use of the new technology.

The interrelationship between growth and unemployment is another structural phenomenon on which Schumpeterian models are beginning to shed light. As Aghion and Howitt (1994) show, a faster-growing economy is not necessarily one with a lower long-run rate of unemployment, because each individual innovation hits a particular subset of the economy and will tend to require a reallocation of resources between sunrise and sunset sectors, between firms with new and old technological capacities, and between occupations that are favoured and not favoured by the innovation. Opposing these forces of creative destruction is a capitalisation effect whereby faster growth tends to encourage the creation of job vacancies to take advantage of more rapidly-growing markets. Aghion and Howitt show that creative destruction tends to dominate at low rates of growth, and capitalisation at high rates, so that unemployment is maximised at intermediate rates of growth.

As the reader will have seen by now, Schumpeterian theory bears on too many structural aspects of growth for us to explain them all in detail in a single chapter. Instead, we have chosen to focus in what follows on what we consider one of the most interesting, namely the relationship between growth and competition. The first Schumpeterian models implied a tradeoff between growth and competition. In a more competitive economy, where innovators could not anticipate as high a level of monopoly profits from their innovations, or for as long a time, innovation would be discouraged and hence growth would be reduced. However, this inverse relationship between growth and competition has not found much empirical support, either from historians or from econometricians (Nickell, 1994; Blundell *et al.*, 1995), who find, on the contrary, a positive affect of competition on growth.

These findings might seem to contradict the basic Schumpeterian approach. What we argue in the following, however, is that, to the contrary, once one begins to add some obviously needed structural detail to the stark preliminary models of Schumpeterian growth theory, one finds a large variety of possible explanations for the apparently positive effect of competition on growth. Thus in what follows we shall first develop a basic general Schumpeterian model, based on Aghion and Howitt (1992), and then show how relaxing the strict assumptions of the model in different directions can produce four separate Schumpeterian explanations for why a more competitive market structure might be conducive to a higher rate of growth.

I   THE SCHUMPETERIAN APPROACH: BASIC FRAMEWORK

1.1   A Basic Setup

The earliest example of the Schumpeterian approach to endogenous growth was that of Segerstrom *et al.* (1990), who modelled sustained growth as arising from a succession of product improvements in a fixed number of sectors, but with no uncertainty in the innovation process. Aghion and Howitt (1992) constructed an endogenous growth model with both product improvements and uncertainty, which we shall now proceed to sketch.

The basic model abstracts from capital accumulation completely.[2] The economy is populated by a continuous mass L of individuals with linear intertemporal preferences: $u(y) = \int_0^\infty y_\tau e^{-r\tau} \cdot d\tau$. Each individual is endowed with one unit flow of labour, so L is also equal to the aggregate flow of labour supply. Output of the consumption good depends upon the input of an intermediate good, x, according to:

$$y = AF(x), \qquad (2.1)$$

where the production function F is increasing and concave. Innovations consist of the invention of a new variety of intermediate good that replaces the old one, and whose use raises the technology parameter, A, by the constant factor, $\gamma > 1$.

Society's fixed stock of labour has two competing uses. It can produce intermediate goods, one for one, and it can be used in research. When the amount n is used in research, innovations arrive randomly with a Poisson arrival rate $\lambda \cdot \varphi(n)$, where $\lambda > 0$ is a parameter indicating the productivity of the research technology, and $\varphi' > 0$, $\varphi'' \leq 0$. The firm that succeeds in innovating can monopolise the intermediate sector until replaced by the next innovator.

As in most endogenous growth models, there are positive spillovers from the activities that generate growth in A, in two senses. The monopoly rents that the innovator can capture are generally less than the consumer surplus created by the intermediate good and, more importantly, the invention makes it possible for other researchers to begin working on the next innovation. However, there is a negative spillover in the form of a 'business-stealing effect', whereby the successful innovator destroys the surplus attributable to the previous generation of intermediate good by making it obsolete.

The research sector is portrayed as in the patent race literature that has been surveyed by Tirole (1988) and Reinganum (1989). The amount of labour devoted to research is determined by the arbitrage condition:

$$w_t = \lambda \cdot \varphi'(n_t) \cdot V_{t+1}, \tag{2.2}$$

where t is not time but the number of innovations that have occurred; w_t the wage; and V_{t+1} the discounted expected payoff to the $(t + 1)^{th}$ innovator. The latter is just:[3]

$$V_{t+1} = \pi_{t+1}/(r + \lambda \cdot \varphi(n_{t+1})), \tag{2.3}$$

where n_{t+1} is the amount of labour devoted to R&D after the $(t + 1)^{th}$ innovation has occurred; and $\pi_{t+1} = A_{t+1} \cdot \tilde{\pi}\left(\dfrac{w_{t+1}}{A_{t+1}}\right)$, $\tilde{\pi}' < 0$, is the flow of profit attainable by the $(t + 1)$ intermediate good monopolist.[4]

The denominator of Equation (2.3), which can be interpreted as the obsolescence-adjusted interest rate, shows the effects of creative destruction. The more research people expect following the next innovation, the shorter the likely duration of the monopoly profits that will be enjoyed by the creator of the next innovation, and hence the smaller the payoff.

Letting $w_t = \dfrac{w_t}{A_t}$ denote the growth-adjusted wage rate after the tth innovation, dividing both sides of Equation (2.2) by A_t, and using Equation (2.3), we obtain the following *arbitrage equation* which reflects the fact that labour can be allocated freely between *manufacturing* and *research*:

(A)

$$w_t = \lambda\varphi'(n_t) \cdot \frac{\gamma\tilde{\pi}(w_{t+1})}{r + \lambda\varphi(n_{t+1})}.$$

The model is then fully characterised by (A) and by a *labour market clearing equation* which reflects the frictionless nature of the labour market, and determines the growth-adjusted wage rate w_t as a function of the residual supply of manufacturing labour $L - n_t$:

(L)

$$L = n_t + \tilde{x}(w_t),$$

where the demand for manufacturing labour $\tilde{x}$ is a decreasing function of the growth-adjusted wage rate w_t.[5]

In steady state the above two equations become:

($\hat{A}$)

$$w = \lambda\varphi'(n) \cdot \frac{\gamma\tilde{\pi}(w)}{r + \lambda\varphi(n)}$$

($\hat{L}$)

$$n + \tilde{x}(w) = L.$$

Positive results   Since the two curves corresponding to ($\hat{A}$) and ($\hat{L}$) in the (n,w) space are respectively downward- and upward-sloping, the steady-state equilibrium $(\hat{n}, \hat{w})$ is unique. Using Figure 2.1 it is easy to see that equilibrium level of research $\hat{n}$ – and therefore the average growth rate $\hat{g} = \lambda\varphi(\hat{n})\ln\gamma$[6] – will be raised by: a lower interest rate r; a larger labour market L; a higher productivity of R&D λ; or a larger size of innovation γ.

In order to analyse the effects of competition on growth, consider the Cobb–Douglas case, where $F(x) = x^\alpha (0 < \alpha < 1)$. Here the parameter α is a measure of the degree of competition, since the derived demand curve faced by an intermediate monopolist (that is, the marginal product schedule) has an elasticity equal to $1/(1 - \alpha)$, which is increasing in α. Accordingly, profits will constitute the fraction $(1 - \alpha)$ of value-added in the intermediate sector, the rest consisting of labour income:

$$\pi = \frac{1 - \alpha}{\alpha} wx \equiv \frac{1 - \alpha}{\alpha} w(L - n).$$

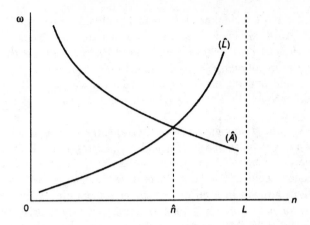

Figure 2.1   The equilibrium level of research $\hat{n}$ is determined by the intersection of a downward-sloping research–arbitrage equation with an upward-sloping labour–market–equilibrium curve

Substituting this expression into $(\hat{A})$ yields the modified research–arbitrage equation:

$(\hat{A}^c)$

$$1 = \lambda\varphi'(\hat{n}) \; \frac{\gamma \cdot \dfrac{1-\alpha}{\alpha} \cdot (L - \hat{n})}{r + \lambda\varphi(\hat{n})},$$

which defines $\hat{n}$ as a decreasing function of α. In other words, product market competition is unambiguously bad for growth: it reduces the size of monopoly rents that can be appropriated by successful innovators, and therefore diminishes the incentive to innovate. This unambiguous – but also somewhat simplistic – prediction of the basic Schumpeterian model will be discussed in Section II.

Growth in the economy is *stochastic*, reflecting the uncertainty of the innovation process. In particular in the steady state, where $n_t \equiv \hat{n}$ and $w_t = w$, the log of output follows a random walk with drift, in accordance with recent empirical studies emphasising the random nature of the economic trend (for example, Campbell and Mankiw, 1987). The Schumpeterian paradigm thus departs from a long-standing tradition of looking at productivity growth and business fluctuations *separately*. It implies, rather, that both growth and fluctuations arise from the same source, namely R&D activity.

That the basic Schumpeterian model outlined above can generate cyclical growth becomes even more transparent once we notice that above system (A)–(L) yields a *continuum* of Perfect Foresight Equilibria including *non-stationary periodic* trajectories in n.[7] In these periodic solutions, the amount of labour devoted to research oscillates regularly between a high and a low level, thereby generating a *cyclical* growth pattern.

However, the following considerations qualify the above conclusion. As shown in Grossman and Helpman (1991), aggregate growth in steady-state ceases to be random if innovations apply to a continuum of uncorrelated sectors. Of course, aggregate fluctuations will persist if productivity growth in a positive mass of sectors hinges on the *same fundamental innovation*. But then an important aspect of innovation-driven cycles is the *diffusion* process of fundamental innovations throughout the economy. The above framework is too simple in this respect: it assumes *instantaneous* diffusion of new discoveries to all firms and sectors.

Normative results   A general presumption that emerges from non-Schumpeterian endogenous growth models is that a *laissez-faire* equilibrium will tend to allocate too few resources to growth-enhancing activities because of the prevalence of positive externalities between researchers or firms that accumulate knowledge. However, this presumption overlooks the *negative* externality that current innovators exert upon previous innovators whose technologies they render obsolete. In particular, the creative destruction (or *business-stealing*) effect pointed out above implies that in some cases a free market economy will devote *too many* resources to growth-enhancing research, because private research firms make no deduction for the loss of surplus to the incumbent when calculating the expected benefits of research, whereas someone trying to maximise social welfare would make such a deduction by considering only the incremental gain from a prospective innovation.

The overall comparison between the *laissez-faire* growth rate $\hat{g} = \lambda\varphi(\hat{n})\ln\gamma$ and the optimal growth rate $g^* = \lambda\varphi(n^*)\ln\gamma$[8] is ambiguous. Growth under *laissez-faire* will be excessive when the size of innovation γ is close to 1 and the degree of monopoly power is large (α close to 0); and it will be insufficient when the size of innovations is large and/or monopoly rents are small (α close to 1) so that the private benefits from innovating (right-hand side of Equation (2.3) are far below the social benefits.

1.2 Multisectors

Consider the following multisector extension – inspired by Caballero and Jaffé (1993) – of the basic model outlined above. Final output is now produced by a continuum of intermediate goods indexed on the unit interval, according to the production function:

$$y = \int_0^1 A_i \cdot F(x_i)di, \qquad (2.4)$$

where x_i is the flow output of intermediate good i; F is again a production function with positive and diminishing marginal product; and A_i a productivity parameter attached to the latest version of intermediate good i. Each intermediate input is still produced from manufacturing labour, according to a one-for-one technology.

Let $A = \max_i A_i$ denote the leading-edge productivity parameter. Growth in the lending-edge occurs from innovations, at rate:

$$A/A = \lambda\varphi(n), \ln \gamma, \qquad (2.5)$$

where n is the aggregate flow of research labour.[9]

We shall again restrict attention to steady-state equilibria in which final output, consumption, the wage rate and the leading-edge all grow at the same constant rate g, and the distribution of relative productivities $a_i = \dfrac{A_i}{A}$ is constant over time. It follows from Equations (2.4) and (2.5) that the growth rate g must equal $\lambda\varphi(n)\ln \gamma$.

Let w denote the (stationary) growth-adjusted wage rate, w_t/A_t. Since individuals are free to choose whether to be employed in manufacturing or in research then, as before, the following arbitrage condition must hold in equilibrium:

$$w = \lambda\varphi'(n) \cdot V, \qquad (2.6)$$

where V is the (growth-adjusted) net present value of a new patent $\left(V = \dfrac{V_i}{A_i}\right)$.

The value V_t of discovering technology A_t is again equal to the expected present value of the rents that will accrue until the intermediate producer is replaced. The time until replacement is distributed exponentially with parameter $\lambda\varphi(n)$. Therefore:

$$V_t = \int_t^\infty e^{-(r+\lambda\varphi(n))(s-t)} \cdot \pi_{s,t} ds, \tag{2.7}$$

where $\pi_{s,t}$ is the flow of monopoly rents earned by a producer with technology A_t at date $s > t$ if the producer has not yet been replaced at that date; that is:

$$\pi_{s,t} = \max \{A_t \cdot F'(x)x - w_s \cdot x\}$$
$$= A_t \cdot \tilde{\pi}(w \cdot e^{g(s-t)}) \text{ where } \tilde{\pi}' < 0. \tag{2.8}$$

Substituting for $\pi_{s,t}$ in Equation (2.7), and for $V = \dfrac{V_t}{A_t}$ in Equation (2.6), we obtain the following arbitrage equation:

(A'):

$$w = \lambda \cdot \varphi'(n) \int_0^\infty e^{-(r+\lambda\varphi(n))s} \cdot \tilde{\pi}(we^{gs})ds.$$

To complete the specification of this multisector model, we have to derive the new labour market clearing condition. Let:

$$\tilde{x}\left(\frac{w_s}{A_t}\right) = \tilde{x}\left(\frac{w}{a_{t,s}}\right)$$

denote the solution to the above maximisation programme in Equation (2.8), where $a_{t,s} = \dfrac{A_t}{As}$. The labour market clearing condition becomes:

(L')

$$n + \int_0^1 \tilde{x}(w/a) \cdot h(a) \cdot da = L,$$

where (see Appendix 1 to this chapter) the unique invariant density function $h(a)$ is given by:

(D)

$$h(a) = a^{\frac{1}{\ln \gamma} - 1} / \ln \gamma.$$

As before, the (A') curve is downward-sloping in (n, w), whereas the (L') curve is upward-sloping. So again there exists a unique steady-state equilibrium to which we can apply the same comparative statics experiments as in the previous section, with some new effects. Consider first an increase in the R&D productivity parameter λ. Since λ does not enter the labour equation (L'), we can treat the adjusted wage rate w as a constant and focus on the arbitrage equation (A'). As in the basic model, increasing λ will increase the arrival rate $\lambda\varphi'(n)$, which is good for research and growth, and will also increase the rate of creative destruction $\lambda\varphi(n)$, which is bad for growth. But a higher λ will also increase the rate at which a producer's profits will fall over time as a result of competing for manufacturing labour with the leading edge. This additional obsolescence effect that reinforces the above creative destruction effect is captured by the term $\tilde{\pi}(we^{gs}) = \tilde{\pi}(we^{\lambda\varphi(n)\ln\gamma s})$ in the right-hand side of (A').

In the Cobb-Douglas case, where $F(x) = x^{\alpha}$, $0 < \alpha < 1$, as before we have:

$$\tilde{\pi}(w/a) = \frac{1-\alpha}{\alpha} \cdot (w/a) \cdot \tilde{x}(w/a) = \frac{1-\alpha}{\alpha} \cdot w \cdot \tilde{x}(w) \cdot a^{\frac{\alpha}{1-\alpha}},$$

so that $(\hat{A}^c)$ becomes:

$$1 = \lambda\varphi'(n) \; \frac{\dfrac{1-\alpha}{\alpha} \cdot x(w)}{r + \underbrace{\lambda\varphi(n)}_{\text{creative destruction}} + \underbrace{\lambda\varphi(n) \dfrac{\alpha}{1-\alpha} \ln\gamma}_{\text{new obsolescence effect}}}. \tag{2.9}$$

Equation (2.9) shows that, in spite of the obsolescence effect, reinforcing the creative destruction effect the overall effect of an increase in λ on research, and growth in steady-state remains positive in the Cobb–Douglas case.

Next, consider the effect of an increased innovation size γ. Recall first that the right-hand side of the research arbitrage equations ($\hat{A}$ or $\hat{A}^c$) in the one-sector model includes a factor γ, indicating a 'productivity effect'. That is, because an innovation would raise all incomes by γ, the expected productivity of research is correspondingly higher relative to the productivity of the alternative activity, manufacturing. It turns out that the multisector model also has a productivity effect, but of a more subtle nature. Specifically, a single innovation will no longer have a measurable effect on income levels at the leading edge; but an increase in γ will nevertheless increase the expected productivity of research, which always takes place on the leading edge, relative to the average productivity of manufacturing across all sectors. That is, an increase γ will tilt the steady-state distribution $h(a)$ of relative productivities towards less efficient manufacturing firms.

To see this modified productivity effect more clearly, notice that, from (L') and (D) above:

$$\tilde{x}(w) = \left[1 + \frac{\ln \gamma}{1 - \alpha}\right] \cdot [L - n].$$

That is, the demand for labour in leading-edge firms will exceed the average demand in manufacturing by the factor $\left[1 + \frac{\ln \gamma}{1 - \alpha}\right]$. Substituting this demand into Equation (2.9) yields the reduced form research-arbitrage equation:

$(\hat{A}^{cm})$

$$1 = \lambda\varphi'(n) \frac{\dfrac{1-\alpha}{\alpha} \overbrace{\left[1 + \dfrac{\ln \gamma}{1 - \alpha}\right]}^{\text{modified productivity effect}} \cdot [L - n]}{r + \lambda\varphi(n) + \dfrac{\alpha}{1-\alpha} \lambda\varphi(n)\ln \gamma},$$

which differs from the one-sector version $(\hat{A}^c)$ not only because of the 'new obsolescence effect' but also because of the 'modified productivity effect'.

Thus, in the multisectoral model, an increase in the size of innovations will still have a positive productivity effect on research and growth, but this will now be mitigated by a negative obsolescence effect similar to that discussed above in connection with a change in λ. It is straightforward, however, to show that the overall effect will still be positive; larger innovations still produce more research and hence generate faster growth.

These two new effects also modify somewhat our analysis of the effects of competition on growth, but without changing the end result. That is, as can be seen directly in $(\hat{A}^m)$, an increase in the 'competitiveness' parameter α will continue to have same negative 'appropriability effect on research as before, working through the term $\dfrac{1 - \alpha}{\alpha}$ in the numerator of $(\hat{A}^m)$. This will now be reinforced by the new obsolescence effect. That is, more competition means that growth in the leading edge will have a more detrimental effect on existing rents. But these two negative effects will now be mitigated by a positive productivity effect. That is, a firm that innovates to put itself on the leading edge will be better able to exploit its productivity gain when it can compete more freely. It is easily seen, however, that the appropriability effect always dominates the productivity effect, so that more competition will still have an unambiguously negative effect on research and on growth.

1.3 Introducing Physical Capital

The endogenous growth models described above assume that technological innovations are not embodied in any *durable* good (that is, physical capital or machinery) that would typically depreciate as the corresponding technology becomes obsolete. On the other hand, recent empirical studies (for example, DeLong and Summers, 1991) have pointed towards a positive relationship between physical capital accumulation and growth. Without entering the debate as to whether investments in machinery should be seen as fundamental or subsidiary[10] to the growth process, we shall simply look for the most straightforward implications of introducing capital goods into the Schumpeterian framework.

Going back to the multisector model of Section 1.2, let us now assume that each intermediate good i is produced according to the production function:

$$x_i = G(K_i^p/A_i, N_i), \tag{2.10}$$

where K_i^p and N_i are the inputs of capital and labour into production in sector i, and G is a regular constant-returns production function.[11] We divide K_i^p by A_i in Equation (2.10) to indicate that successive vintages of the intermediate good are produced by increasingly capital-intensive techniques.

When an intermediate monopolist is replaced, we assume that his or her capital has no secondhand value (in the language of traditional growth theory we assume putty-clay capital). Hence his cost of capital is:

$$\bar{r} = r + \delta_k + \lambda\varphi(n), \tag{11}$$

where δ_k is the proportional rate of capital depreciation, and the last term is the expected rate of (endogenous) obsolescence[12] resulting from being replaced by a new entrant.

Given Equations (2.10) and (2.11) and the fact that the intermediate firm's production function exhibits constant returns to scale, the unit cost $c_{s,t}$ can be written as:

$$c_{s,t} = A_t \, \gamma(\bar{r}, \, we^{g(s-t)}); \; \gamma_1 > 0, \, \gamma_2 > 0,$$

so that the firms' profit flow and manufacturing employment can be expressed respectively as:

$$\pi_{s,t} = A_t \hat{\pi}(\bar{r}, \, we^{g(s-t)}); \; \hat{\pi}_1 < 0, \, \hat{\pi}_2 < 0$$

and

$$N_i = \tilde{x}\left(\bar{r}, \frac{w}{a_i}\right); \; \tilde{x}_1 < 0; \; \tilde{x}_2 < 0.$$

The *arbitrage* and *labour market clearing* equations (A') and (L') thus become:

$$(A') \quad w = \lambda\varphi'(n) \int_0^\infty e^{-(r+\lambda\varphi(n))s} \cdot \hat{\pi}(r + \delta_k + \lambda\varphi(n), \, we^{gs})ds$$

and

$$(L') \quad L = n + \int_0^1 \tilde{x}(r + \delta_k + \lambda\varphi(n), \tfrac{w}{a})h(a)da.$$

Consider now an increase in the R&D productivity parameter λ: in addition to the various effects pointed out in Section 1.1, *this will increase the cost of capital $\bar{r}$* with two opposite effects on research and growth. On the one hand, given w, it will reduce the rents from innovating ($\hat{\pi}_1 < 0$) and thus discourage research and growth.[13] On the other hand, the increased capital cost will also reduce the demand for manufacturing labour ($\tilde{x}_i < 0$), thereby reducing the adjusted wage w. This latter wage effect, in turn, will tend to mitigate the former *capital obsolescence* effect.[14] As shown by Cannon (1995), the *capital obsolescence effect* may sometimes be so strong that growth will actually *slow down* as a result of increasing of R&D productivity.

II MARKET STRUCTURE

2.1 Introduction

Is market competition good or bad for growth? The Schumpeterian answer to this question, as described in Section 1.1 above, appeared to be one-sided: to the extent that monopoly rents are the inducement to innovation, and are therefore the mainspring of growth, product market competition can only be detrimental to growth. By the same token, more intense imitation activities will discourage innovations and growth. Hence the importance of preserving Intellectual Property Rights through an adequate system of (international) patent protection (see Grossman-Helpman, 1991).

On the other hand, recent empirical work (for example, by Nickell (1994) or Blundell *et al.* (1995)) suggests a *positive* correlation between *product market competition* (as measured either by the number of competitors in the same industry or by the inverse of a market share or profitability index) and *productivity growth* within a firm or industry. This evidence, in turn, appears to be more consistent with the view that competition is good for growth.

How can we reconcile the view supported by Nickell *et al.* with the Schumpeterian paradigm developed above? Several tentative answers to this question will be explored in this chapter. A first approach, developed in Section 2.2, is to introduce barriers to entry into research. It is then easy to show that reducing these barriers to competition will raise the growth rate. A second approach, developed in Section 2.3, is to introduce *agency considerations* in the decision-making process of innovating firms, and then investigate the idea that by reducing 'slack' (that is, the amount of free cash available to managers), product market competition combined with the threat of liquidation can act as a disciplinary device that fosters technology adoption and thus growth. A third approach, developed in Section 2.4, is to introduce the idea of 'tacit knowledge'. If firms must engage in R&D to acquire the non-codifiable knowledge embodied in a rival's innovation, then the implicit assumption made earlier that incumbent innovators are automatically leap-frogged by their rivals must be replaced by a more *gradualist* ('*step-by-step*') technological progress assumption. Finally, a fourth approach, developed in Section 2.5 below, will be to decompose R&D activities into *research* (leading to the discovery of new fundamental paradigms or product lines) and *development* (aimed at exploiting the new paradigms and filling up the new product lines).

2.2 Barriers to Entry in Research

Schumpeter's notion of creative destruction projects a view of the 'competitive struggle' somewhat at odds with the standard textbook version, one in which the main instrument of competition is innovation rather than price. Clearly, 'more competition' in this Schumpeterian sense means not a higher price-elasticity of demand faced by a monopolist, but an increased freedom of entry into the competitive innovation sector by potentially rent-stealing rivals. It is relatively straightforward to show that more competition in this sense will lead to higher growth.

2.2.1   The Arrow Effect

Going back to the basic Schumpeterian model of Section 1.1, where the research sector was implicitly assumed to be competitive (with any individual being free to engage in research activities), what would happen to innovations and growth in steady state if the research sector was instead monopolistic? The main difference between the two cases is that, in the latter, research would be done by the incumbent innovator. More formally, Equation (2.2) above would become:

$$w_t = \lambda \varphi'(n_t) \cdot (V_{t+1} - V_t) \qquad (2.12)$$

where

$$rV_t = \pi_t + \lambda \varphi(n_t) \cdot (V_{t+1} - V_t) \qquad (2.13)$$

The right-hand side of Equation (2.12) expresses the fact that the incumbent innovator internalises the business-stealing effect of his/her new innovation: the difference between Equations (2.2) and (2.12) reflects the well-known *replacement effect* of Arrow. The right-hand side of Equation (2.13), in turn, expresses the fact that the incumbent innovator internalises the positive (intertemporal spillover) externality of current innovation on future research activities. In other words, a monopolist researcher will essentially[15] behave like a social planner. The comparison between research (and growth) respectively in the benchmark model with competitive research and in the monopolistic research case will thus boil down to a reinterpretation of the welfare analysis of the benchmark model. Whether or not demonopolising the research sector will create more growth depends upon whether the business-stealing (Arrow) effect exceeds the intertemporal spillover effect.

This apparent ambiguity of the effect of demonopolising research is, however, an artefact of the simplifying assumption that there is only one sector. In the multisector extension of Section 1.2 above the ambiguity disappears, because even if each sector is monopolised, no sector is large enough to internalise the intertemporal spillovers, which benefits all the other local monopolists, not just the monopolist generating the spillovers. In this case, only the Arrow-effect remains, and competition is unambiguously favourable to growth.

2.2.2 The Case of U-shaped Individual R&D Cost Functions

The same result can be demonstrated in the basic (one-sector) model when there exists initially more than one research firm. To show this we must relax the assumption implicitly invoked up to now that there are constant returns to scale in research activities.[16] Instead, assume that each individual firm faces a Poisson probability equal to $\lambda \cdot \theta(z - \phi)$, where the unit cost function corresponding to θ is U-shaped, and where ϕ is an entry fee (expressed in labour units) to be paid by individual firms to the government (thus, if z denotes the research firm's total labour investment, only the fraction $(z - \phi)$ will be directly available for research activities).

Since z is chosen by each research firm so as to minimise the average cost of research, the following must hold in equilibrium:

(C)

$$\frac{\theta(z - \phi)}{z} = \theta'(z - \phi).$$

Let N denote the number of research firms in equilibrium. Since the aggregate arrival rate of new innovations is equal to $\lambda N \cdot \theta(z - \theta)$, the steady-state *arbitrage equation* becomes:

(A)

$$w = \lambda \cdot \theta'(z - \phi)\gamma \frac{\tilde{\pi}(w)}{r + \lambda N \theta(z - \phi)},$$

where z is defined by (C).

The steady-state equilibrium $(\hat{w}, \hat{z}, \hat{N})$ is then fully determined by (C), (A) and the labour *market clearing equation*:

(L)

$$N \cdot z + \tilde{x}(w) = L.$$

How does the steady-state growth rate $g = \lambda \hat{N} \cdot \theta(\hat{z} - \phi) \cdot \ln \gamma$ respond to a reduction in the entry fee ϕ; that is, to making the research sector become more competitive? The answer turns out to be straightforward: consider the change of variables:

$$\tilde{\lambda} = \lambda \, \frac{\theta(z - \phi)}{z} \text{ and } \tilde{n} = N \cdot z.$$

Using (C), we can re-express the above equations (A) and (L) respectively as:

(A)

$$w = \tilde{\lambda} \cdot \gamma \, \frac{\tilde{\pi}(w)}{r + \tilde{\lambda} \cdot \tilde{n}}$$

and

(L)

$$L = \tilde{n} + \tilde{x}(w),$$

which turn out to be identical to (A) and (L) in the basic model, except that λ and n have been replaced by $\tilde{\lambda}$ and $\tilde{n}$, respectively.

A reduction in the entry fee ϕ amounts to increasing $\tilde{\lambda}$ (which is nothing but the arrival rate of innovation per unit of labour spent by a research firm). Now, we know from our comparative statics analysis of the basic model in Section 1.1 that $\frac{d\tilde{n}}{d\lambda} > 0$. Therefore the steady-state growth rate, which is equal to $\tilde{\lambda} \cdot \tilde{n} \cdot \ln \gamma$, will also increase as a result of a lower entry fee. This, in turn, vindicates the Schumpeterian claim that more competition in research activities is growth-enhancing.

2.3 Introducing Agency Considerations[17]

The next three sections all deal with competition in output markets. First, we relax the assumption that innovating firms are profit-maximising. Instead, we assume that managers are mainly concerned with preserving their private benefits of control while at the same time minimising (innovation) costs, an assumption commonly made in the corporate finance literature (innovation costs here refer to the *private* managerial costs – training costs or non-monetary cost of reorganising the firm – of switching to a new technology). Intensifying product market competition may then become growth-enhancing by forcing managers to *speed up* the adoption of new technologies in order to avoid bankruptcy and the resulting loss of control rights. This Darwinian argument is consistent with the view of the role of competition in fostering growth.

More formally, consider the multisector model of Section 1.2, with the final good being produced using a continuum of intermediate inputs of different technological vintages according to the production function.

$$y = \int_i A_i \cdot x_i^\alpha di,$$

where A_i is the productivity parameter in sector i.

Intermediate firms are now involved in two kinds of decision.

2.3.1 Production Decisions (for a Given Technology)

As before, an intermediate firm with technological vintage A_τ will choose its current output flow $x = x_{t,\tau}$ so as to:

$$\max_x \{p_\tau(x)x - w_t x\}$$

where:

$$p_\tau(x) - A_\tau \cdot \alpha x^{\alpha-1}.$$

In steady state, we have: $w_t = A_t \cdot w$, where A_t is the leading-edge; and $A_t = A_0 \cdot e^{gt}$, where g is the steady-state growth rate. Therefore, the output flow of a firm of vintage τ at date t (also the flow demand for labour by that firm) is:

$$x_{t,\tau} = \left(\frac{w}{\alpha^2}\right)^{1/\alpha-1} \cdot e^{-\frac{g(t-\tau)}{1-\alpha}} ;$$

that is, it decreases exponentially with the age of the firm's vintage ($t - \tau$).

Assume that intermediate firms must incur a fixed operating cost (also in terms of labour) equal to $k_{t,\tau} = w_t \cdot k e^{\rho(t-\tau)}$ with $\rho \geq r$. Then the firms' *net* profit flow is given by:

$$\pi_{t,\tau} = \pi(w)e^{-\frac{g(t-\tau)}{1-\alpha}} - wke^{\rho(t-\tau)}e^{gt}$$
$$= \psi(\pi, u) \cdot e^{gt},$$

where $u = t - \tau$ is the age of the firm's vintage and $\pi = \pi(\alpha, w) = s(\alpha) \cdot w^{\alpha/\alpha-1}$ is a profit parameter.

The growth-adjusted profit flow, ψ, is thus positive for $u = 0$ but decreasing in age and negative for u sufficiently large. This, in turn, will play a key role in the Darwinian argument developed below.

2.3.2 Technological Adoption

Departing from the previous sections, let us suppose that new technological vintages result from *sunk adoption* decisions directly made by intermediate firms (rather than from a continuous *flow* of research investments).

Let f denote the sunk cost (in labour units) of adopting the leading-edge technology.[18] Measured in units of final output, the adoption cost at date τ is, $f_\tau = f \cdot w_\tau = f \cdot w e^{g\tau}$. In a steady state each intermediate firm adopts the leading edge technology every T units of time, and the age distribution of firms remains uniform on $[0,T]$. Thus the aggregate flow of new adoptions per unit of time is $1/T$, and the aggregate flow of research labour is $n = f/T$. As in the multisector model of Section 1.2, assume that adoptions lead incrementally to growth in the leading edge, at the rate $\ln \gamma$ per unit of innovation. Then as before, the steady-state growth rate is:

(G)
$$g = \dot{A}/A = \ln \gamma/T.$$

2.3.3 Labour Market Equilibrium

In addition to the flow f/T of research labour there is an aggregate flow $\int_0^T (1/T)\tilde{x}(we^{gu})du = \tilde{x}(w) \int_0^T (1/T)e^{-gu/(1-\alpha)}du$ of manufacturing labour and a flow $\int_0^T (1/T)ke^{\rho u}du$ of 'overhead' labour. Evaluating these integrals using (G) leads to the labour-market clearing condition:

(L)
$$\frac{e^{\rho T} - 1}{\rho T} \cdot k + \frac{f}{T} + \frac{\tilde{x}(w)}{T} \left[\frac{1 - e^{-\ln \gamma/(1-\alpha)}}{\ln \gamma/(1 - \alpha)} \right] = L.$$

For future reference, note that the term in square brackets in (L) represents another 'productivity effect', whereby an increase in γ reduces the aggregate demand for labour relative to the leading-edge demand $x(w)$, as in the multisector model of Section 1.2.

2.3.4 Profit-maximising Firms

First consider an intermediate firm born at date 0 that does *not* face agency problems. Such a firm will, in steady state, choose to switch to the leading-edge at times T_1, $T_1 + T_2, \ldots, T_1 + \ldots + T_k$, and so on, where (T_k) is a solution of the maximisation programme:

$$\rightarrow \max_{(T_k)} [W - fw + \int_0^{T_1} \psi(\pi, u)e^{-(r-g)u}du$$

$$+ e^{-(r-g)T_1}[- fw + \int_0^{T_2} \psi(\pi, u)e^{-(r-g)u}du]$$

$$+ e^{-(r-g)(T_1+T_2)}[- fw + \int_0^{T_3} \psi(\pi, u)e^{-(r-g)u}du]$$

$$+ \ldots],$$

where W is the firm's initial endowment at date 0.

One can easily see that the optimal adoption policy is stationary ($T_k \equiv \hat{T}$ for $k \geq 1$), where:

(A^p):

$$\hat{T} = \operatorname*{argmax}_T \frac{[-f \cdot w + \int_0^T \psi(\pi, u)e^{-(r-g)u}du]}{1 - e^{-(r-g)T}}.$$

This equation will replace the arbitrage equation (A) of the previous sections.

It turns out (see Aghion, Dewatripont and Rey, 1995) that the equilibrium adoption policy $\hat{T}$ defined by (A^p) and (L) satisfies:

$$\frac{d\hat{T}}{d\alpha} > 0.$$

This is, again, the appropriability effect pointed out in the basic Schumpeterian model: more product market competition (that is, a lower π) will discourage technological adoptions ($\hat{T}\nearrow$) and thereby reduce growth.

2.3.5 Non-profit-maximising Firms

A common assumption in the corporate finance literature is that the managers of large companies are mainly concerned with preserving their private benefits of control over the company while at the same time minimising 'effort'. To model this, we assume the following utility function for intermediate firms' managers:

$$U_0 = \int_0^\infty B_t \cdot e^{-\delta t}dt - \sum_{j\geq 1} C \cdot e^{-\delta(T_1+ \ldots +T_j)},$$

where C is the *private cost for the manager to switch* to a new technological vintage (training cost for example); B_t is the *current private benefit of control* at date t, equal to $B > 0$ if the firm has financially survived up to time t and equal to zero otherwise; and δ is the subjective rate at which managers discount future private costs and benefits.

For B and δ sufficiently large, one can show that the above objective function is observationally equivalent to a lexicographic preference ordering whereby the manager always seeks to delay as much as possible the next innovation subject to keeping the firm afloat; that is, with a positive net financial wealth. Consider now an intermediate firm where the manager obeys such a lexicographic preference ordering, and suppose that this firm has entered the market with wealth wf and innovated at date $t = 0$.

If the firm has not innovated thereafter, its accumulated profits at date $t = T$ are equal to:

$$\int_0^T \psi(\pi, u)e^{-(r-g)u} \cdot du.$$

Given that $\psi(\pi, 0) > 0$, $\psi(\pi, u) < 0$ for u large and $\psi_u < 0$, these cumulative profits will be inverted-U shaped with respect to T, being initially increasing and positive for T small and then decreasing and eventually negative for T sufficiently large. This implies that the intermediate firm will necessarily become insolvent (and therefore go bankrupt) if it never innovates after date 0. More precisely, there exists a maximum date $\tilde{T}$ at which the firm's cumulative profits just cover the adoption cost $f \cdot e^{-(r-g)\tilde{T}}$ at that date (evaluated as of date zero), where $\tilde{T}$ is defined by:

$$wfe^{-(r-g)T} = \int_0^T [\pi(w)e^{\frac{-gu}{1-\alpha}} - wke^{gu}] e^{-(r-g)u}du. \qquad (2.14)$$

Intuitively, an increase in competition, by reducing the flow of variable profits $\pi(w)$ will hasten the day when a firm's wealth (the right-hand side) is exhausted by the rising overhead costs $wke^{\rho u}$, thus forcing it to adopt sooner, while it still has enough wealth remaining to do so.

To see this effect more clearly, we again use the fact that, in this Cobb–Douglas world, $\pi = \dfrac{1-\alpha}{\alpha} wx$, along with the labour-market clearing condition (L) and the growth equation (G) to derive from Equation (2.14) the reduced-form arbitrage equation:

(A^F)

$$fe^{-rT+\ln\gamma} = \int_0^T \left\{ \overbrace{\frac{1-\alpha}{\alpha}}^{\text{appropriability}} \cdot \overbrace{\left[\frac{\ln\gamma/(1-\alpha)}{1 - e^{\ln\gamma/(1-\alpha)}} \right]}^{\text{productivity}} T \left[L - \frac{f}{T} - \frac{e^{\rho T} - 1}{\rho T} k \right] \overbrace{e^{\frac{\ln\gamma u}{T(1-\alpha)}}}^{\text{obsolescence}} \right.$$
$$\left. - ke^{\rho u} \right\} e^{-(r-\ln\gamma/T)u}du.$$

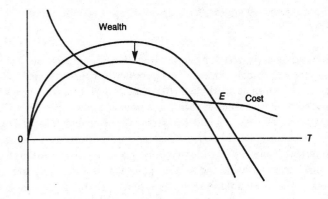

Figure 2.2   An increase in competitiveness, by reducing wealth, forces firms to adopt sooner, thus raising the rate of growth

The two sides of (A^E), adoption cost and wealth, are described in Figure 2.2. Wealth is less than cost for $T = 0$ and again as $T \to \infty$. So the equilibrium, which is the *maximal* delay possible, occurs at a point such as E, where wealth is falling faster than cost. Thus an increase in the competitiveness parameter α will reduce T, and hence raise growth, if it shifts the wealth curve down.

As indicated in (A^F), the same three effects of α will be at work on wealth as we saw at work on the right-hand side of the arbitrage equation ($\hat{A}^{cm}$) in the multisector model. Again, the appropriability and obsolescence effects are negative and the productivity effect is positive, but the appropriability effect dominates the productivity effect. Thus the overall effect of increased competition, as before, is to reduce wealth, but in this case the result is to increase research rather than decrease it, because in this case firms have waited so long that their profits are increasing with respect to the level of research, whereas in the models in Section 1 of the right-hand side of the arbitrage equation was always decreasing in the economy-wide level of research, mainly because of the negative creative-destruction externality.

Remark   Contrary to the basic Schumpeterian model where a higher productivity of R&D has an ambiguously boosting effect on growth, a lower adoption cost f may *slow down* adoptions and growth: indeed, for given wage w, a lower f increases the financial slack of intermediate firms, thereby allowing managers to delay the next technological adoption while keeping their firm solvent.

2.4   From Leap-Frogging to Step-by-Step Technological Progress[19]

An alternative approach for reconciling the Schumpeterian paradigm with recent empirical evidence on productivity growth and product market competition is to replace the *leap-frogging* assumption of the basic Schumpeterian model (with incumbent innovators being over-taken systemically by outside researchers), by a less radical *step-by-step* assumption. That is, a firm that is currently m steps behind the technological leader in its industry must go successively through all m steps and catch up with the leader before becoming a leader itself. This step-by-step assumption can be rationalised by supposing that an innovator acquires tacit knowledge that cannot be duplicated by a rival without engaging in its own R&D to catch up. Once it has caught up, we suppose that no patent protects the former leader from Bertrand competition.

This change leads to a richer analysis of the interplay between product market competition, innovation and growth, by allowing firms in an industry to be *neck-to-neck*. A higher degree of product market competition, by making life more difficult for neck and neck firms, will encourage them to innovate in order to acquire a significant lead over their rivals.

More formally, suppose that final output is produced at any time t using input services from a continuum of intermediate sectors, according to the production function:

$$\ln y_t = \int_0^1 \ln Q_i(t) di.$$

As shown in Grossman and Helpman (1991), this logarithmic technology implies that the same amount $E(t)$ will be spent at any time t by the final good sector on *all* intermediate industries. Choosing current aggregate spending as the numeraire, we then have: $E(t \equiv 1.$

Each sector i is assumed to be *duopolistic* with respect to both production and research activities, with firms A and B, and

$$Q_i = v(q_{Ai}, q_{Bi}),$$

where v is homogeneous of degree one and symmetric is its two arguments.[20]

Let k denote the technology level of a duopoly firm in a given industry. That is, in order to produce one unit of intermediate good, this firm needs to employ γ^{-k} units of labour, where $\gamma > 1$. An industry is thus fully characterised by a pair of integers (l, m), where l is the leader's technology and m is the technological gap between the leader and the follower.

Let π_m (resp. π_{-m}) denote the equilibrium profit flow of a firm m steps ahead of (resp. behind) its rival.[21] For expositional simplicity, we assume that knowledge spillovers between leaders and followers in an industry are such that the maximum sustainable gap is $m = 1$. That is, if a firm one step ahead innovates, the follower will automatically learn to copy the leader's previous technology and will then remain only one step behind.

We now come to the basic feature of the model, namely the *step-by-step* technological assumption. We denote by $\psi(x) = \frac{1}{2}x^2$ the R&D cost (in units of labour) of the leader (resp. the follower) in an industry moving one technological step ahead with Poisson hazard rate x.

Then, if V_m denotes the steady-state, growth-adjusted value of being currently a leader (resp. a follower) in an industry with technological gap m, we have the following Bellman equations:[22,23]

$$rV_1 = \pi_1 + x_{-1}(V_0 - V_1) \qquad (2.15)$$

$$rV_0 = \pi_0 + \bar{x}_{-0}(V_{-1} - V_0) + x_0(V_1 - V_0) - wx_0^2/2 \qquad (2.16)$$

$$rV_{-1} = \pi_{-1} + x_{-1}(V_0 - V_1) - wx_{-1}^2/2. \qquad (2.17)$$

Note that $x_1 = 0$, since our assumption of automatic catchup means a leader cannot get any further advantage by innovating. In Equations (2.15) and (2.16) respectively, x_0 and x_{-1} are chosen to maximize the right-hand side. Thus we have the first-order conditions:

$$w \cdot x_i = V_{i+1} - V_i; \quad i = -1, 0. \qquad (2.18)$$

Equations (2.15)–(2.18) together with the symmetric equilibrium condition $x_0 = \bar{x}_0$ yield the reduced-form research equations:

$$(w/2)x_0^2 + rw \cdot x_0 - (\pi_1 - \pi_0) = 0 \qquad (2.19)$$

$$(w/2)x_{-1}^2 + (r + x_0)wx_{-1} - (\pi_0 - \pi_{-1}) - (w/2)x_0^2 = 0. \qquad (2.20)$$

Given any wage w, these equations solve the unique non-negative values of x_0 and x_{-1}.

We represent an increase in competition as an increase in the elasticity of substitution between the products A and B in each sector in a neighbourhood of the 45° line, which translates into a reduction in the profit level π_0 earned by a firm that is neck-and-neck with its rival.[24] It is then straightforward to show that x_0 will rise, while x_{-1} falls. The latter effect is the basic Schumpeterian effect resulting from reducing the rents that can be captured by a follower who succeeds in catching up with a rival by innovating. The former is the new effect introduced by tacit knowledge; competition reduces the rents in the neck-and-neck status quo, and thus encourages innovation among firms that are even with their rivals, by raising the incremental value of getting ahead.

The model is then closed by a labour market clearing equation which determines w as a function of the xs and the πs.[25] We shall ignore that equation and take the wage rate w as given in our analysis below. It now remains to express the steady-state average growth rate of the economy.

Let μ_1 denote the steady-state fraction of industries with technological gap $m = 1$, and $\mu_0 = 1 - \mu_1$. Thus $\mu_1 = 1 - \mu_0$. During time interval dt, in $\mu_1 x_{-1} \cdot dt$ sectors the follower catches up with the leader; in $2\mu_0 x_0 dt$ sectors one firm acquires a lead. Since the distribution of sectors (the μ_ms) remains stationary over time, we have:

$$\underbrace{\mu_1 x_{-1}}_{\substack{\text{flow of sectors that} \\ \text{become } \textit{levelled}}} = \underbrace{2\mu_0 x_0}_{\substack{\text{flow of sectors that} \\ \text{become } \textit{unlevelled}}}. \tag{2.21}$$

Each industry follows a strict two-stage cycle, alternating between $m = 0$ and $m = 1$. The log of its output rises by $\ln\gamma$ with each completed cycle. The frequency of completed cycles is the fraction μ_1 of time spent in Stage 2, times the frequency x_{-1} of innovations in Stage 2. Hence the average growth rate of each industry is $\mu_1 x_{-1} \ln \gamma$. From Equation (2.21) it follows that the fraction of industries with a leader is $\mu_1 = \dfrac{2x_0}{2x_0 + x_{-1}}$. Hence we have the following expression for the average growth rate of final output:

(G)

$$g = \mu_1 x_{-1} \ln \gamma = \frac{2x_0 x_{-1}}{2x_0 + x_{-1}} \cdot \ln \gamma.$$

From (G) it is clear that increased competition can either raise growth or lower it, depending upon which effect is the stronger: the rise in x_0, which raises g, or the fall in x_{-1}, which lowers g. Just as clearly, however, the effect x_0 will be the dominant one if π_0 is close enough to π_1, because at the limit, as π_0 approaches π_1, x_0 will fall to zero,[26] and hence, according to (G), the growth rate will also fall to zero. Intuitively, if $\pi_1 - \pi_0$ is small, then firms that are behind will have an incentive to catch up but, once even, they will have little incentive to get ahead. Hence most firms in a steady state will be neck-and-neck, doing little R&D. That is, most firms will be in sectors while R&D will be stimulated by an increase in competition. Figure 2.3 shows a numerical example in which $r = .04$; $\pi_{-1} = 0$; $\pi_1 = 10$; $w = 1$; and $\gamma = 1.03$. As π_0 rises, growth rises at first, but then falls as π_0 approaches π_1.

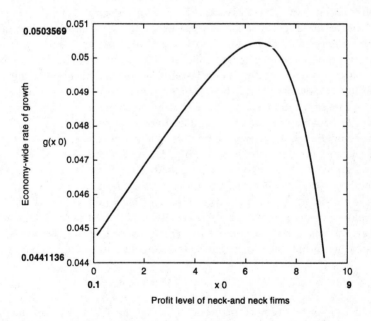

Figure 2.3   As competition decreases, the equilibrium profit level π_0 of neck-and-neck firms increases, resulting eventually in a fall in the economy-wide rate of growth

2.5   Research *and* Development

All the endogenous growth models surveyed above represent R&D activities as homogeneous, performed by only one kind of researcher, and generating just one kind of innovation and/or one kind of knowledge. However, whether growth will be enhanced by a subsidy to R&D may depend not only upon the *size* of the subsidy but also upon its *allocation*, for example, to *basic* versus *applied* research or to *independent* research labs versus *integrated* industries.

In this section we distinguish between two kinds of innovative activity: research and development. Research opens up new windows of opportunity by inventing new product lines. Development realises those opportunities by inventing concrete plans that allow the products to be produced. We show that the level of research, and therefore the growth rate, are increased if developers become more *adaptable*; that is, if the rate at which they are able to switch from developing old lines to developing new ones increases. This result supports Lucas's (1993) claim to the effect that the key to success of some newly-industrialised countries is their ability to move skilled workers quickly from sectors where learning is beginning to slow down to those where new ideas can more fruitfully be developed. When we endogenise this adaptability parameter we also find that the same result implies a *positive effect of competition on growth*. That is, an increase in the substitutability between new and old product lines, which implies an increase in competitiveness between them, will induce developers to leave old lines more rapidly, with the effect of inducing a higher level of research and growth. Contrary to the basic Schumpeterian model of Part I, this implies that *increased competition may again lead to faster growth*.

We consider a variant of the multisector model above, in which the sectors are distinguished by the age u of their fundamental technology. In this variant an innovation creates a new sector, without destroying an old one. Aggregate output at date t in a steady state is:

$$y_t = A_t \int_0^\infty e^{-gu} F(x_u) \cdot S_u du,$$

where S_u is the number of products of age u, and x_u the amount of labour allocated to producing each of them.

To focus on the relationship between research and development we suppose that there are two kinds of worker; L (unskilled workers) can produce goods, and H (skilled workers) can engage in innovative activity – either research or development. At each date, labour will be allocated across vintages so as to satisfy the equilibrium conditions:

$$e^{-gu} \{F')(x_u) + x_u F''(x_u)\} = w \text{ for all } u \qquad (2.22)$$

$$\int_0^\infty x_u \cdot S_u du = L,$$

where the left-hand side of Equation (2.22) is the marginal revenue product of labour in sector u, and w is the economy-wide wage, divided by the leading edge A_t.

The intermediate goods in sector u embody the technology A_{t-u} that was on the leading age at $t - u$. But they were almost all invented after $t - u$. Instead, each one comes from a 'product line' that was invented at $t - u$. Product lines are the result of research, and arrive continually at the flow rate $\lambda^r H^r$, where H^r is the amount of skilled labour allocated to research and λ^r the Poisson arrival rate per researcher. New goods on any product line arise from the discoveries of developers who attach themselves to that line.

For expository purposes we suppose initially that developers attach themselves only to lines of the most recent vintage, but that once attached they remain so until they are 'freed' to go into research, or to develop a newer line, by an exogenous event with a constant Poisson arrival rate σ for each worker. The 'relocation rate' σ will play a major role in what follows, and will eventually be endogenised.

We suppose that the Poisson arrival rate of secondary innovations to any developer depends upon the number η_u of developers on the same line, according to: $\lambda^d \eta_u^{-v} (0 < v < 1)$. Let h^d be the flow of skilled workers into developing new lines per period. Since there are $\lambda^r H^r$ new lines per period, $\eta_u = (h^d/\lambda^r H^r) e^{-\sigma u}$ and:[27]

$$S_u = (\lambda^r H^r)^v \lambda^d (h^d)^{1-v} (1 - e^{-\sigma(1-v)u})/\sigma \cdot (1 - v). \qquad (2.23)$$

The leading edge A_t embodies the general knowledge available to all. Everyone takes it as being exogenous. Its growth rate will become the economy's growth rate g in a steady state. We assume that general knowledge is created only by research.[28] Thus we have the growth equation:

(G)

$$g = \lambda^r H^r.$$

Since the stock of developers changes over time according to the relocation equation: $H_t^d = h_t^{\dot{d}} - \sigma H_t^d = h_t^d - \sigma(H - H_t^r)$, in steady-state the flow of skilled workers into developing new lines will be constant and equal to:

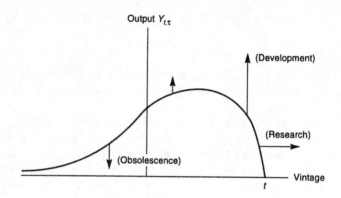

Figure 2.4 The profile of output across lines of difference vintages, at date *t*

(R)
$$h^d = \sigma(H - H^r).$$

Figure 2.4 shows the structure of output in the economy at any given date *t*. Because nothing can be produced on lines that have not yet been invented, therefore $Y_{t,\tau} = 0$ for all $\tau \geq t$. Because older vintages are less efficient, output of very old lines will be very low. Hence the profile will tend to have the wave form depicted by Figure 2.4. Over time, the profile will shift to the right, as research opens up new product lines. Near the leading edge the profile will be shifting up, as development creates new goods. But far back from the leading edge the profile will be shifting down, as the rise in real wages associated with growth draws labour from old product lines, and the reallocation of old developers into new lines reduces the rate at which new goods are being introduced on old lines. However, there will always be some development taking place no matter how old the line.[29]

For both kinds of innovative activity to coexist in a steady state, skilled workers who have just been upgraded must be indifferent between research and development on a new line. To specify the arbitrage equation that reflects this indifference we must describe how each kind of innovative activity is compensated. Each plan (to produce a new intermediate good) on a line is implemented by a company formed by the researcher who discovered the line and the developer who found the plan. When the developer first begins work on the line it is agreed that a certain fraction of *K* of each company's profits will go to the researcher, with $1 - K$ going to the developer. At each date t there will be $\lambda^r H^r$ researchers with new lines of vintage t competing for developers, using K as their strategic variable. As we show in Appendix 2, this competition defines a unique equilibrium value of κ, namely $K = v$. That is, as in any model of perfect competition, the developers' share of rents will be the Cobb–Douglas exponent of development in producing rents on a line, since the arrival rate of new products on a line with η developers is proportional to η^{1-v}.[30]

Let $V_t^r = V^r e^{gt}$ denote the expected present value of the income that a researcher will receive until his or her alternative choice as a developer is upgraded to a new line. That is, V_t^r is the value of a claim to all the researcher's rents from fundamental innovations made over the time period (of stochastic length) during which s/he could have been developing a line of vintage t. Let $V_t^d = V^d \cdot e^{gt}$ denote the value of the income the researcher would have received in development over the same period. Since a newly-upgraded skilled worker can choose either activity freely, a steady state with both research and development requires:

$$V^r = V^d.$$

In a steady-state the value V_t^r grows at rate g and capitalises flow payoffs (per unit of time) equal to the flow probability of discovering a new line λ^r times the researcher's share of a new product line KW_t (where W_t denotes the capitalised value of rents generated by the intermediate plans on each product line opened up at date t). Since upgrading occurs at Poisson rate σ, the Bellman equation defining the steady-state value of V^r is:

$$r \cdot V^r - \lambda^r \cdot K \cdot W - \sigma \cdot V^r + g \cdot V^r.$$

Since each developer receives the fraction $1/\eta$ of $(1 - k) \cdot W$, we have:

$$V^d = (\lambda^r \cdot H^r/h^d) \cdot (1 - k) \cdot W.$$

The previous three equations, together with the steady-state condition (R) and the fact that $K = v$, yield the arbitrage equation:

(A)

$$r + \sigma - g = \frac{v}{1 - v} \sigma \frac{(H - H^r)}{H^r}.$$

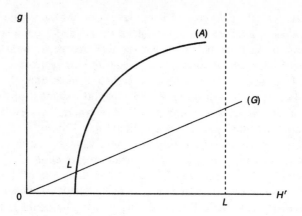

Figure 2.5

According to (A), an increase in the growth rate will result in a larger equilibrium level of research. This positive effect of growth on research is clearly a reflection of the more forward-looking nature of research when compared with development.

The steady-state values of g and H^r are jointly determined by the arbitrage equation (A) and the growth equation (G), shown in Figure 2.5. As we have seen, both are upward-sloping. An increase in the relocation rate σ will increase both the amount of research H^r and the growth rate g, by shifting the (A) curve to the right.

The positive effect of the upgrading rate σ on research and growth can be explained as follows: Holding the total supply of skilled workers H constant, an increase in σ implies an increase in the initial flow of developers into newly-discovered lines. It also increases the speed at which current lines are being depleted of their developers, but time-discounting implies that the former effect dominates the latter; that is, a higher σ increases the value of being a researcher relative to that of being a developer. Hence the positive effect of the upgrading rate σ on research and thus on growth by equation (G). This is the '*Lucas effect*' referred to above, whereby adaptability increases growth. (Although, contrary to Lucas (1993), a higher mobility of developers across lines enhances growth not so much because it increases aggregate learning by doing but rather because it increases the steady-state mass of researchers.) As we show below, the same effect translates into a positive effect of competition on growth when we endogenise σ.

Remark The above analysis may convey the wrong impression that the positive effect of σ on g is essentially driven by our extreme assumption about the growth equation (G), namely that only fundamental innovations (that is, ultimately research) generate new general knowledge. However, we can show (see Aghion and Howitt, 1996) that the above comparative statics results carry over to the general case where *both* fundamental *and* secondary innovations contribute to the growth of general knowledge. The main reason is that, because of its more forward-looking nature relative to development, research has a larger marginal product than development in generating *either* kind of innovation, fundamental *or* applied.[31]

Suppose now that developers are free at each instant to engage in research or to do development on any line. To keep the model tractable we restrict attention to the Cobb–Douglas case, where $F(x) = x^\alpha$ ($0 < \alpha < 1$). It turns out that an analogous arbitrage equation results, because developers will again relocate at a constant rate in the steady-state equilibrium, except that the rate of upgrading is now endogenous. The positive results are identical to those obtained under an exogenous σ, except that the Cobb–Douglas paramater α now matters for positive results, because it affects the endogenous upgrading rate.

Let $W_{t,\tau}$ denote the value at date t of a plan of vintage τ: $\int_t^\infty e^{-r(s-t)}\pi_{s,\tau}ds$, where $\pi_{s,\tau}$ is the flow of profits to the producer of an intermediate goods of vintage τ. In the Cobb–Douglas case it is easily shown that $\pi_{s,\tau} = \delta A_\tau^{1/(1-\alpha)} w_s^{\alpha/(\alpha-1)}$, where δ is a positive constant. Since A_τ grows at the constant rate g in a steady state, therefore:

$$W_{t,\tau} = W_{t,t}e^{-g(t-\tau)/(1-\alpha)}.$$

Since all skilled workers are mobile across all innovative activities, they must all earn the same expected income x_t at date t. In particular, a researcher who has a line of vintage τ at date t will have to pay x_t to each developer s/he employs at that date. Thus s/he will choose $\eta_{t,\tau}$ so as to maximise his or her flow of new development royalties:

$$Max\{\lambda^d\eta_{t,\tau}^{1-v}W_{t,\tau}e^{g(t-\tau)/(1-\alpha)} - x_t\eta_{t,\tau}\}.$$

(Recall that each developer's arrival rate is $\lambda^d\eta_{t,\tau}^{-v}$). The solution to this maximisation problem is:

$$\eta_{t,\tau} = [x_t/(1 - v)\lambda^d W_{t,t}e^{-g(t-\tau)/(1-\alpha)}]^{-1/v} = \eta_{t,t}e^{-g(t-\tau)/v(1-\alpha)}.$$

This shows that the unique candidate for an endogenous steady-state relocation rate is: $\sigma = \dfrac{g}{v(1-\alpha)}$.

It turns out that this endogenous rate satisfies the same arbitrage equation (A) as before,[32] but with σ being replaced by the endogenous relocation rate $\dfrac{g}{v(1-\alpha)}$; that is:

(A')

$$r + [g/v(1 - \alpha)] - g = \frac{v}{1 - v}[g/v(1 - \alpha)]\frac{(H - H')}{H'}$$

A steady-state equilibrium occurs when the growth equation (G) and the modified arbitrage equation (A') are both satisfied. It is straightforward to verify that the curve representing (A') in Figure 2.5 would be upward-sloping and would be affected by parameter changes in exactly the same direction as is the curve representing (A), except that now the Cobb–Douglas parameter α will shift it to the right because it has a direct effect on the endogenous upgrading rate $[g/v(1 - \alpha)]$, whereas neither α nor any parameter of the general production function F had an effect when the upgrading rate was exogenous.

Thus the only effect which endogenising the upgrading rate has on the comparative-statics results of the model is to add an effect of α. In particular, since an increase in α has the effect of increasing the upgrading rate, it will work through the 'Lucas effect' described earlier to shift the modified arbitrage curve to the right, resulting in more research and more growth. That is, the effect on the overall level of development of the fact that innovators will be choosing to remain for a shorter time on old lines outweighs the effect created by more of them going into lines of the most recent vintage, with the result that there will be fewer people in development, and hence more in research, in the new steady state.[33]

We have thus obtained a fourth 'explanation' for the observed positive correlation between product market competition and productivity growth, which again relies upon extending the basic Schumpeterian model of Section I.

III CONCLUSION

We began this chapter by claiming that Schumpeterian models of endogenous growth are shedding new substantive light on structural aspects of growth, because of their specificity concerning the details of the innovation process. We then went on to illustrate this claim by showing how these models can help to explain the apparent fact that competition and growth are positively correlated, even though this fact contradicts the most elementary Schumpeterian models, which embody only the appropriability effect of competition.

We end by observing that the various Schumpeterian explanations of this apparent fact provide a number of empirical hypotheses that are worth pursuing, and which suggest a potential empirical test of the Schumpeterian approach. First, the argument of Section 2.2 suggests that competition in research, as opposed to product market competition, is almost always likely to be favourable to growth. As for product market competition, the various explanations presented above suggest that the correlation between competition and growth is more likely to be positive in subgroups of the economy where the various factors introduced in each of the explanations is prevalent to a large enough extent that the positive effects derived from them might outweigh the negative appropriability effect that is always present.

Thus, for example, if industries were classified into two subgroups characterised respectively by strong and weak control of managers by shareholders, one ought to find a stronger positive effect of competition on growth within the latter group than within the former, since the agency problems at the heart of our Darwinian argument of Section 2.3 above are more likely to prevail in the latter group. Similarly, there should be a stronger positive effect of competition on growth between sectors where tacit knowledge is the limiting barrier to imitation, relative to the effect between sectors where patent protection is the limiting barrier, since patent protection reduces the scope for the neck-and-neck competition shown in Section 2.4 to be favourable to growth. By the same token, the positive effect of competition on growth should show up more strongly within a group of sectors or countries where developers are mobile across product lines than where heavy technology-specific fixed investments limits their ability to move in response to increased competition, since it is this response which gives rise to the positive effect shown in Section 2.5 above. Our hope is that empirical work aimed at testing these various propositions will allow econometricians not only to confront Schumpeterian growth theory with evidence, but also to sharpen our understanding of how competition affects growth.

Appendix 1

This appendix derives (D) of Section 1.2. Let $F_A(\cdot t)$ denote the cumulative distribution of the absolute productivity parameters A across sectors in a steady state at date t. Pick $\bar{A} > 0$ and define $\Phi(t) \equiv F_A(\bar{A}, t)$, $t_0 \equiv \ln \bar{A}/g$. Then:

$$\Phi(t_0) = 1; \text{ and}$$
$$\Phi(t) = -\lambda \cdot \varphi(n) \cdot \Phi(t) \text{ for all } t \geq t_0.$$

That is, $\bar{A}$ is by construction the leading-edge at t_0, and after t_0 the fraction of sectors behind $\bar{A}$ falls at the aggregate rate of innovations, each of which leaves the innovating sector ahead of $\bar{A}$, multiplied by the fraction of innovations occurring in sectors behind $\bar{A}$ at the time. Thus:

$$\Phi(t) = e^{-\lambda\varphi(n) \cdot (t-t_0)} \text{ for all } t \geq t_0.$$

Since $t \equiv \ln A_t/g$, $t_0 \equiv \ln\bar{A}/g$ and $g = \ln \gamma \cdot \lambda \cdot \varphi(n)$:

$$F_A(\bar{A},t) \equiv \Phi(t) = (\bar{A}/A_t)^{1/\ln \gamma}.$$

By definition, the cumulative distribution of relative productivities a is:

$$F_a(a) \equiv F_A(aA_t, t).$$

Hence:

$$F_a(a) = a^{1/\ln \gamma}.$$

The density h is the derivative of F_a which the above equation shows is given by (D) in the text.

Appendix 2

This appendix shows that $k = v$, as asserted in Section 2.5. Let W_t denote the capitalised value of the anticipated rents generated by each product line of vintage t, at date t. Since there are $\lambda^r H^r$ product lines of each vintage, and S_u goods across all lines of age u, in a steady state $W_t = e^{gt}.W$, where:

$$W = \int_0^\infty e^{-ru} S_u \tilde{\pi}(we^{gu}) du/\lambda^r H^r.$$

This equation, Equation (2.23) and the definition $\eta \equiv h^d/\lambda^r H^r$ together yield:

$$W = \eta^{1-v} \cdot \lambda^d \int_0^\infty e^{-ru} \tilde{\pi}(we^{gu})(1 - e^{-\sigma(1-v)u})du/\sigma(1 - v)$$
$$= \eta^{1-v} \times \text{constant}$$

Perfect competition implies that each developer is paid his or her marginal contribution to W:

$$V^d = \partial W/\partial \eta = (1 - v)W/\eta.$$

Thus the fraction $1 - k$ of W going to developers is $\eta V^d/W = 1 - v$; that is, $k = v$.

Notes

1. For example, Segestrom *et al.* (1990); Aghion and Howitt (1992); Corriveau (1991); Romer (1990); Grossman and Helpman (1991); and Young (1993a, 1993b).
2. Some implications of introducing physical capital accumulation are discussed in Section 1.3.
3. This follows from the following asset equation for the annuity value of innovation $(t + 1)$:

$$rV_{t+1} = \pi_{t+1} - \lambda \cdot \varphi(n_{t+1}) \cdot V_{t+1},$$

   (with probability $\lambda \cdot \varphi(n_{t+1})$ the $(t + 1)^{\text{th}}$ innovator will be replaced by the following innovation, therefore the second term on the right–hand is the annual expected loss for the $(t + 1)^{\text{th}}$ innovator).
4. More precisely, we have:

$$\pi_t = \max_x [A_t \cdot F'(x) - w_t/x,$$

   where $A_tF'(x) = P_t$ is the inverse demand curve facing the tth innovator and w_t is the wage. (We assume that innovations are big enough so that the monopolist need not worry about competition from the previous generation of intermediate goods; that is, that innovations are 'drastic'. No significant differences arise in the 'non-drastic' case – see Aghon and Howitt, 1992)

   When the production function $F(x)$ is such that the marginal revenue function is downward-sloping, then it can immediately be seen that π_t and the solution x_t to the above programme are decreasing functions of the growth-adjusted wage rate, $w_t = w_t/A_t$ with $x_t = \tilde{x}(w_t)$ and $\pi_t = A_t \cdot \tilde{\pi}(w_t)$).
5. See Note 4 above.
6. In a steady state the flow of final (consumption) output produced during the time interval between the tth and the $(t + 1)^{\text{th}}$ innovation is: $y_t = A_tF(\hat{x}) = A_tF(L - \hat{n})$. Thus $\ln y_{t+1} = \ln y_t + \ln \gamma$. In real time, we then have: $\ln y(\tau + 1) = \ln y(\tau) + (\ln \gamma)\varepsilon(\tau)$, where $\varepsilon(\tau)$ is the number of innovations between τ and $\tau + 1$. Given that $\varepsilon(\tau)$ is distributed Poisson

with parameter $\lambda\varphi(\hat{n})$ we have $E(\ln y(\tau + 1) - \ln y(\tau)) = \lambda\varphi(\hat{n})\ln \gamma$, where the left-hand side is nothing but the average growth rate.

7. To see this, notice that if we substitute for w_t and w_{t+1} using (L) [or equivalently: $w_t = \tilde{x}^{-1} (L - n_t)$], the arbitrage equation (A) becomes:

$$n_t = \psi(n_{t+1}), \quad \psi' < 0.$$

In addition to the steady-state $\hat{n} = \psi(\hat{n})$, this difference equation can also have periodic solutions of order two.

8. The optimal labor allocation between research and manufacturing activities is determined as the solution to the programme:

$$\underset{x,n}{\text{Max}} \int_0^\infty e^{-rt} \sum_{t=0}^\infty \pi(t, \tau) \cdot A_t \cdot F(x)d\tau$$

$$s.t.: \quad x + n = L,$$

where $\pi(t, \tau) = (\lambda n \tau)^t \cdot e^{-\lambda n \tau}/t!$ is the Poisson probability that t innovations occur during the time interval $[0, \tau]$.

9. A natural interpretation for this growth equation is that there is an infinite list of techniques, each embodying a productivity parameter whose log equals that technique's number on the list multiplied by $\ln \gamma$, and that R&D consists in discovering these techniques one at a time. Each discovery is implementable only in the chosen sector of the innovator, but its discovery allows the next innovator to discover a slightly better technique in another sector.

10. See Grossman and Helpman (1991, ch. 5) for another extension of the basic Schumpeterian model in Section 1.1, where physical capital enters as an additional input for producing final output but otherwise does not interact at all with the innovation process and therefore with long-run growth.

11. We were previously assuming $G(K^p_i/A_i, N_i) \equiv N_i$.

12. See also Redding (1993).

13. This effect was first pointed out by Cannon (1995).

14. Note that the same two opposite effects on research and growth will follow from an increase in the exogenous rate of depreciation δ_k.

15. Except for the fact that a monopolist maximises profits, whereas a social planner will seek to maximise intertemporal consumption.

16. That is, we have implicitly assumed that individual firms have Poisson innovation rates of the form: $\lambda\psi(z,k)$, where z is the firm's R&D effort, k is a complementary input into research (for example, capital), and ψ is homogeneous of degree one in z and k. We have implicitly taken k as being fixed.

17. See Aghion, Dewatripont and Rey (1995) from which this section is drawn.

18. We thus posit a deterministic innovation process at the firm level, which in turn can be interpreted as assuming either that each intermediate firm hires a large number (continuum) of researchers subject to uncorrelated Poisson processes, or simply that a firm adopts existing new inventions.

19. See Aghion, Harris and Vickers (1995).

20. A particular case is when $Q_i = q_A + q_B$; that is, when the two intermediate

inputs produced in industry i are perfect substitutes.

21. The above logarithmic final good technology, together with the linear production cost structure $c(q) = q \cdot \gamma^{-k}$, imply that the equilibrium profit flows of the leader and the follower in an industry depend only upon the technological gap m in that industry.

22. Where r still denotes the individual rate of time preference. The πs and Vs in this and following equations are obviously expressed in units of numeraire, where the numeraire is current total expenditures.

23. In words, the annuity value of being a technological leader in an industry with technological gap m is equal to the current profit flow π_m, plus the expected capital gain if the leader makes a further innovation and thereby increases the gap from m to $m + 1$, minus the expected capital loss if the follower makes an innovation and thereby reduces the gap from m to $(m - 1)$, minus the R&D cost.

24. For simplicity, we assume that π_1 and π_{-1} are unaffected by a change in competitiveness, although the analysis goes through essentially unmodified if π_1 is increased and/or π_{-1} is reduced.

25. See Aghion, Harris and Vickers (1995).

26. From Equation (2.19), $x_0 = \sqrt{r^2 + 2 \cdot (\pi_1 - \pi_0)/w} - r$.

27. That is, S_u is the number of lines times the integral of the flow of secondary innovations per line: $S_u = \lambda^r H^r \int_0^u \lambda^d \cdot (h_e^{d - \sigma\alpha}/\lambda^r H^r)^{1-v} d\alpha$.

28. In Aghion and Howitt (1996) we derive the same result as below, assuming that both research *and* development contribute to the growth of general knowledge.

29. Hence the model exhibits at least part of what economic historians sometimes call the 'sailing-ship effect', whereby development continues even on obsolescent lines.

30. In particular if $v = 0$; that is, if there are constant returns to development on a product line, Bertrand competition for developers among the researchers who discovered the newest lines will drive the equilibrium share K of the researchers down to zero. In other words, this is a case where no research will ever take place in steady-state equilibrium, and thus where the growth process, if any, will be driven entirely by horizontal product development on the initial lines. This is why, in order for both research and development to coexist in a steady state, we must assume $v > 0$.

31. The difference in marginal products of research and development in the production function for secondary innovations is proportional to:

$$\frac{v}{H^r} - \frac{1 - v}{H - H^r},$$

whereas the arbitrage equation (A) can be rewritten as:

$$r - g = \sigma \cdot \left[\frac{H - H^r}{1 - v}\right] \cdot \left[\frac{v}{H^r} - \frac{1 - v}{H - H^r}\right].$$

Thus research has a larger marginal product than development in generating secondary innovations. Research also has a larger marginal product

than development in producing fundamental innovations, since the marginal product of development is simply equal to zero.
32. See Aghion and Howitt (1996) for a detailed proof.
33. Of course, if there was a variable sum for research and development, we would expect to find both our effect and the traditional Schumpeterian effect at work.

References

Aghion, Philippe and Peter Howitt (1992) 'A Model of Growth through Creative Destruction', *Econometrica*, vol. 60 (March), pp. 323–51.

Aghion, Philippe and Peter Howitt (1994) 'Growth and Unemployment', *Review of Economic Studies*, vol. 61, pp. 477–94.

Aghion, Philippe and Peter Howitt (1996) 'Research and Development in the Growth Process', *Journal of Economic Growth*, no. 1.

Aghion, Philippe, Mathias Dewatripont and Patrick Rey (1995) 'Competition, Financial Discipline and Growth', Unpublished paper, April.

Aghion, Philippe, Christopher Harris and John Vickers (1995) 'Competition and Growth with Step-by-Step Technological Progress', Unpublished paper, January.

Atkeson, Andrew and Pat Kehoe (1993) 'Industry Evolution and Transition: The Role of Information Capital', Unpublished paper, University of Pennsylvania.

Blundell, R., R. Griffiths and J. Van Reenan (1995) 'Dynamic Count Data Model of Technological Innovations', *Economic Journal* (March) pp. 333–44.

Bresnahan, Timothy F. and Manuel Trajtenberg (1995) 'General Purpose Technologies: "Engines of Growth?"', *Journal of Econometrics*, vol. 65, pp. 83–108.

Caballero, Ricardo J. and Adam B. Jaffé (1993) 'How High are the Giants' Shoulders: An Empirical Assessment of Knowledge Spillovers and Creative Destruction in a Model of Economic Growth', in *NBER Macroeconomics Annual* (Cambridge, Mass.: MIT Press).

Campbell, John Y. and N. Gregory Mankiw (1987) 'Are Output Fluctuations Transitory', *Quarterly Journal of Economics*, vol. 102 (November), pp. 857–80.

Cannon, Edmund (1995) 'Endogenous Growth and Depreciation of Physical Capital'. Mimeo, Nuffield College, Oxford.

Corriveau, L. (1991) 'Entrepreneurs, Growth, and Cycles', Ph.D. dissertation, University of Western Ontario.

Crafts, N. (1996) 'Economic History and Endogenous Growth', in David Kreps and Ken Wallis (eds) *Advances in Economics and Econometrics: Theory and Applications*, (London: Cambridge University Press).

DeLong, B.J. and Lawrence H. Summers (1991) 'Equipment Investment and Economic Growth', *Quarterly Journal of Economics*, vol. 106 (May), pp. 445–502.

Galí, Jordi and M. Hammour (1991) 'Long-Run Effects of Business Cycles', Unpublished paper, Columbia University.

Grossman, G. M. and E. Helpman (1991) *Innovation and Growth in the Global Economy* (Cambridge, Mass.: MIT Press).

Helpman, E. and M. Trajtenberg (1994) 'A Time to Sow and a Time to Reap: Growth Based on General Purpose Technologies', CIAR Working Paper No. 32 (August).

Jovanovic, Boyan and Yaw Nyarko (1994) 'The Bayesian Foundations of Learning by Doing', Unpublished paper, New York University (April).

Lucas, Robert E., Jr (1993) 'Making a Miracle', *Econometrica*, vol. 60 (March) pp. 251–72.

Nickell, S. J. (1994) 'Competition and Corporate Performance', Institute of Economic Studies, Oxford (March).

Redding, Stephen (1993) 'Invention, Innovation and Technical Progress', M. Phil. thesis, Oxford University.

Reinganum, Jennifer (1989) 'The Timing of Innovation: Research, Development and Diffusion', in R. Schmalensee and R. Willig (eds) *Handbook of Industrial Organization*, vol. I (Amsterdam: North-Holland).

Romer, Paul M. (1990) 'Endogenous Technological Change', *Journal of Political Economy*, vol. 98, pp. S71–102.

Segerstrom, Paul S., T. C. A. Anant and E. Dinopoulos (1990) 'A Schumpeterian Model of the Product Life Cycle', *American Economic Review*, vol. 80, pp. 1077–91.

Shleifer, Andrei (1986) 'Implementation Cycles', *Journal of Political Economy*, vol. 94 (December), pp. 1163–90.

Stadler, George (1990) 'Business Cycle Models with Endogenous Technology', *American Economic Review*, vol. 80 (September) pp. 763–8.

Stiglitz, Joseph (1993) 'Endogenous Growth and Cycles'. NBER Working Paper No. 4286 (March).

Tirole, Jean (1988) *The Theory of Industrial Organization* (Cambridge, Mass.: MIT Press).

Young, Alwyn (1993a) 'Invention and Bounded Learning by Doing', *Journal of Political Economy*, vol. 101 (June), pp. 443–72.

Young, Alwyn (1993b) 'Substitution and Complementarity in Endogenous Innovation', *Quarterly Journal of Economics*, vol. 108 (August) pp. 775–807.

3 Innovation and Growth: The Relationship between Short- and Long-term Properties of Processes of Economic Change

Mario Amendola and Jean Luc Gaffard

I BEYOND ENDOGENOUS GROWTH

Endogenous growth theory focuses on changes in input–output relations in order to bring to light the endogenous sources of growth. This is so whether an increase in the saving rate and hence in the fraction of output invested is considered, as in the simplest models, or a diversion of resources into R&D so as to speed up the process of innovation is instead taken into account, as in the most sophisticated ones. Different productive structures are required to sustain different growth rates, but the appearance of a productive capacity with a different structure, or the production of a new technology, are not simply the matter of a different input/output relationship: allocation of resources is just the preliminary step of a process through which these changes will be brought about: 'The hard part is to model what happens then' (Solow, 1994, p. 52). A shift of resources, which equilibrium models automatically identify with the result that it should bring about, may instead generate a very complex dynamics that can even lead the economy to a collapse.

Endogenous growth models are not suited to bringing this to light. As a matter of fact, they are equilibrium models where the appropriate choice of the relevant conditions (preference parameters, coefficients of the equations and so on), guaranteed by perfect foresight, makes the economy jump immediately to its steady growth rate. This allows a comparative analysis of different endogenous steady growth paths (in the same way as with standard neoclassical models) but not to focus thoroughly on transitional dynamics problems. Although, of course, comparison is here more interesting than in standard analysis, as the association of different growth paths with different preference parameters opens up the possibility of policy interventions that had no essential role in that analysis.

A change from one productive structure to another can only take place through a transition process which must be explicitly taken into account, with the specific problems that it entails. No complementarity and/or co-ordination problems (which necessarily come about during a transition) can arise in economies which are always in equilibrium. Thus, notwithstanding 'that many endogenous growth models produce the characteristic result of coordination failures models: multiple suboptimal equilibria' and 'although the techniques of endogenous growth models have helped to uncover many coordination and adjustment problems, the theory is ultimately rooted in a conventional equilibrium analysis that assumes most of them away' (Howitt, 1994, p. 764). And conventional analysis identifies co-ordination problems only, with co-ordination failures at equilibrium: which is not the real issue in transition processes.

Endogenous growth models, like all equilibrium growth models, are aimed at identifying growth factors and measuring their respective contribution to growth, so as to be able to derive policy implications (in particular through a change in the value of preference parameters). However, there is no attempt to understand the working of the growth mechanism, that is assumed in the model. The actual working of this mechanism may have important bearings on the effective evolution of the economy, though, and on policy implications.

We need, then, a different type of model, which is the expression of a different analytical approach, to deal properly with phenomena that are in the nature of sequential processes in time, such as acceleration of growth or innovation. In particular, we need a representation of the process of production which puts the accent on its time articulation, so as to make the problems of intertemporal complementarity that arise when a structural change implies a break of the existing equilibrium state appear at the analytical level. On the other hand, we also need to stress the co-ordination problems that characterise out-of-equilibrium processes of change and which interact sequentially with the intertemporal complementarity of production, thus sketching out the actual evolution path of the economy.

In this perspective we substitute a sequentially articulated decision process for the optimising behaviour of standard theory. As a consequence, instantaneous price adjustments no longer allow markets to clear systematically, but their functioning obeys stock-flow mechanisms which mediate transactions among agents using periodic price-adjustment rules. These mechanisms show to what extent co-ordination problems arise.

What we can do then is to consider specific working rules and calculate the behaviour of the resulting model, keeping in mind, however, that 'such calculations are of illustrative value only' (Hicks, 1985, p. 87). The model proposed appears thus as an heuristic tool which makes it possible to explore different evolutionary paths of the economy associated with any kind of original shock, in the aim to unveil sequential causality relations which represent the backbone of processes of economic change.

II A SEQUENTIAL MODEL

We shall now present a model (see Amendola and Gaffard, 1988) that gives structure to the above argument, starting from the representation of production carried out by means of production processes of a neo-Austrian type, using a homogeneous primary human resource (labour) to obtain a homogeneous final output used as consumption good. An elementary process of production j is defined by the input vectors:

$$\mathbf{a}_j^c = [a_0, a_1, \ldots, a_n]_j$$
$$\mathbf{a}_j^u = [a_{n+1}, \ldots, a_{n+N}]_j, \tag{3.1}$$

whose elements represent the quantities of labour required in the successive periods of the phase of construction c (from 0 to n) and, following it, of the phase of utilisation u (from $n + 1$ to $n + N$) of the productive capacity of commodity j, and by the output vector:

$$\mathbf{a}_j = [a_0, a_1, \ldots, a_{n+N}]_j, \tag{3.2}$$

whose elements represent the quantities of commodity j obtained in the successive periods of the phase of utilisation of the same productive capacity.

At each given moment t, the productive capacity of commodity j is represented by the intensity vectors:

$$\mathbf{x}_j(t) = [\mathbf{x}_j^c(t); \mathbf{x}_j^u(t)]$$

$$\mathbf{x}_j^c(t) = [x_0(t), x_1(t), \ldots, x_n(t)]_j \qquad (3.3)$$

$$\mathbf{x}_j^u(t) = [x_{n+1}(t), \ldots, x_{n+N}(t)]_j,$$

each element of which is a number of elementary production processes of a particular age, still in the construction phase or already in the utilisation phase.

On the other hand, as a consequence of ageing and of scrapping, the actual number of production processes of type j of different ages carried out at the same moment t is such that:

$$x_{(i)j}(t) = \hat{x}_{(i)j}(t) - u_{(i)j}(t) \; ; \; i = 1, \ldots, n + N \qquad (3.4)$$

$$\hat{x}_{(i)j}(t) = x_{(i-1)j}(t - 1) \; ; \; \hat{x}_{(0)j}(t) = u_{(0)j}(t) \qquad (3.5)$$

where $u_{(0)j}(t)$ is the rate of start of new processes of type j and $u_{(i)j}(t)$ the number of processes of the same type which have been scrapped.

Scrapping of production processes occurs when human or financial resource constraints are so stringent as not to allow all the processes inherited from the past to be carried on.

The 'productive structure' of the economy can then be defined in terms of the age structure of its productive capacity. It has a *horizontal* dimension which, in the case of a plurality of commodities, is expressed at time (t) by the vectors of elementary production processes of the various commodities at different stages of their life – still in the phase of construction $\Sigma_j \mathbf{x}_j^c(t)$ or already in the phase of utilization $\Sigma_j \mathbf{x}_j^u(t)$ – being carried on; which also implies a *vertical* dimension: the time pattern of production associated with this age structure of productive capacity. These, in equilibrium, must be consistent with each other: then, together with construction and utilisation, also investment and consumption, and supply and demand of final output, are harmonised at each given moment of time and over time. An equilibrium age structure of productive capacity also implies a given and stable relation between the relevant economic magnitudes.

We consider two classes of agent: firms and households. All exchanges between them are intermediated by a financial asset – call it 'money' – which is the only one considered in the model; the resources required to carry out production and to sustain consumption are therefore financial resources, not physical output. These resources, for both producers and consumers, come from their participation in current productive activity. External financial resources (that is, resources coming not from productive activity: fiat money and overdrafts, for example) are required when productive activity is expanding, and at the rate at which this expansion takes place. These resources (call them $f(t)$) usually depend on the choices of the monetary authority and/or the banks. In the model they are determined exogenously and dealt with as a control variable.

In each period the firms' level of activity is constrained by available financial resources or, alternatively, by labour supply. Let $m(t - 1)$ be the money proceeds from the sales of final output of the previous period, $f(t)$ the external financial resources, $w(t)$ the wage fund – that is, the resources devoted to finance labour employed on production processes of all kind – $c(t)$ the 'take out' – that is, the resources (consumption by producers, transfer and so on) withheld from the financing of production – also dealt with as a control variable in the model, $h^f(t)$ the monetary idle balances held by firms (desired $h^f_d(t)$, and undesired $h^f_{nd}(t)$). Then the firms' finance constraint which determines $w(t)$ can be written:

$$\tilde{w}(t) = m(t - 1) + h^f(t - 1) - c(t) - h^f_d(t), \qquad (3.6)$$

with $w(t) \equiv \tilde{w}(t)$ if firms are not constrained in their activity by human resources. Otherwise $w(t) \equiv \hat{w}(t)$ where $\hat{w}(t)$ is the wage fund 'constrained' by lack of human resources. In this case we have the appearance of non-desired idle balances:

$$h^f_{nd}(t) = \tilde{w}(t) - \hat{w}(t) > 0, \qquad (3.7)$$

that is, the amount of available financial resources it was impossible to use up in production because of the existence of a human constraint.

Desired idle balances are defined as:

$$h^f_d(t) = \rho(t)[m(t - 1) + h^f(t - 1) + f(t)], \qquad (3.8)$$

and appear when the function $\rho(t)$, which represents the fraction of available financial resources that firms intend to withhold from production because of a loss of confidence in the existing state of affairs, takes a positive value.

Total expenditure by households in period (t) also depends on financial resources available to them; that is, on wages received at the beginning of the period $w(t)$, and on the idle balances $h^h(t - 1)$ (desired

h_d^h and non-desired h_{nd}^h) carried over from the preceding period. If we add to this the 'take out' we obtain, the money value of current demand for final output $y(t)$ is:

$$y(t) = w(t) + c(t) + h^h(t - 1) - h_d^h(t). \qquad (3.9)$$

Desired idle balances, as with producers, pile up when there is a loss of confidence in the existing state of affairs and the function $\sigma(t)$ takes a positive value in the expression:

$$h_d^h(t) = \sigma(t)[w(t) + c(t) + h^h(t - 1)]. \qquad (3.10)$$

Within the sequential setting considered, all prices, including the wage rate, are fixed within each given period and can only change at the junction of one period and the next.

As a consequence, we have:

$$m(t) = \sum_j \min[\, p_j(t)s_j(t);\; p_j(t)d_j(t)], \qquad (3.11)$$

that is, money proceeds are determined by the minimum between the value of current demand d and that of current supply s of final output, which can differ, since we cannot count on price changes to bring demand and supply back into balance within each given period.

Real and monetary stock changes are a substitute for the price changes which cannot take place within each period. Thus excess demand for final output (if any) results in the appearance of undesired idle balances for households:

$$h_{nd}^h(t) = \sum_j p_j(t)[d_j(t) - s_j(t)] \text{ for any } d_j(t) > s_j(t), \qquad (3.12)$$

while excess supply results in an accumulation of undesired stocks o for the firms:

$$o_j(t) = s_j(t) - d_j(t) \text{ for any } s_j(t) > d_j(t). \qquad (3.13)$$

Total labour supply, in each given period t, can be written:

$$L^s(t) = L^s(t - 1)(1 + \iota), \qquad (3.14)$$

where ι is the rate of growth of population.

Total demand for labour, on the other hand, is determined by the activity of construction and utilisation of productive capacity of the different commodities; that is:

$$L^D(t) = \sum_j L^D_j. \tag{3.15}$$

The intensity of productive activity, in turn, depends on available financial resources (the wage fund $w(t)$) and on the wage rate w, which is fixed, as are all prices, for the whole current period. When, because of full employment, labour demand is limited by labour supply, a human constraint stronger than the financial constraint can appear. In this case, productive activity is determined by a 'constrained' wage fund, given by:

$$\hat{w}(t) = w(t)\hat{L}^D_d(t), \tag{3.16}$$

where $\hat{L}^D_d(t)$ is the demand for labour 'constrained'.

The demand for commodity j at time (t), in real terms, can be written

$$d_j(t) = [y_j(t)/p_j(t)]. \tag{3.17}$$

Supply of commodity j at time (t), in real terms, is determined as follows:

$$s_j(t) = [y^*_j(t)/p_j(t)], \tag{3.18}$$

where

$$y^*_j(t) = y_j(t-1)[1 + g_m(t-1)] \tag{3.19}$$

is the money value of final demand expected in the current period, obtained by extrapolating the trend of money proceeds from the sales of final output in the previous period.

Current final production of commodity j will then be:

$$q_j(t) = s_j(t) - \eta[O_j(t-1)]; \; 0 < \eta < 1, \tag{3.20}$$

where η represents the fraction of total real stocks O (if any) put back on the market. Moreover,

$$q_j(t) \le \sum_{i=n+1}^{n+N} b_{(i)j} x_{(i-1)j}(t-1). \tag{3.21}$$

Thus we determine the vectors of production processes in the phase of utilization $\mathbf{x}_j^u(t)$, $\forall_j$, given the scrapping rule, and the fraction of the wage fund required to finance the carrying out of these processes, that is:

$$w^u(t) = \sum_j w(t)\mathbf{a}_j^u\mathbf{x}_j^{u'}(t) \tag{3.22}$$

The resources available for financing construction processes will then be:

$$i(t) \equiv w^c(t) = w(t) - w^u(t), \tag{3.23}$$

and these resources, given the scrapping rule, will determine the vectors of production processes in the phase of construction $\mathbf{x}_j^c(t)$, $\forall_j$, that is:

$$w^c(t) = \sum_j w(t)\mathbf{a}_j^c\mathbf{x}_j^{c'}(t). \tag{3.24}$$

In determining $\mathbf{x}_j^c$ and $\mathbf{x}_j^u$ for the various commodities, the processes scrapped must also be taken into account. This, in each period, depends on the magnitude of final demand related to the utilisation processes, and on the available financial resources as regards construction processes. In other words, there is never a voluntary scrapping of construction processes, which only occurs as a result of a lack of financial resources, while the scrapping of utilisation processes is the result of decisions taken on the basis of given expectations. When there is a final demand constraint, the first processes in the utilisation phase to be cut are the older ones; when there is a financial constraint, the first to be cut is the rate of starts of new processes, then the processes still in the construction phase (first the younger, then the older). This reflects a flexibility criterion that focuses on expected final output (both in its amount and in its nearness in time), and hence on expected profits, as an index of a less stringent expected finance constraint.

The evolution path followed by the economy put out of equilibrium by the attempt to carry out a qualitative change is in fact determined by the behaviour of the control variables $f(t)$ and $c(t)$ and by the adjustment mechanisms represented by changes in prices and wages.

Let the operator g be defined by:

$$g_z(t) = [z(t) - z(t - 1)]/z(t - 1)\forall z(t). \tag{3.25}$$

Then market determined wage rate changes can be written:

$$g_w(t) = v\psi(t - 1) \tag{3.26}$$

where

$$\psi(t) = [l^D(t) - l^s(t)]/l^s(t) \tag{3.27}$$

is the rate of excess demand for labour, and v a reaction coefficient.

On the other hand, market-determined price changes can be written:

$$g_{pj}(t) = \kappa_j\phi_j(t - 1) \tag{3.28}$$

where

$$\phi_j(t) = [d_j(t) - s_j(t)]/s_j(t) \tag{3.29}$$

is the rate of excess demand for the j commodity, and K is a reaction coefficient that can differ for the different commodities. Different values of the coefficients K and v stand for different regulating mechanisms which can be made to represent alternative market organisations.

Money supply is alternatively determined as:

$$f^s(t) = f^s(t - 1)[1 + g_m(t - 1)] \tag{3.30}$$

$$f^s(t) = f^s(t - 1)[1 + g_m(0)], \tag{3.31}$$

that is, its growth rate is set equal to the current growth rate of the economy, or to the original steady growth rate.

Consumption out of profits (the 'take out') is determined as:

$$c(t) = c(t - 1)[1 + g_m(t - 1)\varepsilon^{t-tc}], \mu \geq \bar{\mu} \tag{3.32}$$

$$c(t) = c(t - 1)[1 + g_m(t - 1)], \mu < \bar{\mu}, \tag{3.33}$$

that is, its growth rate is determined in such a way as to increase gradually the amount of resources devoted to finance the construction of new production processes. The reduction in the growth rate of the 'take out' which begins at date t_c goes on until the fraction of resources 'taken out' reaches the value of $\bar{\mu}$.

III VIABILITY OF INNOVATION

Greater resources are required to grow at a higher rate or to sustain innovation, but simple availability of these resources is not a sufficient condition for obtaining the above results. Processes may be stirred by a different allocation of resources, which cast doubts on the viability of the economy rather than conduce it smoothly to the new equilibrium state sought for. The model presented in the preceding section makes it possible to investigate the out-of-equilibrium processes resulting from all types of original shocks. We shall consider in this section the specific case of an innovation that consists in the adoption of a new technique characterised by higher construction costs more than offset by the cost reductions obtained in the phase of utilisation of the new productive capacity.

Take a system that is growing at a steady rate (namely, 2 per cent) which guarantees full employment of labour. Consider the introduction of a new, more efficient in the above sense, technique which takes place at the period $t = 20$ and associate it with a decrease in the 'take out' (from a fraction of 0.3 of firms' proceeds to one of 0.2) in order to channel to production the greater resources required by the innovation process. Assume at the same time an increase in the liquidity preference of both firms and households (rendered in the model by the appearance of desired idle balances as the result of ρ and σ passing from zero to a positive value – that is, 0.01) because of the uncertainty surrounding the innovation process.

With positive but weak price and wage reaction coefficients (0.1 for both) innovation is successful in that the initial fluctuations caused by the introduction of the new technique damp down and the economy converges to a new quasi-regular state where the temporary unemployment brought about by a 'machinery effect' à la Ricardo (see Hicks, 1973) is fully reabsorbed and both the nominal and the real wage increase, together with the share of wages out of income (see Figure 3.1).

This result depends mainly on the co-ordination mechanism represented by the way in which price and wage rate react to disequilibria arriving on the respective markets during the process of innovation. In fact, the different ways of this mechanism's functioning rendered by higher values of the reaction coefficients lead to different results. We have performed twenty simulations corresponding to values of the reaction coefficients, increasing regularly from 0.1 to 2. The fluctuations of the growth rate of the economy, of the wage rate, of the rate of unemployment, of the rate of inflation are stronger the higher the value

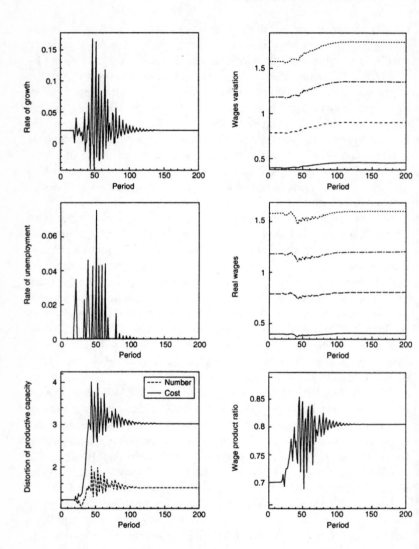

Figure 3.1

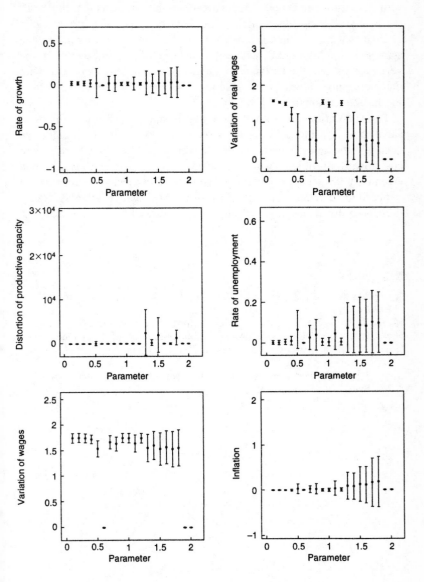

Figure 3.2

of the reaction coefficients. Beyond certain values (1.8 is the threshold) the economy is no longer viable: the distortion of productive capacity is such that all production processes in the phase of construction are scrapped (see Figure 3.2, where the mean values are measured on the vertical axis, and the variance of the different variables associated with the increasing values of the reaction coefficients are measured along the horizontal axis).

The simulations performed show that in the case of a technological shock (but it is the same for all sorts of shocks implying a qualitative change), the interdependence of disequilibria over time bring about co-ordination problems which are a strong threat to viability. It is then essentially the adequate working of co-ordination mechanisms that make it possible to reduce the incoming imbalances which affect not only the market for final output but also the structure of productive capacity.

References

Amendola M. and J. L. Gaffard (1988) *The Innovative Choice* (Oxford: Basil Blackwell).
Hicks, J. R. (1973) *Capital and Time* (Oxford University Press).
Hicks, J. R. (1985) *Methods of Dynamic Economics* (Oxford: Clarendon Press).
Howitt, P. (1994) 'Adjusting to Technical Change', *Canadian Journal of Economics*, vol. 4, pp. 763–75.
Solow R. (1994) 'Perspectives on Growth Theory', *Journal of Economic Perspectives*, vol. 8, pp. 45–55.

4 The 'New' Growth Theory: Old Wine in New Goatskins*

Heinz D. Kurz and Neri Salvadori

> Everything important has already been said
> by someone who did not discover it.
>
> (A. N. Whitehead)

With the inception of systematic economic analysis in the time of the classical economists the problem of what determines the dynamism and growth performance of the economy became a major focus of research in social sciences. Since that time it has always been felt that in order to understand the nature and causes of the wealth of nations and its growth one ought to study first and foremost the 'causes of improvement in the productive powers of labour', as Adam Smith put it, or the factors affecting the development of the 'productive powers of society', to use Karl Marx's concept. It has also always been understood that there is an endogenous side to this process of improvement in social productivity. Reading authors such as Smith, Charles Babbage, Marx or Alfred Marshall one indeed gets the impression that there is no such thing as a purely exogenous change in productive powers. These are seen to rather depend on the actions of individuals and the impact these actions have in fostering economic growth. These actions and their 'growth effectiveness' are envisaged as being shaped by a variety of factors including cultural norms, social institutions, and a nation's policy.[1] In these authors' works, technological and organisational change is portrayed consistently as being essentially endogenous. For example, in Smith's concept of the division of labour, the pace at which capital accumulates (and thus markets expand) is singled out as the factor that is most important for the growth in labour productivity and income per capita (see Smith (1976) bk I, chs I–III; see also Negishi, 1993). The endogeneity of technological progress was also stressed in more recent times by authors such as Allyn Young and, particularly, Nicholas Kaldor, who even attempted – albeit with only limited success – to put the relationship between productivity growth and capital accumulation into algebraic form, in his so-called 'technical progress function'. It was clear to these authors that 'human capital' and 'technological knowledge' do matter, and that improvements in the 'skill, dexterity, and judgment with which labour is applied in any nation' (Smith) are favourable to growth.

Following the boom of interest in growth theory within the economics profession in the 1950s and 1960s, there was a slump in the 1970s and early 1980s, but the second half of the 1980s saw a swift revival of interest in this theory. Robert Solow recently spoke of a 'boomlet' (see Pasinetti, 1994, p. 354). Given the burst of activity which is reflected in a large and still mounting wave of publications on growth, this has now become a fully-fledged boom. In this chapter, emphasis will be on the so-called 'new' or 'endogenous' growth rate theory (henceforth NGT) which presents itself in a bewildering variety of 'new' growth models (henceforth NGMs). The NGT purports to provide, to use Hicks's term, a 'theory of economic history' (see Hicks, 1969), as far as the growth and development of economies is concerned.[2]

There is no objection, in principle, to the elaboration of a theory of economic history or, somewhat less demanding, a model of endogenous technological progress. The question is whether the story told by the NGT is interesting and illuminating, and whether and by how much it goes beyond what we already know. In other words, the question is whether the NGT stands up to its bold claims, or can be expected to do so in the near future. In this chapter we shall, however, ask simpler questions, namely in what sense is the theory really 'new', and in what sense is growth explained 'endogenously'? More specifically, we shall analyse some models of endogenous growth and show how they relate to earlier theories.

The meaning of *endogenous growth* in the 'new' growth literature is that output grows faster than exogenous factors alone would make it grow.[3] The innovation of these contributions relative to the Solovian model is that the rate of technological change, and, a fortiori, the rate of growth, is no longer taken as given from outside, but is envisaged as depending on the 'behaviour' of agents; that is, on their preferences or tastes. In the formalisations this influence is commonly reduced to that of the rate of time discount, or time preference, and the elasticity of substitution between present and future consumption. In some contributions to the NGT the emphasis is on positive exeternalities of the actions of agents. Hence, it can be claimed that the NGT attempts, albeit in a limited sense only, to come to grips with Adam Ferguson's dictum that what is happening in history is 'the result of human action, but not the execution of any human design' (Ferguson, 1793, p. 205). With different preferences, the technological and demographic parameters being the same, the steady-state growth rate will generally be different, essentially because the positive externalities are exploited to a smaller or larger degree: there is a problem of 'market failure'. This is one of the basic messages of one class of NGMs.[4]

The structure of this chapter is as follows. Section I deals with how, in our view, endogenous growth is generated in the NGMs. The following sections verify this view with respect to some NGMs. Given the amount of literature devoted recently to this area of theoretical and applied research, these sections can only deal with a small subset of this literature. Emphasis will be on those contributions that triggered the literary avalanche, since they defined the confines within which much of the later work was carried out. Broadly speaking, the different NGMs analysed in these sections will be scrutinised in an ascending order of difficulty or sophistication; as will become clear, this order deviates from the chronological one. We shall discuss, in Sections II–IV respectively:

(i) 'Linear models', in which our view of how endogenous growth is generated is most easily recognised (Rebelo, 1991; King and Rebelo, 1990);

(ii) The model by Lucas (1988), which focuses attention on the accumulation of human capital; and

(iii) The model by Romer (1986), which emphasises the generation of new knowledge in research and development activities of firms.

Section II also contains a generalisation of the Rebelo model which will be formally expounded in a further publication by us; and Section III makes suggestions about how land and scarce natural resources may be introduced in the Lucas model. Section V introduces some critical remarks, methodoligical and otherwise, on the NGT. Section VI offers some conclusions.

I HOW ENDOGENOUS GROWTH IS GENERATED

The core of every growth theory is the relationship between saving and investment, or the saving–investment mechanism. In the neoclassical model advocated by Robert Solow (1956, 1963), Trevor Swan (1956) and James Meade (1961), this relationship is given by

$$sf(k) = gk,$$

where s is the (marginal and average) propensity to save; $f(k)$ is the per unit of labour production function; k is the capital–labour ratio (labour is measured in terms of efficiency units); and g is the steady-state growth rate of capital (and labour and income). Since in the one-commodity analysis used by these economists the rate of profit r equals the marginal productivity of capital,

$$r = f'(k),$$

the two equations are able to determine a relationship between the rate of profit and the growth rate. In these models the growth rate was conceived as being given exogeneously, and these equations were used to determine the rate of profit – that is, the income distribution.[5] Alternatively, had income distribution been taken as given, the relationship between saving and investment would have determined the growth rate.

The exogenously given saving rate was taken to reflect a multiplicity of factors shaping consumer behaviour. Most of the NGMs have done away with this approach. In the alternative approach, a 'microfoundation' of that behaviour is attempted. A closer look reveals, however, that the microfoundations are rather sparse. It is assumed that there exists an immortal 'representative agent' who is concerned with maximising an intertemporal utility function, $u = u(c(t))$, over an infinite horizon. Choosing the path that maximises consumption involves maximising the integral of instantaneous utility.

$$\int_0^\infty e^{-\rho t} u(c(t)) dt, \tag{4.1}$$

where ρ is the discount rate. As will be seen in Section V, this formulation leads to various difficulties, logical and otherwise, which raise serious doubts about its usefulness. Solow, for perfectly good reasons it would seem, does not think highly of the optimising versions of the new theory: 'the use made of the intertemporally-optimizing representative agent . . . adds little or nothing to the story anyway, while encumbering it with unnecessary implausibilities and complexities' (Solow, 1994, p. 49). Moreover, the adoption of one of these hypotheses about saving is neither a necessary nor a sufficient condition in orter to obtain endogenous growth. This can be seen from the fact that treating the saving rate as a parameter in the NGMs renders these models no more exogenous growth models than the adoption of the representative agent approach rendered some earlier models endogenous growth models (see the review of the earlier models by Lucas, 1988, pp. 6–11).

Different as the three NGMs scrutinshed here may look at first sight, their common feature is the way in which endogenous growth is generated: they determine income distribution; that is, the rate of profit, by technology, profit maximisation, and nothing else. The task to be accomplished by the saving–investment mechanism then consists of nothing else but the determination of the rate of growth.

It is perhaps useful to compare the idea that the rate of profit can be determined by technology (and profit maximisation) alone to the way in which the 'classical' economists, from Adam Smith to David Ricardo, saw how the rate of profit is determined in given circumstances. These economists took the *real* wage rate as given and reckoned wages among the capital advanced at the beginning of the production period. Therefore, real wages were considered 'on the same footing as the fuel for the engines or the feed for the cattle'. In this perspective, labour was seen to be in some sense 'producible': in the simplest case, providing a larger amount of commodities to be distributed in the form of wages, given the real wage rate, may be seen to be equivalent to providing a proportionally larger amount of labour. Taking the real wage rate as given involves adding an extra equation to the price equations and allowed the classical economists to determine the rate of profit. If the 'technology' that 'produces labour' – that is, the real wage rate – is incorporated in the technology producing material commodities, the rate of profit and prices may be *thought of* as being purely 'technologically' determined. In contradistinction, in several of the NGMs the technological determinism of the rate of profit is arrived at by eliminating labour altogether as an 'original' or 'primary' – that is, non-accumulable – factor of production: in its place one finds instead the accumulable factor *human capital*.[6]

It is maintained frequently that the original novelty of the NGMs is that they manage to deal with increasing returns to scale. However, scrutiny shows that this is not the case. What really matters is that returns to scale *with respect to the accumulable factors are at least constant*. This can mean two things: either there are no scarce inputs such as labour or natural resources, as in the models by Rebelo (1991), King and Rebelo (1990), and Lucas (1988); or some externality is introduced in order to obtain that returns to scale *with respect to the accumulable factors* are increasing or, at least, constant, as in the model by Romer (1986) and in a variant of the model by Lucas (1988) here suggested at the end of Section III.

As is well known, a major concern of Ricardo's was the problem of the scarcity of land and the emergence and gradual increase in rents because of intensive and extensive diminishing returns in agriculture. The rise in rents would be detrimental to profits, and with profits as the main source of savings and investment, this would decelerate accumulation and growth. Seen from this perspective, the NGMs, with constant returns to scale with respect to accumulable factors, are comparable to a Ricardian corn model in which *land is a free good*. As a consequence of the lack of scarcity, the rate of profit is constant over time and thus the accumulation rate is also constant over time. On the other side, those NGMs that avoid dealing with scarce natural resources completely could be given the following interpretation: natural resources are taken to be non-scarce – that is, 'free goods', as in J. von Neumann's growth model (von Neumann, [1937] 1945). However, with the system growing for a sufficiently long period of time, the point will surely come where some natural resource(s) will become scarce. In order to avoid this, one has to assume that natural resources are kept in a state of abundance by a sufficiently rapid *exogenous* technological change which reduces the required inputs of natural resources yet leaves unchanged the required inputs of capital. While this assumption is hardly less compelling than the previous one, seen from the vantage point of Ricardo's analysis it seems to be the only one compatible with the NGMs that set aside the problem of scarce natural resources. Put another way, in order for the 'endogenous' growth models to work, a lot of exogenous change, technological and otherwise, has to be presupposed.

The sort of perpetual motion generated by a technology using only inputs produced by themselves bears a close resemblance to Frank Knight's Crusonia plant model (see Knight, 1944).[7] Knight introduced the model as follows:

> We may think of our Crusonia as living on the natural growth of some perennial which grows indefinitely at a constant (geometric) rate, except as new tissue is cut away for consumption. We assume that it requires no cultivation or other care, and we must ignore any 'labour' which may be involved in gathering or simply 'eating' the product.

He stressed that 'The resource must, of course, be of the nature of capital' and added: 'In an economy of the type postulated, the only problem of choice presented to the 'management' will be the determination of the rate of consumption, which is the same as saying the rate of saving and investment or of disinvestment' (ibid., p. 30). In the simplest version contemplated by Knight there are constant returns to investment. In this case the marginal product of investment is independent of the size of the capital stock. However, Knight also discussed the case of decreasing returns to investment. In this case, the growth of the plant (and thus of the economy) would vanish over the course of time. As regards the 'real world', he saw a reason to assume that there are no diminishing returns to investment so long as some part of investment is devoted to the creation of new knowledge (ibid., pp. 41–3).[8] In a nutshell, the research programme of the NGT may be viewed as an attempt to garb Knight's ideas in the cloth of modern long-period intertemporal equilibrium theory. It should be noted, however, that Knight considered the Crusonia plant model only as a pedagogical device that must not be taken too seriously.

II LINEAR MODELS

The simplest way to determine the rate of profit by technology alone is set aside all factors of production that are non-accumulable and to assume that there is a linear relationship between total output, Y, and a broad measure of the accumulable factor, K, both consisting of the *same* commodity:

$$Y = AK, \qquad (4.2)$$

where $1/A$ is the amount of that commodity required to produce one unit of itself. Because of the linear form of the aggregate production function, these models are also known as 'linear models', or with reference to the letters used in Equation (4.2), as 'AK models'. The rate of return on capital r is given by:

$$r + \delta = \frac{Y}{K} = A,$$

where δ is the exogenously given rate of depreciation. There is a large variety of models of this type in the literature. In the two-sector version in Rebelo (1991) it is assumed that the capital good sector produces the capital good by means of itself and nothing else.[9] It is also assumed that there is only one method of production to produce the capital good. Hence the rate of profit is determined by technology alone. The consumption good is produced by means of the capital good and nothing else. Then the saving–investment equation, jointly with the assumption of a uniform rate of growth – that is, a steady-state equilibrium – determines a relationship between the growth rate, g, and the rate of profit, r. Rebelo (1991, pp. 504 and 506) obtains either

$$g = \frac{A - \delta - \rho}{\sigma} = \frac{r - \rho}{\sigma}, \qquad (4.3)$$

or

$$g = (A - \delta)s = sr. \qquad (4.4)$$

Equation (4.3) is obtained when savings are determined on the assumption that the immortal representative agent maximises function (4.1) subject to constraint (4.2), where $Y = c(t) + K$ and

$$u(c(t)) = \frac{c(t)^{1-\sigma}}{1 - \sigma}.$$

Equation (4.4) is obtained when the average propensity to save s is given. Formally, it is identical to the famous 'Cambridge equation' of the post-Keynesian theory of growth and distribution, advocated by Kaldor, Robinson and Pasinetti.[10] Its interpretation, however, is different: the direction of causality is the reverse. Post-Keynesians regard the growth rate as determined by 'animal spirits' of investors; the profit rate is then determined by the saving–investment equation, where savings are taken to adjust to investment through changes in income distribution (see, for example, Kurz (1991) and the papers collected in Panico and Salvadori, 1993). Rebelo assumes, on the contrary, that what is not consumed will be invested, and since the rate of profit is determined by technology alone, the saving–investment equation determines the growth rate.[11]

Essentially the same avenue was followed by King and Rebelo (1990). The characteristic feature of their model is that instead of one kind of 'capital' there are two kinds, real and human, both of which are accumulable. There are two lines of production, one for the social product and the real capital, which consist of quantities of the same commodity, and one for human capital. The production functions relating to the two kinds of capital are given by:

$$H = H(H_H, K_H) \qquad (4.5a)$$

and

$$K = K(H_K, K_K). \qquad (4.5b)$$

Both functions are assumed to be homogeneous of degree one and strictly concave. There are no diminishing returns to (composite) capital, for the reason that there is no non-accumulable factor such as simple or unskilled labour entering into the production of the accumulable factors, investment goods and human capital.[12] As in Rebelo's model, the rate of profit is uniquely determined by the technology (and the maximisation of profits, which implies that only one technique can be used in the long run); the growth rate of the system is then endogenously determined by the saving–investment equation. The larger the propensity to accumulate human and physical capital, the larger the growth rate. This is the essence of the King–Rebelo model. Maximisation of profits implies that (for simplicity, the exogenously given rate of depreciation δ has been set equal to 0):

$$\frac{\partial H}{\partial H_H} = r \qquad (4.6a)$$

$$\frac{\partial H}{\partial K_H} = \frac{r}{p} \qquad (4.6b)$$

$$\frac{\partial K}{\partial H_k} = rP \qquad (4.6c)$$

$$\frac{\partial K}{\partial K_K} = r, \qquad (4.6d)$$

where r is the rate of profit and p is the price of human capital in terms of the commodity which is consumed or accumulated as physical capital. Since functions (4.5a and 4.5b) are homogeneous of degree one, their first derivatives are homogeneous of degree zero, and hence the four equations (4.6a to 4.6d) are enough to determine the four unknowns r, p, $H_H/K_H/H_K/K_K$.[13]

It is not difficult to generalise this model to a case with any number of capital goods. We shall proceed in two steps. We first assume that there is no 'substitution' in production – that is, there is only one technique available. Then the possibility of a choice of technique will be introduced.

Technology is defined by the input–output matrix $\mathbf{A}$ and by a uniform rate of depreciation δ of capital goods.[14] In steady state the rate of profit, r, and the price vector, $\mathbf{p}$, are then determined by the equation:

$$\mathbf{p} = (\delta + r)\mathbf{A}\mathbf{p},$$

that is,

$$r = \frac{1 - \delta\lambda}{\lambda}, \qquad (4.7)$$

where λ is the Perron–Frobenius eigenvalue of matrix $\mathbf{A}$, $0 < \lambda < 1$, and $\mathbf{p}$ is the right-hand eigenvector associated with λ. If only Commodity 1 is consumed and the free disposal assumption holds, then the intensity vector, $\mathbf{x}_t$ and consumption, C_t, both functions of time, must satisfy the inequalities:

$$\mathbf{x}_t^T(\mathbf{I} - \delta\mathbf{A}) \geqq C_t\mathbf{e}_1^T + \dot{\mathbf{x}}_t^T\mathbf{A}, \qquad (4.8a)$$

$$\mathbf{x}_t \geqq \mathbf{0}, \, C_t \geq 0, \qquad (4.8b)$$

where $\mathbf{e}_1$ is the first unit vector and $\dot{\mathbf{x}}_t$ is the vector of the derivatives with respect to time of the vector function $\mathbf{x}_t$. If, following Rebelo, the consumption path is obtained by maximising

$$U = \int_0^\infty e^{-\rho t} \frac{C_t^{1-\sigma}}{1 - \sigma} \, dt$$

subject to the constraints (4.8a) and (4.8b) and the initial condition $\mathbf{x}_0 = $ given, one obtains (see Kurz and Salvadori, 1996) that a steady state with $C_t = C_0 e^{gt}$ and $\mathbf{x}_t = \mathbf{x}_0 e^{gt}$ holds if and only if

$$g = \frac{1 - \delta\lambda - \rho\lambda}{\lambda\sigma}$$

$$\frac{1 - \delta\lambda - \rho\lambda}{1 - \delta\lambda} < \sigma$$

and there is a scalar $\theta > 0$ such that:

$$\bar{\mathbf{x}}^T = \theta\mathbf{e}_1^T[\mathbf{I} - (\delta + g)\mathbf{A}]^{-1}.$$

Hence, because of Equation (4.7):

$$g = \frac{r - \rho}{\sigma} < r.$$

If, alternatively, savings equal s times the income $0 < s < 1$, then in steady-state inequality Equation (4.8a) holds as an equation, inequality Equation (4.8b) holds as a strict inequality, and

$$s\mathbf{x}_t^T(\mathbf{I} - \delta\mathbf{A})\mathbf{p} = \dot{\mathbf{x}}_t^T\mathbf{A}\mathbf{p},$$

which can be stated as

$$s(1 - \delta\lambda)\mathbf{x}_t^T\mathbf{p} = \lambda\dot{\mathbf{x}}_t^T\mathbf{p}.$$

Hence

$$\mathbf{x}_t^T\mathbf{p} = Be^{gt}, \tag{4.9a}$$

where B is a constant depending on the initial conditions and

$$g = \frac{s(1 - \delta\lambda)}{\lambda} = sr. \tag{4.9b}$$

Postmultiplying Equation (4.8a) by $\mathbf{p}$, and taking into account Equations (4.9a) and (4.9b), we obtain

$$C_t = \frac{(1 - s)(1 - \delta\lambda)B}{\mathbf{e}_1^T\mathbf{p}} e^{gt} = C_0e^{gt}.$$

Allow now for 'substitution' in production, but retain the assumptions that returns to scale are constant and that each process produces only one commodity (single production). In this case it suffices to refer to the so-called Nonsubstitution Theorem (Arrow, 1951; Koopmans,

1951a; Samuelson, 1951)[15] to argue that under the given conditions (i) the profit rate and the price vector are uniquely determined; and (ii) if the technology is strictly convex, then in a steady state exactly n processes will be operated (that is, the number of commodities equals the number of processes operated), whereas if the technology is convex but not strictly convex (as in the case of a finite number of processes for each commodity to be produced), then the number of processes that can be operated may be $m \geq n$, but $m - n$ of these processes can be neglected.

III ACCUMULATION OF HUMAN CAPITAL

An early attempt to generate sustained growth at an endogenous rate in a neoclassical framework was that of Uzawa (1965). In his model, the scale factor A in the Cobb–Douglas production function

$$Y = AK^\beta N^{1-\beta}$$

is interpreted as representing human capital per worker. Its growth depends on the amount of labour services allocated to education. Emphasis is in optimal growth paths. With a linear utility function, Uzawa was able to show that the optimal path required that initially all investment be channelled into either physical or human capital until, after some time, a steady state was reached, characterised by uniform exponential growth in both physical and human capital per worker. Uzawa's model was the starting point of several contributions to the NGT.

Lucas (1988) assumed that the economy's representative agent maximises the following utility function:

$$\int_0^\infty e^{-\rho t} \frac{1}{1 - \sigma} [c(t)^{1-\sigma} - 1] \, dt,$$

where $\sigma > 0$ and σ^{-1} is the elasticity of substitution between present and future consumption. In this model agents have a choice between two ways of spending their non-leisure time: to contribute to current production or to accumulate human capital (ibid., p. 17). There is no other way of using one's time. It is essentially the allocation of time between the two alternatives contemplated that decides the growth rate of the system. This is a very peculiar assumption. It implies that leisure time per unit of time is exogenously given. Hence, leisure is not a good of which the amount can be chosen at will. More important, in a model which does not allow for (involuntary) unemployment, the above premise implies that all people that are idle are engaged in the production of human capital. That is, it takes those *not* employed in production as building up their human capital and thus contributing to a larger future output. When applied to interpreting real growth processes, this model misreads reality in a fundamental way: rather than increasing their skills and dexterity, the majority of those on the dole can safely be assumed gradually to lose them. In a sense, Lucas has put Arrow's concept of learning by doing (Arrow, 1962) into reverse: *learning by not doing*.

Lucas's conceptualisation of the process by means of which human capital is built up is simple. Let h be the stock of human capital per unit of labour available at a given moment of time; $1 - u$ the fraction of time spent studying; and v a positive constant, then the change of h over time is assumed to be given by:[16]

$$\dot{h} = vh(1 - u). \tag{4.10}$$

Agents decide according to their preferences about the allocation of their time, that is, fix u, and therefore determine the growth rate of output. For example, a decrease in u involves a reduction in current output growth; at the same time it speeds up the formation of human capital and thereby increases future output growth.

The production of the single good in the economy is given by the following macroeconomic production function:

$$Y = AK^{\beta}(uhN)^{1-\beta}h^{*\gamma}, \tag{4.11}$$

where the labour input consists of the number of workers, N, multiplied by the fraction of time spent working, u, multiplied by h, which gives the labour input in efficiency units. Finally, there is the term h^*. This is designed to represent an external effect associated with the accumulation of human capital: the more human capital society as a whole has accumulated, the more productive each single member will be. The single agent takes h^* as a parameter in his or her optimising by choice of c and u. However, for society as a whole, the accumulation of human capital increases output both directly and indirectly; that is, through the externality. Here we are confronted with a variant of a *public good* problem, which may be expressed as follows. The individual optimising agent faces constant returns to scale in production: the sum of the partial elasticities of production of the factors he or she can control – that is, his or her physical and human capital – is unity. Yet, for society as a whole, the partial elasticity of production of human capital is not $1 - \beta$, but $1 - \beta + \gamma$.

Interestingly, it can be shown that endogenous growth in Lucas's model is obtained in essentially the same way as in the models by Rebelo (1991) and King and Rebelo (1990): the rate of profit is determined by technology and profit maximisation alone; and for the predetermined level of the rate of profit the saving–investment equation determines the rate of growth. Moreover – as Lucas himself has pointed out – the endogenous growth is positive, independently of the fact that there is the above-mentioned externality, that is, independently of the fact that γ is positive. To drive home our point, we shall first deal with the case in which $\gamma = 0$. In a second step we shall then consider the case in which γ is positive.

With the production functions (4.10) and (4.11), and $\gamma = 0$, profits are maximised when

$$w_e = p\upsilon \tag{4.12a}$$

$$r = \beta A \left(\frac{K}{uhN} \right)^{\beta-1} \tag{4.12b}$$

$$w_e = (1 - \beta)A \left(\frac{K}{uhN} \right)^{\beta}, \tag{4.12c}$$

where w_e is the wage per efficiency unit of labour (if w_h is the hourly wage of a worker of skill h, then $w_h = w_e h$), p is the price of human capital in terms of the single commodity that is consumed or accumulated as physical capital, and r is the rate of profit. In conditions of free competition the rate of profit tends to be uniform across the two sectors. This implies that the existing human capital times the rate of profit equals the income obtained from that human capital, that is,

$$rNhp = w_e uNh + \dot{N}hp + N\dot{h}p + Nh\dot{p} \tag{4.13}$$

Since the Non-substitution Theorem holds, p and w_e are uniquely determined in the long run and, therefore, in steady states $\dot{p} = 0$. Then, from Equations (4.10), (4.12a) and (4.13) we obtain:

$$r = \upsilon + \lambda,$$

where λ is the *exogenous* rate of growth of population. There is only one meaning that can be given to the dependence of r on λ: it is a consequence of the remarkable fact that in Lucas's model the growth of 'population' means simply that the immortal consumer grows 'bigger' at rate λ. (Otherwise one would have to assume the existence of another type of externality: costless cultural transmission – that is, the existing knowledge is a free good to new generations.) Thus, as in Rebelo's model, the rate of profit is determined by technology (and profit maximisation) alone. Equations (4.12b) and (4.12c) determine the technique utilised in the commodity sector and the wage rate:

$$\frac{K}{uhN} = \left(\frac{\upsilon + \lambda}{\beta A}\right)^{(\beta - 1)^{-1}}$$

$$w_e = (1 - \beta)A\left(\frac{\upsilon + \lambda}{\beta A}\right)^{\beta(\beta - 1)^{-1}}$$

Hence, if u is constant over time, and K, h and N grow at rates that are also constant over time (that is, the economy is in a steady state), then:

$$\frac{\dot{K}}{K} = \frac{\dot{h}}{h} + \frac{\dot{N}}{N}.$$

Finally, as in the models of Rebelo (1991) and King and Rebelo (1990), the behaviour of consumers (and investors) reflected in the saving–investment equation determines a relationship between the rate of profit and the rate of growth, and since the profit rate is determined by technology (and the choice of technique), the growth rate is *endogenously* fixed. With Lucas's assumptions about saving:

$$\frac{\dot{h}}{h} = \frac{r - \rho}{\sigma} = \frac{\upsilon + \lambda - \rho}{\sigma},$$

which implies that:

$$u = \frac{\upsilon(\sigma - 1) + \rho - \lambda}{\upsilon\sigma},$$

and since $0 \leq u \leq 1$

$$0 \leq \frac{\upsilon + \lambda - \rho}{\sigma} \leq \upsilon.$$

If, contrary to Lucas, savings are taken to be proportional to income, with s as the proportionality factor, then:

$$\frac{\dot{K}}{K} = \frac{\dot{h}}{h} + \frac{\dot{N}}{N} = sr,$$

which implies that:

$$u = \frac{(1 - s)(\upsilon + \lambda)}{\upsilon},$$

and since $0 \leq u \leq 1$

$$\frac{\lambda}{\upsilon + \lambda} \leq s \leq 1.$$

Let us now assume a positive γ. In this case, returns to scale are not constant. Hence, the Non-substitution Theorem does not apply, and this is the reason why neither the profit maximising technique, nor w_e, nor p are determined by technology and profit maximisation alone. As a consequence, r also is not so determined. The simple 'recursive' structure of the model is thereby lost. Nevertheless, technology and profit maximisation still determine, in steady states, a *relationship* between the rate of profit and the rate of growth. This relationship, together with the relationship between the same rates obtained from the saving–investment equation, determines both variables. Thus, although the analysis is more complex, essentially the same mechanism applies.

In fact, if $\gamma > 0$, Equation (4.12) becomes:

$$w_e = p\upsilon \qquad (4.14a)$$

$$r = \beta A h^\gamma \left(\frac{K}{uhN}\right)^{\beta - 1} \qquad (4.14b)$$

$$w_e = (1 - \beta)A h^\gamma \left(\frac{K}{uhN}\right)^\beta. \qquad (4.14c)$$

From Equations (4.14a) and (4.14c) we obtain:

$$\frac{\dot{w}_e}{w_e} = \frac{\dot{p}}{p}$$

$$\frac{\dot{w}_e}{w_e} = (\gamma - \beta)\frac{\dot{h}}{h} + \beta\left(\frac{\dot{K}}{K} - \lambda\right).$$

From the production function Equation (4.11) we obtain that, in steady states,

$$\frac{\dot{Y}}{Y} = \frac{\dot{K}}{K} = \frac{1 - \beta + \gamma}{1 - \beta}\frac{\dot{h}}{h} + \lambda.$$

Hence,

$$\frac{\dot{p}}{p} = \frac{\dot{w}_e}{w_e} = \frac{\gamma}{1 - \beta}\frac{\dot{h}}{h},$$

which, substituted in Equation (4.13) and taking account of Equations (4.10) and (4.14a), gives

$$r = \upsilon + \lambda + \frac{\gamma}{1 - \beta}\frac{\dot{h}}{h}.$$

Before concluding this section we want to show briefly that the Lucas model can easily be generalised to take into account non-produced means of production. If land, Q, is introduced so that the production function in Equation (4.11) becomes:

$$Y = AK^{\beta}(uhN)^{\alpha}Q^{1-\alpha-\beta}h^{*\gamma}, \tag{4.15}$$

by following the same procedure we obtain:

$$r = \upsilon + \frac{\alpha}{1 - \beta}\lambda + \frac{\alpha + \beta + \gamma - 1}{1 - \beta}\frac{\dot{h}}{h}.$$

Note that if $\alpha + \beta + \gamma = 1$ – that is, if returns to scale with respect to accumulable factors are constant – then the rate of profit is determined by technology and profit maximisation alone; otherwise, technology and profit maximisation determine a linear relationship between the rate of profit and the rate of growth.

IV   ENDOGENOUS TECHNOLOGICAL CHANGE

The NGT has singled out, in addition to Uzawa (1965), a paper by Arrow (1962) as an important earlier contribution that anticipated some of the ideas that are prominent with the NGMs. In his paper on 'learning by doing', Arrow related the state variable 'level of technology' of a single firm to another state variable: the amount of capital accumulated in the economy as a whole. In a simplified form, output of firm i can be written as:

$$Y_i = A(K)F(K_i, L_i),$$

where K gives the aggregate stock of capital, and K_i and L_i denote the amounts of capital and labour employed in firm i. In this model, the increase in A is an unintended by-product of the experience accumulated while producing new capital goods. This learning by doing is taken to be purely external to the firms producing and those using the new capital goods.

Romer (1986) took Arrow's model as a starting point. Attention now focuses on the role of a single state variable: 'knowledge' or 'information'. The basic idea is that the information contained in inventions and discoveries (which have become innovations) has the property of eventually being available to anybody to make use of it at the same time. In other words, information is considered to be essentially a non-rival good. However, it is not taken to be totally non-excludable. It is around the two different aspects of 'publicness' (non-rivalry and non-excludability) that the argument revolves. Discoveries are made in research and development departments of firms.[17] This requires that resources be withheld from producing current output. The basic idea of Romer's model is 'that there is a trade-off between consumption today and knowledge that can be used to produce more consumption tomorrow' (Romer, 1986, p. 1015). To this effect he postulates that there exists a (single) 'research technology' that produces 'knowledge' from forgone consumption. Interestingly enough, Romer conceives of 'knowledge' as a magnitude which does not depreciate and can be measured on a single scale as a continuous variable.[18] In other words, it is like non-depreciating Knightian capital.

As regards the conceptualisation of research activities, Romer stipulates a research technology that is concave and homogeneous of degree one,

$$\dot{k_i} = G(I_i, k_i),$$

where k_i is the current stock of private knowledge, I_i is an amount of forgone consumption in research by firm i, and $\dot{k_i}$ is the induced increase in the firm's knowledge.[19] The production function of the consumption good relative to firm i is:

$$Y_i = F(k_i, K, \mathbf{x}_i),$$

where K denotes the accumulated stock of knowledge in the economy as a whole and $\mathbf{x}_i$ are all inputs different from knowledge. These inputs are assumed to be given and constant over time: 'factors other than knowledge are in fixed supply' (Romer, 1986, p. 1019). This premise is comprehensible with respect to labour, since 'a key distinguishing feature of this model is that population growth is not necessary for unbounded growth in per capita income. For simplicity it is left out' (ibid.). The premise is also clear with respect to land of a single (or of different) qualities, whose powers, following Ricardo's approach, could be taken as being 'indestructible'. But the premise would not apply to exhaustible and renewable resources or to capital goods. The amounts available at each moment of time of these factors depend on the decisions of consumers and investors. Hence their amounts cannot be kept constant by assumption. Strictly speaking, Romer's assumption above implies that there are neither exhaustible and renewable resources nor capital goods in the model. Put differently, there exists only labour, Ricardian land, and 'knowledge'. That is, 'knowledge' is the only existing capital utilised in the production of the consumption good. (The forgone consumption good is, on the contrary, a capital good utilised in the production of 'knowledge'.) Spillovers from private research and development activities cause improvements in the public stock of knowledge K. It is assumed that the function is homogeneous of degree one in k_i and $\mathbf{x}_i$ and is homogeneous of degree $\gamma > 1$ in k_i and K.[20]

In order to analyse Romer's 1986 model we shall first assume that $\gamma = 1$. As we have just seen, this was *not* the assumption entertained by Romer. In a second step we shall then take γ to be larger than unity. With $\gamma = 1$ the diminishing returns to k_i are just balanced by the external improvements in technology associated with capital accumulation, such that the marginal product of capital remains unchanged. In fact, profit maximisation requires that

$$p \frac{\partial G}{\partial I_i} = r \qquad (4.16a)$$

$$\frac{\partial G}{\partial k_i} = r \qquad (4.16b)$$

$$\frac{\partial F}{\partial k_i} = rp \qquad (4.16c)$$

$$\frac{\partial F}{\partial x_{ij}} = w_j, \qquad (4.17)$$

where p is the price of 'knowledge' in terms of the consumption good; and w_j is the rental of the jth fixed factor.[21] The derivative of $F(k_i, K, \mathbf{x}_i)$ with respect to k_i is homogeneous of degree zero in k_i and K. Then it depends only on the given vector $\mathbf{x}_i$ and the ratio K/k_i, which, since all firms are taken to be equal to one another, coincides with the (given) number of firms S. That is, since $\mathbf{x}_i$ is a given vector, and since function $G(I_i, k_i)$ is homogeneous of degree one, the three equations in Equation (4.16) involve only three unknowns: r, p, I_i/k_i. As in the models previously dealt with, the rate of profit is determined by technology and profit maximisation alone, so that the saving–investment relationship can determine the growth rate *endogenously*. Once again, endogenous growth is *not* generated by any assumption about increasing returns with regard to accumulable factors, for here returns are constant. (Equations (4.17) determine the rentals of the fixed factors.)

In the case in which $\gamma > 1$, the analysis is much more complicated. First, a steady-state equilibrium cannot exist. From the production function of the consumption good we obtain that:

$$\frac{\dot{Y}_i}{Y_i} = \gamma \frac{\dot{k}_i}{k_i},$$

which, in a steady state, should equal the growth rate of consumption and of forgone consumption. Then the ratio I/k should increase over time and therefore the profit rate r should also increase (see Equation (4.16b)), and this is inconsistent with a steady state.

Romer (1986) is, of course, interested in the existence of an equilibrium.

A priori theorising cannot help much in determining the existence of the equilibrium, but some speculation is possible. Since forgone consumption I_i grows more quickly than 'knowledge' k_i, the rate of profit r, and therefore the growth rate of the consumption good, increases over time. Hence an equilibrium may exist only if r is bounded from above. Romer is in fact forced to assume 'a strong form of diminishing returns in research' (ibid., p. 1019), otherwise consumption would grow too fast and discounted utility would go to infinity.[22] To prevent this from happening he assumes that $G(I_i/k_i, 1) < \alpha$ for each I_i/k_i, $0 \leq I_i/k_i < \infty$, where α is a given constant. If $\lim_{I/k \to \infty} G(I/k, 1) = \alpha$, then also $\lim_{I/k \to \infty} r = \alpha$. Obviously, in this way also the growth rate of consumption, which is related to r by the saving–investment relationship, is bounded. As a consequence, all other growth rates are bounded and an equilibrium could obtain. Romer (1986) has indeed proved that such an equilibrium exists. It deserves to be mentioned, however, that if $\gamma < 1$, then the rate of profit and all the growth rates would decrease indefinitely.

V LIMITATIONS AND DEFICIENCIES OF THE NGMs

The NGMs are designed to contribute to a better understanding of actual growth processes, of both industrialised and developing countries. These models revolve around a few broad and rather obvious ideas that were spelt out time and again in the history of economic thought. What is new is the bold attempt to formalise these ideas within a macroeconomic steady-state framework. However, it can be doubted that the formalisations add significantly to our understanding of growth processes. This section points out what we consider to be some of the most important shortcomings of the NGT.

Nobody could sensibly deny that *structural aspects* play an important role in processes of economic growth and development. These include (i) the endogenous change of the economy's institutional framework in the course of its growth and development; (ii) distributional shifts in output and employment between different sectors of the economy; and (iii) different forms of technological and organisational change. None of these aspects plays a role in the NGT.[23]

As regards *preferences*, in most contributions to the NGT consumption is taken to be the sole end of economic activity. In some formulations, not even leisure is considered to be a good that contributes to the consumer's utility. In these models, saving is thus carried out, in a world of perfect foresight, solely for the purpose of changing the time pattern of the flow of consumption. Many eminent economists have provided reasons for doubting the validity of that crucial assumption (see for example, Steedman, 1981). Even Irving Fisher, whose emphasis on a 'preference for early enjoyment income over deferred enjoyment income' (Fisher, 1977, p. 65) is frequently referred to in textbook treatments of time preference, was well aware of the existence of non-consumption enjoyments. As regards 'the benefits' deriving from 'property and wealth', Fisher expounded:

> a man may include in the benefits of his wealth the fun of running the business, or the social standing he thinks it gives him, or political or other power and influence, or the miserly sense of possession or the satisfaction in the mere process of further accumulation. (ibid., p. 17)

When it is allowed that the holding and accumulation of wealth are desired for their own sakes, then certain familiar results of time-preference theory that underlie most of the NGMs cease to hold. It is only recently that an attempt has been made to take into account the fact, emphasised by generations of economists from Smith, Marx, Max Weber, Frank Knight and Schumpeter to Keynes, that individuals derive satisfaction also from accumulating wealth (see Cole *et al.*, 1992).[24] This is somewhat surprising since the striving to accumulate wealth, or some similar desire, would lead directly to an 'endogenous' explanation of growth, as is the case, for example, with Keynes' 'animal spirits'.

The process of economic growth is indissolubly intertwined with the emergence of *new methods of production and new goods*, the co-existence of different methods of production and the gradual disappearance of presently-known methods and goods. This fact is acknowledged in some versions of the theory of endogenous growth and is given special attention in others. Yet the way this is done involves reducing a world with heterogeneous goods, the variety of which may change, to a world with only a single good. Indeed, using Lancaster's term (Lancaster, 1969), all the different goods produced and consumed represent different amounts of a single *characteristic* only. For example, if a changing (increasing) variety of commodities arising from product innovations is sought to be covered, however imperfectly, by intertemporal utility maximisation it would have to be assumed that all goods to be invented only in the future are already allowed for in the current utility function. Alternatively, there must not be any genuinely new goods but only new products representing different amounts of a single characteristic.

An *aggregate production function* is designed to represent complex microrelations of production in simple terms. The quest for simplicity is most certainly laudable. It should be noted, however, that from contributions to aggregation theory we learn that the conditions for consistent aggregation of microrelations of production to a macrorelation are excessively restrictive, such that the aggregation conditions can safely be assumed never to be realised in reality; as Franklin Fisher (1971) pointed out, the conditions for any such derivation are 'far too stringent to be believable' (see also the papers collected in Fisher, 1993). Despite this finding, the NGT uses aggregate production functions. Sometimes this use is defended on the grounds that these functions fit the data fairly well and their estimated marginal products approximate closely the observed 'factor prices', the wage rate and the profit rate (which is a highly dubious claim). However, this must not be interpreted as rendering some *empirical* credibility to the aggregate production function. According to Fisher (1971) the seemingly good fit is simply an artefact of the constancy of the profit (and thus the wage) share. Hence there is neither theoretical nor empirical support for the aggregate production functions used in many NGMs.

It is an outstanding feature of many contributions to the NGT that they heavily stress *capital*, whether physical or human, as a factor of production, downplaying and sometimes neglecting the role of simple labour and natural resources. In some models there is even only a single factor of production: 'capital'. The overwhelming weight attributed to that factor, its accumulation and incessant qualitative revolution consequent upon the growth in technological knowledge would seem to have as a prerequisite the elaboration of a coherent long-period notion of capital. However, nothing even remotely resembling a serious attempt to come to grips with this problem is to be found in the NGT. On the contrary, the representatives of that theory seem simply to ignore the results of aggregation theory and of the controversy in the theory of capital in the 1960s and 1970s. (For a discussion of that controversy, see Kurz and Salvadori, 1995, ch. 14.)

In his 1956 paper, Solow made it very clear that his analysis was based on extremely simplifying assumptions. In the concluding section of his paper, entitled 'Qualifications', he emphasised:

All the difficulties and rigidities which go into modern Keynesian income analysis have been shunted aside. It is not my contention that these problems don't exist, nor that they are of no significance in the long run. My purpose was to examine what might be called the tight-rope view of economic growth and to see where more flexible assumptions about production would lead to a simple model. Underemployment and excess capacity or their opposites can still be attributed to any of the old causes of deficient or excess aggregate demand, but less readily to any deviation from a narrow 'balance'. (Solow, 1956, p. XXX)

The NGMs share this 'tight-rope view of economic growth' – that is, they set aside economic fluctuations and assume that the economy follows a path characterised by the *full employment of labour and full capital utilisation*.

Solow has repeatedly expressed uneasiness about the general usefulness of this view.[25] Indeed, it is not only *vis-à-vis* current unemployment figures in the OEEC that the assumption of full employment (and full capacity utilisation) appears to be difficult to sustain. As Edmond Malinvaud stressed a few years before the proper take-off of the NGT:

Students of economic growth will easily accept two ideas put forward . . . namely that some disequilibria may be sustained over rather long periods, and that the existence of these disequilibria significantly reacts on the growth process, to speed it up, slow it down or change its course. (Malinvaud, 1983, p. 95)

However, what could easily be accepted by students of economic growth is not actually accepted by many practitioners of growth theory. The main problem with regard to much of growth theory, including the NGMs, is to be seen in the absence of a proper analysis of investment behaviour. As Malinvaud stressed:

an essential part of any theory of economic growth should be the representation of investment, and it seems to me that both excess capacity and profitability have an important role to play in this representation. The investment equation . . . should be the final outcome of the explanation. (ibid, pp. 95–6)

It is a major shortcoming both of the Solovian and of the NGT that no serious attempt is made to represent investment and to analyse the interplay between investment and saving. To assume that 'Say's Law of Markets' holds good is just not satisfactory (see also Sen, 1970).

VI CONCLUDING REMARKS

This chapter has shown how endogenous growth is generated in some of the best-known NGMs. It is a striking common feature of these models, notwithstanding their many differences, that the rate of profit is determined by technology alone, or, if there is a choice of technique, by the profit-maximising behaviour of producers. With the rate of profit determined in this way, the task of the saving–investment mechanism is restricted to the determination of the steady-state growth rate. With a given saving rate, the growth rate is simply the profit rate multiplied by the saving rate. With intertemporal utility maximisation things are slightly more complicated, and the saving rate is endogenously determined.

Two earlier contributions to the theory of growth and distribution have been singled out as anticipating ideas that have become prominent with the NGT. First, there is the 'corn model', in which production is conceived of as being a circular flow, and income net of wages is given by the surplus product which obtains after the requirements of reproduction have been taken care of. Depending on how much of this surplus is consumed and how much is saved and invested, the rate of capital accumulation is smaller or larger. Ricardo's analysis draws attention to the important fact that with diminishing returns resulting from a non-accumulable factor such as land (and setting aside technological progress) the system is bound to end up in a stationary state. Second, there is the Crusonia plant model that Frank Knight introduced for pedagogical reasons. In this model, all non-accumulable factors are set aside. Seen from the vantage point of these two approaches, the NGMs can be grouped as follows. Either all non-accumulable factors are set aside, as in Knight's model, or, if there is (are) non-accumulable factor(s), its (their) efficiency is increased within the economic system such that any tendency of the marginal product of capital to fall with the accumulation of capital is offset exactly. Hence any diminishing returns to capital are effectively banned from the economic system. Given the anticipation of the central ideas of the NGT in earlier authors one may indeed speak of old wine in new goatskins.

Finally, it should be noted that the NGT has revitalised *long-period* analysis, centred around the concept of a uniform rate of profit. In our view this is to be welcomed. At the same time it should be noted that the kind of long-period argument put forward in the NGT falls far behind the present state of the art in this field of research. In particular, it appears to us to be anachronistic to attempt to develop a theory of growth that focuses on product innovations, new 'industrial designs' and so on in terms of a model that does not allow for the heterogeneity of goods, including capital goods, and the diversity of behaviour. The NGT has indeed preserved several of the disquieting features of the neoclassical growth theory of the 1950s and 1960s, which the latter shares with Knight's Crusonia plant, in particular, a homogeneous capital jelly. There is no need, and indeed no justification whatsoever, to continue to dwell on such fairy tales. Modern long-period theory of 'classical' derivation might offer an alternative that allows a better understanding of the phenomena under consideration. In other words, we hope to have shown that many of the interesting aspects of the NGMs are related to the classical perspective on growth they (unwittingly) take. Furthermore, some of their shortcomings derive from the lack of solutions to the problems of the neoclassical theory of growth which were put into sharp relief during the 1960s. It has also been hinted that in some non-neoclassical approaches to the theory of accumulation and growth, the endogeneity of the growth rate has always been taken for granted. A brief look into the history of economic thought shows that from Adam Smith via David Ricardo, Robert Torrens, Thomas Robert Malthus and Karl Marx up to Evsey Domar and Roy Harrod, both the equilibrium and the actual rate of capital accumulation – and thus both the equilibrium and the actual rate of growth of output as a whole – were seen to depend on agents' behaviour.

Notes

* This chapter is a considerably revised version of the paper given by one of its authors at the workshop 'Endogenous Growth and Development' held at The International School of Economic Research, University of Siena, Italy, 3–9 July 1994. Thanks are due to Pompeo Della Posta, Meghnad Desai, Stan Metcalfe, Robert Solow, Ian Steedman and the participants of the workshop for useful discussions, and to the Organising Board and its secretary, JoAnna Warren, for their effective organisation and assistance. Neri Salvadori thanks the MURST (the Italian Ministry of the University and Technological and Scientific Research) and the CNR (the Italian National Research Council) for financial support.
1. In Smith we read about the role of policy: 'Nations tolerably well advanced as to skill, dexterity, and judgment, in the application of labour,

have followed very different plans in the general conduct or direction of it; and those plans have not all been equally favourable to the greatness of its produce' (Smith (1776) 1976, p. 11).

2. Different authors have made this claim with different degrees of circumspection. While some appear to be aware of at least some of the limitations of the NGT, others seem to believe that these limitations can eventually be overcome (see, for example, Grossman and Helpman, 1994, p. 42).

3. The reference is conventionally to the growth in output per capita. However, as we shall see below, in some of the NGMs the notion of output per capita is difficult to ascertain.

4. See, in particular, Romer (1986) and Lucas (1988). This then leads to a discussion of the possibility that economic policy may increase permanently the pace at which income (per capita) grows.

5. The 1950s and 1960s saw the confrontation of two approaches: the post-Keynesian and the neoclassical. According to the former, championed by Nicholas Kaldor (1955–6), Joan Robinson (1956) and Luigi Pasinetti (1962), savings tend to adjust to investment through changes in income distribution, since workers and capitalists are assumed to have different saving habits. Yet despite the difference in the route chosen, both schools of economic thought obtained a relationship between the growth rate on the one hand and income distribution on the other. Since in both of them the growth rate was considered as given from outside the system – that is, was taken to be exogenous – in both theories what was to be determined was income distribution.

6. In these models all income is seen as returns on capital invested.

7. As Dewey (1965, p. 52) pointed out, the properties of the Crusonia plant 'were completely, though cryptically, described by W. S. Jevons as early as 1871'. Reference is to Jevons (1871, pp. 244–9).

8. Knight was, in fact, of the opinion that any kind of investment was to some extent innovative: 'It is practically impossible to imagine any investment activity in the real world which is not in some degree rationally experimental, in the sense of being reasonably expected to lead to new knowledge having some enduring economic significance. That is, all investment consists, in part, of investment in new knowledge' (ibid., p. 40). This was also stressed by Scott (1989).

9. This is reminiscent of Ricardo's famous 'corn model'. In this model 'it is the profits of the farmer which regulate the profits of all other trades' (Ricardo, *Works VI*, p. 104). According to Sraffa's interpretation of this proposition (see Sraffa's Introduction in Ricardo, *Works I*, pp. xxxi–ii) Ricardo assumed that in agriculture the same commodity (corn) forms both the capital (conceived of as consisting of the subsistence necessary for workers plus some seed corn) and the product. The rate of profit in agriculture can therefore be determined as the ratio of the 'surplus product' (net output) and capital advanced at the beginning of the production period – that is, as a ratio between two quantities of corn without any question of valuation. With other sectors employing corn as capital (in the form of wages or as a raw material), and assuming free competition, a uniform rate of profit across sectors would emerge – equal to the agricultural rate – via the adjustment of the prices of the products of these sectors relative to corn.

10. See also Bertola's observation: 'A relaxation of the representative-individual assumption to allow for heterogeneous income sources reveals a striking similarity between these models and post-Keynesian models of income distribution and growth' (Bertola, 1993, p. 1196).

11. It should also be noted that Rebelo assumes a single capital good, whereas post-Keynesian economists generally allow for any number of capital goods; see once again the papers in Panico and Salvadori, 1993. This shortcoming of Rebelo's analysis can easily be remedied, however, as will be shown below.

12. The assumption that the formation of human capital does not involve any unskilled labour as an input is not convincing: the whole point of education processes is that a person's capacity to perform unskilled labour is gradually transformed into his or her capacity to perform skilled labour. For an analytical treatment of the problem of human capital, taking Adam Smith's discussion as a starting point, see Kurz and Salvadori (1995, ch. 11).

13. It is easily checked that if the production functions (4.5) are 'well-behaved', then there is one and only one solution to system (4.6).

14. Here a sketch of the argument must suffice. Rigorous mathematical proofs are provided in Kurz and Salvadori (1996). We assume that matrix $\mathbf{A}$ is invertible and that there is a non-negative vector $\mathbf{z}$ such that $\mathbf{z}^T > \mathbf{z}^T \mathbf{A}$.

15. Since no original factor of production is assumed to exist, differently from the early formulations of the Non-substitution Theorem, we need to assume in addition that there is a commodity that will be produced whatever is the net output of the economy; see Kurz and Salvadori (1994).

16. Lucas actually states function (4.10) as

$$\dot{h} = \upsilon h^{\zeta}(1 - u).$$

where ζ is a positive constant. He hastens to add that it is not sufficient to assume $\zeta > 0$, because 'if we take $\zeta < 1$ in this formulation, so that there is diminishing returns to the accumulation of human capital, it is easy to see that human capital cannot serve as an alternative engine of growth to the [Solovian] technology term $A(t)$.... This formulation would simply complicate the original Solow model without offering any genuinely new possibilities' (ibid., p. 19). Hence, it has to be assumed that $\zeta \geq 1$. Without much further discussion Lucas postulates $\zeta = 1$. It deserves to be stressed that setting $\zeta = 1$ is not just a very special assumption consistent with endogenous growth, but the only assumption consistent with steady-state growth in Lucas's model. For if ζ were to be larger than unity, the growth rate would go up over time. See also Solow (1992).

17. This idea can be traced back to Adam Smith, who observed that 'All the improvements in machinery ... have by no means been the inventions of those who had occasion to use the machines [learning by using]. Many improvements have been made by the ingenuity of the makers of the machines, when to make them became the business of a peculiar trade; and some by that of those who are called philosophers or men of speculation, whose trade it is, not to do any thing, but to observe every thing; and who, upon that account, are often capable of combining together the powers of the most distant and dissimilar objects. *In the progress of so-*

ciety, philosophy or speculation becomes, like every other employment, the principal or sole trade and occupation of a particular class of citizens' (Smith (1776) 1976, p. 21; emphasis added).

18. These assumptions are difficult to sustain. Knowledge is not a variable that can be measured on a single scale; it is in any case not cardinally measurable. It is intrinsically heterogeneous. Different kinds of knowledge are differently useful in production. New knowledge often renders previous knowledge obsolete.

19. The building up of such a function requires that knowledge is cardinally measured.

20. As Romer later admitted, this formulation is inconsistent with the assumption that research is a non-rival good (see Romer, 1994, p. 15). He added that this

> 'may seem like a trifling matter in an area of theory that depends on so many other short cuts. After all, if one is going to do violence to the complexity of economic activity by assuming that there is an aggregate production function, how much more harm can it do to be sloppy about the difference between rival and nonrival goods?' (ibid., pp. 15–16).

(It goes without saying that it is unclear where to stop this process.)

21. It hardly needs to be emphasised that Equations (4.16b) and (4.16c) are meaningless if 'knowledge' is an ordinal concept.

22. In his discrete-time model of growth with only two periods he assumes a simple linear research technology by means of which one unit of forgone consumption produces one unit of knowledge; see Romer (1986, section IV). Obviously, this technology has constant returns.

23. While institutions, cultural norms and so on play no role in the formal part of the NGMs, they are invoked frequently in the interpretative part. For example, different numerical values assigned to the rate of time preference are taken to reflect differences in the cultural setting. However, next to nothing is offered that would explain how these numerical values are arrived at. There is an abundance of *ad hoc* reasoning or, put less favourably, of prejudices garbed in scientific vocabulary.

24. Marx's 'Accumulate, accumulate! This is Moses and the prophets' is perhaps the most emphatic statement of a propensity to accumulate that is not consumption driven. Yet, as Marx stressed, the 'obsession' with capital accumulation is not characteristic of all forms of society, but limited to particular forms only. As Meghnad Desai has impressed on us, Marx, by paraphrasing Luke, referred to old and dated knowledge, or rather mores, thereby implying that the classical economists had no explanation of the motives for accumulation. In private correspondence, Professor Solow pointed out to us that the assumption of a separate desire to accumulate wealth may be interpreted as yet another invitation to *ad hoc* models and that it may be that *ad hoc* models are the best we can provide.

25. In his lecture delivered in Stockholm when he received the Nobel Prize in Economic Science, Solow admitted, with regard to his growth theory: 'I think I paid too little attention to the problems of effective demand' (Solow, 1988, p. 309). He also spoke of 'a standing temptation to sound

like Dr. Pangloss, a very clever Dr. Pangloss. I think that tendency has won out in recent years' (ibid.).

References

Arrow, K. J. (1951) 'Alternative Proof of the Substitution Theorem for Leontief Models in the General Case', in Koopmans (1951b), pp. 155–64.

Arrow, K. J. (1962) 'The Economic Implications of Learning by Doing', *Review of Economic Studies*, vol. 29, pp. 155–73.

Bertola, G. (1993) 'Factor Shares and Savings in Endogenous Growth', *American Economic Review*, vol. 83, pp. 1184–98.

Cole, H., G. Mailath and A. Postlewaite (1992) 'Social Norms, Savings Behavior, and Growth', *Journal of Political Economy*, vol. 100, pp. 1092–125.

Dewey, D. (1965) *Modern Capital Theory* (New York and London: Columbia University Press).

Ferguson, A. (1793) *An Essay on the History of Civil Society*, 6th edn (1st edn 1767), reprinted 1966 (Edinburgh University Press).

Fisher, F. M. (1971) 'Aggregate Production Functions and the Explanation of Wages: A Simulation Experiment', *Review of Economics and Statistics*, vol. 53, pp. 305–25; reprinted in Fisher (1993).

Fisher, F. M. (1993) *Aggregation: Aggregate Production Functions and Related Topics. Collected Papers by Franklin M. Fisher*, J. Monz (ed.) (Cambridge, Mass.: MIT Press).

Fisher, I. (1977) *The Theory of Interest* (Philadelphia); originally published 1930.

Grossman, G. M. and E. Helpman (1994) 'Endogenous Innovation in the Theory of Growth', *Journal of Economic Perspectives*, vol. 8, pp. 23–44.

Hicks, J. R. (1969) *A Theory of Economic History* (Oxford: Clarendon Press).

Jevons, W. S. (1871) *The Theory of Political Economy* (London: Macmillan) reprinted 1965 (New York: Kelley).

Kaldor, N. (1955–6) 'Alternative Theories of Distribution', *Review of Economic Studies*, vol. 23, pp. 83–100.

King, R. G. and S. Rebelo (1990) 'Public Policy and Economic Growth: Developing Neoclassical Implications', *Journal of Political Economy*, vol. 98, pp. 126–50.

Knight, F. H. (1944) 'Diminishing Returns from Investment', *Journal of Political Economy*, vol. 52, pp. 26–47.

Koopmans, T. C. (1951a) 'Alternative Proof of the Substitution Theorem for Leontief Models in the Case of Three Industries', in Koopmans (1951b), pp. 147–54.

Koopmans, T. C. (ed.) (1951b) *Activity Analysis of Production and Allocation* (New York: John Wiley).

Kurz, H. D. (1991) 'Technical Change, Growth and Distribution: A Steady-state Approach to "Unsteady" Growth on Kaldorian Lines', in E. J. Nell and W. Semmler (eds), *Nicholas Kaldor and Mainstream Economics, Confrontation or Convergence?* (London: Macmillan) pp. 421–48.

Kurz, H. D. and N. Salvadori (1994) 'The Non-Substitution Theorem: Making Good a Lacuna', *Zeitschrift für Nationalökonomie*, vol. 59, pp. 97–103.

Kurz, H. D. and N. Salvadori (1995) *Theory of Production. A Long-period Analysis* (Cambridge, Melbourne and New York: Cambridge University Press).

Kurz, H. D. and N. Salvadori (1996) 'A Multisector "AK Model" of Endogenous Growth', Mimeo.

Lancaster, K. (1969) *Introduction to Modern Microeconomics* (Chicago: Rand McNally).

Lucas, R. E. (1988) 'On the Mechanics of Economic Development', *Journal of Monetary Economics*, vol. 22, pp. 3–42.

Malinvaud, E. (1983) 'Notes on Growth Theory with Imperfectly Flexible Prices', in J.-P. Fitoussi (ed.), *Modern Macroeconomic Theory* (Oxford: Basil Blackwell), pp. 93–114.

Meade, J. E. (1961) *A Neoclassical Theory of Economic Growth* (London: Allen & Unwin).

Negishi, T. (1993) 'A Smithian Growth Model and Malthus's Optimal Propensity to Save', *The European Journal of the History of Economic Thought*, vol. 1, pp. 115–27.

Neumann, J. von (1945) 'A Model of General Economic Equilibrium', *Review of Economic Studies*, vol. 13, pp. 1–9. English translation of John von Neumann (1937) 'Uber ein ökonomisches Gleichungssystem und eine Verallgemeinerung des Brouwerschen Fixpunktsatzes', *Ergebnisse eines mathematischen Kolloquiums*, vol. 8, pp. 73–83.

Panico, C. and N. Salvadori (eds) (1993) *Post Keynesian Theory of Growth and Distribution* (Aldershot: Edward Elgar).

Pasinetti, L. L. (1962) 'Rate of Profit and Income Distribution in Relation to the Rate of Economic Growth', *Review of Economic Studies*, vol. 29, pp. 267–79.

Pasinetti, L. L. (1994) 'The Structure of Long-Term Development', in L. L. Pasinetti and R. M. Solow (eds), *Economic Growth and the Structure of Long-Term Development*, Proceedings of the IEA Conference held in Varenna, Italy (London: Macmillan), pp. 353–62.

Rebelo, S. (1991) 'Long Run Policy Analysis and Long Run Growth', *Journal of Political Economy*, vol. 99, pp. 500–21.

Ricardo, D. (1951 ff.) *The Works and Correspondence of David Ricardo*, vols I and VI (referred to as *Works* I and VI), ed. Piero Sraffa with Maurice H. Dobb (Cambridge University Press).

Robinson, J. V. (1956) *The Accumulation of Capital* (London: Macmillan).

Romer, P. M. (1986) 'Increasing Returns and Long-Run Growth', *Journal of Political Economy*, vol. 94, pp. 1002–37.

Romer, P. M. (1994) 'The Origins of Endogenous Growth', *Journal of Economic Perspectives*, vol. 8, pp. 3–22.

Samuelson, P. A. (1951) 'Abstract of a Theorem Concerning Substitutability in Open Leontief Models', in Koopmans (1951b), pp. 142–6.

Scott, M. F. (1989) *A New View of Economic Growth* (Oxford: Clarendon Press).

Sen, A. (1970) 'Introduction', in A. Sen (ed.), *Growth Economics* (Harmondsworth: Penguin), pp. 9–40.

Smith, A. (1976) *An Inquiry into the Nature and Causes of the Wealth of Nations*, first published 1776, *The Glasgow Edition of the Works and Correspondence of Adam Smith*, vol. I (Oxford University Press).

Solow, R. (1963) *Capital Theory and the Rate of Return* (Amsterdam: North-Holland).

Solow, R. M. (1956) 'A Contribution to the Theory of Economic Growth', *Quarterly Journal of Economics*, vol. 70, pp. 65–94.

Solow, R. M. (1988) 'Growth Theory and After', *American Economic Review*, vol. 78, pp. 307–17.

Solow, R. M. (1992) *Siena Lectures on Endogenous Growth Theory* (Siena: Collana del Dipartimento di Economia Politicà, No. 6, Università degli Studi di Siena).

Solow, R. M. (1994) 'Perspectives on Growth Theory', *Journal of Economic Perspectives*, vol. 8, pp. 45–54.

Steedman, I. (1981) 'Time Preference, the Rate of Interest and Abstinence from Accumulation', *Australian Economic Papers*, vol. 20, pp. 219–34, reprinted in I. Steedman (1989) *From Exploitation to Altruism* (Cambridge: Polity Press).

Swan, T. W. (1956) 'Economic Growth and Capital Accumulation', *Economic Record*, vol. 32, pp. 334–61.

Uzawa, H. (1965) 'Optimum Technical Change in an Aggregate Model of Economic Growth', *International Economic Review*, vol. 6, pp. 18–31.

Part II

Growth and Development

5 The Contributions of Endogenous Growth Theory to the Analysis of Development Problems: An Assessment*

Pranab Bardhan

The 'old' growth theory influenced the theory of economic development in several ways. Starting with the basic Harrod–Domar structure of capacity growth, development economists paid attention to the constraints posed by savings and the efficiency with which savings are utilised. The basic model was extended to incorporate structural rigidities constraining the capacity to convert exportables into imports of capital and intermediate goods (leading to the foreign exchange gap as an additional constraint) and the capacity to shift once-installed capital intersectorally (leading to a growth premium on investment allocation in favour of machine-making as in the Fel'dman–Mahalanobis planning model). The optimum growth literature led to a sophisticated discussion of terminal capacity constraints and social time discount rates in the context of development planning. Given the persistence of unemployment and underemployment, and the precapitalist organisation of production in some sectors, the classical growth model (to which Arthur Lewis had drawn attention) was often considered to be more appropriate than the Solow–Swan neoclassical growth model for studying development problems.

Contrary to the claim sometimes made in the literature on the 'new' growth theory, many of the growth models of the 1960s endogenised technical progress in significant ways: apart from Arrow's (1962) celebrated learning by doing model, where learning emanated from the dynamic externalities of cumulated gross investment, and Uzawa's (1965) model of investment in human capital generating technical change, there are the Kaldor–Mirrlees model (1962) where investments is the vehicle of technical progress and Shell's (1967) model of inventive activity.

97

Learning by doing, particularly in the form of acquisition of tacit knowledge and interfirm spillover effects of cumulated gross output influenced development theory by providing a formal rationale for an old argument for support of 'infant' industry producing import-substitutes (or new exports), as in the models of Bardhan (1970) and Clemhout and Wan (1970). In general, the old literature on the microeconomics of technological progress has emphasised the pervasiveness of externalities in the innovation process in the transfer, absorption, development and adaptation of new technologies, and the discussion in development economics of the problems posed by the catching-up process in the developing countries reflected this.

Where, then, are the distinctive contributions of the 'new' growth theory that may be particularly useful for understanding development problems? They certainly do not lie in the so-called convergence controversy which has spawned a large part of published output in the literature.[1] The main result, reached on the basis of dubious cross-country regressions and even more dubious data quality, that the lack of convergence in per capita income growth rates across countries beliefs the standard presumption of the availability of similar technological opportunities in all countries of the world is not particularly earthshaking from the point of view of development economics. As Solow (1994) comments on this body of empirical work: 'I do not find this a confidence-inspiring project. It seems altogether too vulnerable to bias from omitted variables, to reverse causation, and above all to the recurrent suspicion that the experiences of various national economies are not to be explained as if they represent different "points" on some well-defined surface.' In any case, a development economist ploughing through this literature gets hardly any clues (and a lot of red herrings) about the factors determining the crucial international differences in factor productivity growth.

A more substantive contribution of the 'new' growth theory is to formalise endogenous technical progress in terms of a tractable imperfect-competition framework in which temporary monopoly power acts as a motivating force for private innovators. The leading work in this area of what has been called neo-Schumpeterian growth theory is by Romer (1990), Grossman and Helpman (1991), Segerstrom (1991), and Aghion and Howitt (1992). Growth theory has now been liberated from the confines of the competitive market framework of earlier endogenous growth models in which dynamic externalities played the central role (even considering the models of Kaldor, who repeatedly emphasised the importance of imperfect competition in the context of endogenous technical progress, the current models drawing upon the advances in industrial organisation theory are more satisfactory). The major impact of this literature on development theory has been in the area of trade and technological diffusion in an international economy.

* * *

The East Asian success stories have given credence[2] to the belief of many economists in a positive relationship between 'outward-orientation' and economic development (although a rigorous empirical demonstration of the *causal* relationship between some satisfactory measure of outward-orientation and the rate of growth is rather scarce). Standard neoclassical growth theory did not provide any such general theorem on the effect of trade on the long-run growth rate.

A major result in the new literature is to show how economic integration in the world market, compared to isolation, helps long-run growth by avoiding unnecessary duplication of research and thus increases aggregate productivity of resources employed in the R&D sector (characterised by economies of scale). World market competition gives incentives to entrepreneurs in each of these countries to invent products that are unique in the world economy – see the models of Rivera-Batiz and Romer (1991), and Grossman and Helpman (1991), ch. 9. One has, of course, to keep in mind the fact that sometimes these products are unique in the sense of product differentiation but not in the sense of any genuine technological advance (it is well known, for example, that in the pharmaceutical industry a majority of the so-called new products are really recombinations of existing ingredients with an eye to prolonging patent protection, and that they are new, not therapeutically, but from the marketability point of view). Of course, trade often helps transmission of useful ideas in production engineering and information about changing product patterns. But the presumption in many of the models of a common pool of knowledge capital created by international spillovers of technical information is sometimes not relevant for a poor country. When knowledge accumulation is localised largely in the rich country and the poor country is also smaller in (economic) size, particularly in the size of its already accumulated knowledge capital (which determines research effectiveness), the rich country captures a growing market share in the total number of differentiated varieties, and the entrepreneurs in the poor country, foreseeing capital losses, may innovate less rapidly in long-run equilibrium with international trade than it does under autarky, as shown by Feenstra

(1990) and Grossman and Helpman (1991), ch. 9. Trade reduces the profitability of R&D in the poor country as it places local entrepreneurs in competition with a rapidly expanding set of imported, differentiated products and may drive the country to specialise in production rather than research, and within production from high-tech products to traditional, possibly stagnant, industries which use its relatively plentiful supply of unskilled workers – thus slowing innovation and growth.[3] Of course, slower growth does not necessarily mean that the consumer loses from trade: apart from usual static gains from trade, consumers may have access to more varieties innovated abroad. But trade may sometimes cause a net welfare loss, since in the poorer country it accelerates a market failure (underinvestment in research in the initial situation) by allocating resources further away from research.

One should note that the relevant R&D for a poor country is, of course, more in technological adaptation of products and processes invented abroad and in imitation. But even this kind of R&D sector is usually so small that major changes in aggregate productivity and growth on the basis of the trade-induced general-equilibrium type reallocation of fully-employed resources into or away from the R&D sector, as emphasised by Grossman and Helpman, seem a little overdrawn if applied in the context of poor countries.[4] In any case, the ambiguity in the relationship between trade expansion and productivity growth in these general-equilibrium models only confirms similar conclusions in careful partial-equilibrium models, particularly when entry and exit from industries are not frictionless – see, for example, Rodrik (1992).

In the Grossman–Helpman model of the innovating North and the imitating South, with all firms in Bertrand competition with one another, labour costs form the only component of the cost of entry into the imitative-adaptive R&D activity in the South. So, armed with cheaper labour the Southern firms can keep on targeting Northern products relentlessly for imitation, unhampered by many of the formidable real-world non-labour constraints on entry (for example, those posed by the lack of a viable physical, social and educational infrastructure, or that of organisational expertise in a poor country). Also, the Grossman–Helpman models, by adopting Dixit–Stiglitz-style consumer preferences, assume a uniform price elasticity and a unitary expenditure elasticity for each of the differentiated products which enter symmetrically in the utility function. This, of course, immediately rules out what has been a major preoccupation of the trade and development literature: to explore the implications of sectoral demand asymmetries for trade relationships between rich and poor countries. The assumption of monopolistic competition and contestable markets in the models also precludes any serious examination of the impact of trade on growth through the lowering of entry barriers in oligopolistic industries, industry rationalisation and reduction of the gap between actual and best practice international technology that foreign competitive pressure may induce. The Dixit–Stiglitz functional form also narrows the operation of scale economies to take the form of expansion of variety, not in the scale of output.

The slow diffusion of technology from rich to poor countries is often interpreted in the literature as reflecting the frequent laxity in the enforcement of patents in poor countries, and innovators in rich countries are thus compelled to protect their ideas through secrecy. This brings us to the controversial issue of intellectual property rights (IPR), which has sometimes divided the rich and poor countries, as notable in the recent Uruguay Round discussions. Rich countries often claim that a tighter IPR regime encourages innovations (by expanding the duration of the innovator's monopoly) from which all countries benefit. Poor countries often counter this by pointing to their losses following upon increased monopoly power of the larger companies of rich countries, Since the poor countries provide a very small market for many industrial products, the disincentive effects of lax patent protection in those countries may be marginal on the rate of innovation in rich countries, and as such attempts at free riding by the poor countries may make sense, as Chin and Grossman (1990) suggest. To this, Diwan and Rodrik (1991) add the qualification that the disincentive effects may be very significant in the case of innovation in technologies or products that are particularly appropriate for poor countries (for example, drugs against tropical diseases). But both of these theoretical models use a static partial-equilibrium framework. Helpman (1993) recently constructed a dynamic general-equilibrium model of innovation and imitation to discuss the question of IPR. In the long-run equilibrium of his model, a tighter IPR (reducing the rate of imitation by the lower-wage poor country) increases the fraction of the total number of products produced unchallenged by the rich country, but *lowers* the long-run rate of innovation of new products[5] (this works through the rise in the price-earning ratio of the R&D firm in the rich country, consequent upon the general-equilibrium labour reallocation effect of a larger range of manufactured products produced in the rich country).[6] Even apart from this effect on the rate of innovation, a tighter IPR, by shifting production from the lower-wage (and therefore lower-price) country to the higher-wage country makes consumers in both countries worse off.

The discussion advocating a tighter IPR regime also ignores the cases of restrictive business practices of many multinational companies (such as pre-emptive patenting and 'sleeping' patents, where new patents are taken out in poor countries simply to ward off competitors but are seldom used in local production).[7] Furthermore, the flow of technology through direct investments by multinational enterprises to a poor country is often constrained not so much by restrictive government policy in the host country as by its lack of infrastructure (the development of which in turn is constrained by the difficulty of raising large loans in a severely imperfect international credit market).

In fact, while the new models of trade and growth bring into sharp focus the features of monopolistic competition (particularly in the sector producing intermediate products) and, in some models, the Schumpeterian process of costly R&D races with the prospect of temporary monopoly power for the winner – aspects that were missing in most of the earlier macroeconomic growth models – there are other important aspects of imperfect competition (such as the case of 'sleeping' patents discussed earlier, or how international credit market imperfections shape the pattern of comparative advantage)[8] which need formalising in the literature on trade and development.

In another respect, the new literature marks a substantial advance over the old. This relates to the dynamic economies of scale associated with learning by doing. An important extension of the models of Bardhan (1970) and Clemhout and Wan (1970) has been carried out by Krugman (1987) and Boldrin and Scheinkman (1988), where the learning effects (emanating from production experience measured by cumulated industry output) enhance over time the existing sectoral patterns of comparative advantage; this may call for a deliberate trade policy that can orchestrate a breakout from such a historical 'lock-in'.[9]

But these models of learning share with the earlier ones the unrealistic feature of continued learning at a given rate on a fixed set of goods. As Lucas (1993) comments, evidence about learning on narrowly-defined product lines often shows high initial learning rates, declining over time as production cumulates, and for on-the-job learning to occur in an economy on a sustained basis it is necessary that workers and managers continue to take on tasks that are new to them, to continue to move up the quality ladder in goods. The major formulations that try to capture this in the context of an open economy are those of Young (1991) and Stokey (1991). On the basis of learning by doing that spills over across industries, although bounded in each industry, Young's model endogenises the movement of goods out of the learning sector into a mature sector in which learning no longer occurs and thus gives a plausible account of an evolving trade structure. Stokey has a model of North–South trade, based on vertical product differentiation and international differences in labour quality; the South produces a low-quality spectrum of goods and the North a high-quality spectrum. If human capital is acquired through learning by doing and so is stimulated by the production of high-quality goods, free trade (as opposed to autarky) will speed up human capital accumulation in the North and slow it down in the South. A similar result is obtained by Young. (Of course, it does not follow that the South would be better off under autarky.) It also indicates why a policy of subsidising infant export industries is sometimes more growth-promoting in the long run than that of protecting infant import-substitute industries, since in the former case the opportunities for learning spillover into newer and more sophisticated goods are wider than when one is restricted to the home market. Export growth encourages accumulation of technological capability not only in the producer firms but also in the specialised supplier firms through vertical linkage. A high level of skills in the labour force, as in some of the East Asian cases, facilitates this process. The rapid growth of exports also enabled these countries, as Pack (1992) points out, to overcome imperfections in technology markets, such as monopolistic licensing fees, that limit the diffusion of proprietary knowledge and hinder a move towards international best practice.

While the new literature has sharpened analytical tools and made our ways of thinking about the relationship between trade and growth more rigorous, it is high time that more attention is paid to the extremely difficult task of empirical verification of some of the propositions in the literature. While some beginnings have been made – see, for example, the study by Feenstra *et al.* (1992) on the basis of a sample of Korean industries – to confirm the hypothesis of the new growth models that the creation of new inputs generates continuous growth in total factor productivity, the evidence on the link between trade and productivity growth is still scanty and rather mixed. On the basis of a sample of semi-industrial countries in the World Bank project on 'Industrial Competition, Productivity and their Relation to Trade Regimes', Tybout (1992) observes: 'the lack of stable correlations (between trade and productivity) in sectoral and industry-level data is matched by a surprising diversity in the processes of entry, exit and scale adjustment'. From the policy point of view, the new literature on learning and spillover effects, like the earlier development literature on externalities, underestimates the difficulty of identifying the few sectors and locations where the spillover effects may be large and particularly difficult to internalise. Learning is often highly localised and project-specific. Besides, the extent of spillovers depends crucially on the nature of competition that the policy environment promotes and its interaction with the nature of the physical, social and organisational infrastructure in the country.

* * *

While the emphasis in the new growth theory is to search for the factors that perpetuate growth, it is not directly concerned with an older question of development theory: how underdevelopment often tends to persist, and how does a poor country get out of a poverty trap? Yet a fallout of the recent formalisations and explorations of dynamic externalities has been to revive interest in the older question. In the immediate postwar florescence of development economics one idea that was particularly prominent was that of how co-ordination of investments across sectors is essential for industrialisation. The literature that grew out of the famous paper of Rosenstein–Rodan (1943) emphasised that when domestic markets are small (and foreign trade is costly), simultaneous expansion of many sectors can be self-sustaining through mutual demand support, even if by itself no sector can break even (primarily because firms in a sector may not by themselves be able to generate enough sales to render adoption of modern increasing-returns technologies with large fixed costs profitable). There was a presumption in this literature of multiple equilibria and the essential problem was posed as one of escaping a 'low-level equilibrium trap' to a higher-income equilibrium with industrialisation.

To capture the full flavour of this problem of strategic complementarity of industries in terms of market size, one needs a full-scale model of plant-level economies of scale in production (with the associated imperfections in market competition) which can be tapped with large demand spillovers. This formalisation was done in a recent model by Murphy *et al.* (1989). One common objection to such models is that in an open economy where an industry faces the world market, the size of the domestic market cannot plausibly limit the adoption of increasing returns technologies. Such objections usually underestimate how the size of the domestic market matters even in an open economy. In any case, the idea of intersectoral complementarities in investment can be reformulated for an open economy with tradable final outputs, but where jointly used infrastructure (such as roads, railways, power stations or training facilities) and other non-traded support services and specialised inputs (such as repair and maintenance, some ancilliary parts and components, and financial, communication or distribution services) are indispensable for the production and distribution of the final goods. One variant of the models in Murphy *et al.* (1989) shows how in the case of shared infrastructure each industrialising firm that uses it contributes to the large fixed cost of building it and thus indirectly helps other users, hence making their industrialisation more likely. In one of the equilibria of the model the infrastructure will make money on its first-period investment if the economy industrialises, but will incur a large loss if no industrialisation takes place and there are no users of its services. Thus the infrastructure is not built lest an insufficient number of firms industrialise, and this in turn ensures that firms do not make the large-scale investments needed to industrialise. This is an underdevelopment trap caused by a co-ordination failure.

Alternatively, Rodríguez (1993) has a model of multiple equilibria arising from sectoral complementarity and cumulative processes generated by increasing returns in the production of support services and inputs. The tradable final goods require these non-traded intermediate inputs and services readily available in close proximity. The domestic availability of a wide variety of such specialised inputs enhances the productive efficiency of the manufacturing sector, but the extent of input specialisation (or division of labour in their production) is limited by the extent of the market. In such a situation the economy may get stuck in an equilibrium where the division of labour in the input-producing sector is shallow, and the final goods production remains confined to the use of low-productivity techniques that do not require a wide variety of inputs.[10] The task of development policy here is to compensate for an historical handicap (in the form of a trap of low-productivity specialisation), either by trade policy or a policy of subsidisation of fixed costs, or of other ways of encouraging appropriate linkages between the finals goods sector and the intermediate inputs sector. In the model of the preceding paragraph, on the other hand, co-ordination of investments between sectors is the key, and the role of expectations (about investment by other firms) and self-fulfilling prophecy become more important. The task of development policy is to co-ordinate expectations around high investment. This 'history versus expectations' dichotomy in the dynamic processes of how a particular equilibrium gets established has been further analysed by Krugman (1991) and Matsuyama (1991) and the relative importance of the past and expected future is shown to depend on some parameters of the economy (such as the discount rate and the speed of adjustment).

The idea of strategic complementarities between sectors generated by increasing returns must be one of the early examples in the flowering of the general literature on co-ordination failures in economics. It was central to the development economics of the 1950s. Yet it lost much of its intellectual force in subsequent decades, not so much because it lacked, until recently, a firm anchoring in a formal model using tools of imperfect markets equilibrium analysis, as Krugman (1992) suggests, but more because, at the policy level, the difficulties of aggregate co-ordination were underestimated (particularly at the existing levels of administrative capacity and political coherence in the developing countries), and the incentive and organisational issues of micromanagement of capital were underappreciated. The resulting government failures diverted the profession's attention from what nevertheless remains an important source of market failure discovered by early development economics.

Another by-product of the recent formalisations of market size, increasing returns and imperfect competition has been in the area of economic geography, which throws some light on the problem of urban concentration and uneven regional development in the developing countries. Krugman (1994) has a model of the endogenous determination of agglomeration economies out of the interaction among economies of scale at the plant level, transportation costs and factor mobility. (There economies may be particularly important in poor countries, where basic manufacturing using the transport system is still more important than the new footloose service industries, and where the small market size makes the issue of scale economies significant.) The pattern of urban growth and regional inequality are shaped by a tension between centripetal forces that tend to pull population and production into agglomerations, and the centrifugal forces that tend to break up such agglomerations. On the one hand, firms want to locate close to the large market provided by other firms' workers, and workers want to live close to the supply of goods provided by other firms; but on the other hand, commuting costs and urban land rent (not to speak of congestion and pollution) tend to generate diseconomies of city size. While this is no doubt a promising line of enquiry and opens the door for more sophisticated formalisation, here, as in other aspects of the new growth theory, the theoretical models have a long way to go before they can catch up with the complexity of the empirical reality, particularly in developing countries.

Robert Lucas (1988), pondering over the questions of differential development performance of poor countries and what can be done about it, says: 'The consequences for human welfare involved in questions like these are simply staggering: Once one starts to think about them, it is hard to think about anything else.' Coming from a leading economist in the mainstream, which has long marginalised development economics, this is indeed reassuring. But notwithstanding popular impressions to the contrary, the advances made so far in the new literature on growth theory (over and above its rediscovery, with great fanfare, of some of the insights of the old development literature)[11] have barely scratched the surface, and let us hope that the new interest in necessary model-building in this area does not divert us from the tough organisational, institutional and historical issues of underdevelopment which are less amenable to neat formalisation.

Notes

* This chapter is based on the paper written for Workshop VIII organised by the International School of Economic Research at Centosa di Pontignano, Siena, Italy, 3–9 July 1994.

1. For an evaluation of the empirical literature, see Levine and Renelt (1992) and Pack (1994). For an examination of the data quality, see the symposium on Database for Development Analysis in the *Journal of Development Economics*, June 1994.

2. It should, however, be noted that the export boom in manufactures for Korea and Taiwan in the 1960s came *before* any significant trade liberalisation. As Rodrik (1992) suggests, a realistic exchange rate policy and a generous programme of export subsidies, rather than trade liberalisation *per se*, may be the key ingredients for successful export performance.

3. This is at least consistent with the view in the historical studies of Japan's innovation system that restrictions on imports and foreign direct investment may have played a major positive role in regard to R&D effort until the early 1970s. See Odagiri and Goto (1993).

4. It may also be noted that in the Grossman–Helpman (1991, ch. 11) model of imitation, where the poor country grows faster with imitation and trade than without them, it is the process of imitation rather than the integration of product markets *per se* that contributes to a more rapid pace of innovation in the poor country.

5. This result may not be robust for the case where direct foreign investment as well as imitation acts as a channel of technology transfer, as Lai (1993) shows.

6. In a different context, Mookherjee and Ray (1991) have shown that when a dominant firm decides on the adoption of a sequence of potential cost-reducing innovations with Bertrand competition in the product market, a faster rate of diffusion of the latest technology to a competitive fringe

may, over some range, increase the competitive pressure on the leader, quickening the latter's pace of innovations.

7. Some estimates by UNCTAD (1975) suggest that 90–95 per cent of foreign-owned patents in developing countries are not used in those countries.

8. Kletzer and Bardhan (1987) show how more costly credit under imperfect information may drive a poor country away from specialising in sophisticated manufactured products which require more selling and distribution costs than traditional primary products.

9. A similar model of hysteresis, based on self-reinforcing advantages, not of learning but of headstarts in R&D, is developed in Grossman and Helpman (1991), ch. 8.

10. A low initial average level of human capital plays a similar trapping role in the model of Ciccone (1994), where the interdependence between individual human capital accumulation and the supply of specialised physical capital goods may lead to equilibria with no potential for technical progress or growth. Earlier, Azariadis and Drazen (1990) had emphasised the threshold effects of human capital and the multiple balanced growth paths induced by the externalities in the technologies of human capital accumulation.

11. See, on this, Bardhan (1993).

References

Aghion, P. and P. Howitt (1992) 'A Model of Growth through Creative Destruction', *Econometrica*, vol. 60, pp. 322–52.

Arrow, K. J. (1962) 'The Economic Implications of Learning by Doing', *Review of Economic Studies*, vol. 29, pp. 155–173.

Azariadis, C. and A. Drazen (1990) 'Threshold Externalities in Economic Development', *Quarterly Journal of Economics*, 105, (May), pp. 501–526.

Bardhan, P. (1970) *Economic Growth, Development and Foreign Trade: A Study in Pure Theory* (New York: Wiley–Interscience).

Bardhan, P. (1993) 'Economics of Development and the Development of Economics', *Journal of Economic Perspectives*, vol. 7, pp. 129–42.

Bardhan, P. and K. Kletzer (1984) 'Dynamic Effects of Protection on Productivity', *Journal of International Economics*, vol. 16, pp. 45–57.

Boldrin, M. and J. A. Scheinkman (1988) 'Learning by Doing, International Trade and Growth: A Note', in P. W. Anderson, K. J. Arrow and D. Pines (eds), *The Economy as an Evolving Complex System* (Reading, U.K.: Addison-Wesley), pp. 285–300.

Chin, J. C. and G. M. Grossman (1990) 'Intellectual Property Rights and North–South Trade', in R. W. Jones and A. O. Krueger (eds), *The Political Economy of International Trade: Essays in Honor of Robert E. Baldwin* (Cambridge: Basil Blackwell), pp. 90–107.

Ciccone, A. (1994) 'Human Capital and Technical Progress: Stagnation, Transition, and Growth', mimeo, Stanford University.

Clemhout, S. and H. Wan (1970) 'Learning by Doing and Infant Industry Protection', *Review of Economic Studies*, vol. 37, pp. 33–56.

Diwan, I. and D. Rodrik (1991) Patents, Appropriate Technology, and North–South Trade', *Journal of International Economics,* vol. 30, pp. 27–47.

Feenstra, R. C. (1990) 'Trade and Uneven Growth', NBER Working Paper No. 3276 (Cambridge, Mass: NBER).

Feenstra, R. C., J. R. Markusen and W. Zeile (1992) 'Accounting for Growth with New Inputs: Theory and Evidence', *American Economic Review,* vol. 82, pp. 415–21.

Grossman, G. M. and E. Helpman (1991) *Innovation and Growth in the Global Economy* (Cambridge, Mass.: MIT Press).

Helpman, E. (1993) 'Innovation, Imitation, and Intellectual Property Rights', *Econometrica,* vol. 61, pp. 1247–80.

Kaldor, N. and J. A. Mirrlees (1962) 'A New Model of Economic Growth', *Review of Economic Studies,* vol. 29, pp. 174–92.

Kletzer, K. and P. Bardhan (1987) 'Credit Markets and Patterns of International Trade', *Journal of Development Economics,* vol. 27, pp. 57–70.

Krugman, P. (1987) 'The Narrow Moving Band, the Dutch Disease, and the Competitive Consequences of Mrs Thatcher: Notes on Trade in the Presence of Dynamic Scale Economies', *Journal of Development Economics,* vol. 27, pp. 41–55.

Krugman, P. (1991) 'History versus Expectations', *Quarterly Journal of Economics,* vol. 106, pp. 651–67.

Krugman, P. (1992) 'Toward a Counter-Counterrevolution in Development Theory', *Proceedings of the World Bank Annual Conference on Development Economics, 1992,* pp. 15–38.

Krugman, P. (1994) 'Urban Concentration: The Role of Increasing Returns and Transport Costs', *Proceedings of the World Bank Annual Conference on Development Economics, 1994.*

Lai, E. L. C. (1993) 'International Intellectual Property Rights Protection and the Rate of Product Innovation', Unpublished paper.

Levine, R. and D. Renelt (1992) 'A Sensitivity Analysis of Cross-Country Growth Regressions', *American Economic Review,* vol. 82, pp. 942–63.

Lucas, R. E. (1988) 'On the Mechanics of Economic Development', *Journal of Monetary Economics,* vol. 22, pp. 3–42.

Lucas, R. E. (1993) 'Making a Miracle', *Econometrica,* vol. 61, pp. 251–72.

Matsuyama, K. (1991) 'Increasing Returns, Industrialization and Indeterminacy of Equilibrium', *Quarterly Journal of Economics,* vol. 106, pp. 616–50.

Mookherjee, D. and D. Ray (1991) 'On the Competitive Pressure Created by the Diffusion of Innovations', *Journal of Economic Theory,* vol. 54, pp. 124–47.

Murphy, K., A. Shleifer and R. Vishny (1989) 'Industrialization and the Big Push', *Journal of Political Economy,* vol. 97, pp. 1003–26.

Odagiri, H. and A. Goto (1993) 'The Japanese System of Innovation: Past, Present and Future', in R. R. Nelson (ed.), *National Innovation Systems: A Comparative Analysis* (New York: Oxford University Press).

Pack, H. (1992) 'Technology Gaps between Industrial and Developing Countries: Are There Dividends for Latecomers?' *Proceedings of the World Bank Annual Conference on Development Economics, 1992,* pp. 283–302.

Pack, H. (1994) 'Endogenous Growth Theory: Intellectual Appeal and Empirical Shortcomings', *Journal of Economic Perspectives,* vol. 8, pp. 55–72.

Quah, D. and J. E. Rauch (1990) 'Openness and the Rate of Economic Growth', Mimeo, University College of San Diego.

Rivera-Batiz, L. A. and P. M. Romer (1991) 'Economic Integration and Endogenous Growth', *Quarterly Journal of Economics*, vol. 106, pp. 531–55.

Rodríguez, A. (1993) 'The Division of Labor and Economic Development', Mimeo, Stanford University.

Rodrik, D. (1992) 'Closing the Productivity Gap: Does Trade Liberalization Really Help?', in G. Helleiner (ed.), *Trade Policy, Industrialization and Development: New Perspectives* (Oxford: Clarendon Press).

Romer, P. M. (1990) 'Endogenous Technological Change', *Journal of Political Economy*, vol. 98, pp. S71–102.

Rosenstein-Rodan, P. (1943) 'Problems of Industrialization of Eastern and Southeastern Europe', *Economic Journal*, vol. 53, pp. 202–11.

Segerstrom, P. S. (1991) 'Innovation, Imitation and Economic Growth', *Journal of Political Economy*, vol. 99, pp. 807–27.

Shell, K. (1967) 'A Model of Inventive Activity and Capital Accumulation', in K. Shell (ed.), *Essays in the Theory of Optimal Economic Growth* (Cambridge, Mass.: MIT Press), pp. 67–86.

Solow, R. M. (1994) 'Perspectives on Growth Theory', *Journal of Economic Perspectives*, vol. 8, pp. 45–54.

Stokey, N. (1991) 'The Volume and Composition of Trade between Rich and Poor Countries', *Review of Economic Studies*, vol. 58, pp. 63–80.

Tybout, J. R. (1992) 'Linking Trade and Productivity: New Research Directions', *World Bank Economic Review*, vol. 6, pp. 189–211.

UNCTAD (United Nations Conference on Trade and Development) (1975) *The Role of the Patent System in the Transfer of Technology to Developing Countries* (New York: United Nations).

Uzawa, H. (1965) 'Optimal Technical Change in an Aggregative Model of Economic Growth', *International Economic Review*, vol. 6, pp. 18–31.

Young, A. (1991) 'Learning by Doing and the Dynamic Effects of International Trade', *Quarterly Journal of Economics*, vol. 106, pp. 369–405.

6 Development and Theories of Endogenous Growth*

T. N. Srinivasan

I THE DEVELOPMENT PROCESS

J. Schumpeter (1961) contrasted mere growth of the economy (that is, growth of its population and wealth) with development, which he viewed as 'a distinct phenomenon, entirely foreign to what may be observed in the circular flow or in the tendency towards equilibrium. It is spontaneous and discontinuous change in the channels of flow, which forever alters and displaces the equilibrium existing' (p. 69). He emphasised the role of innovations and the concomitant private anticipation of entrepreneurial profit as major factors explaining development. While Schumpeter had the development of contemporary developed or industrialised countries in mind, economists writing after the Second World War on development of contemporary developing countries described them variously as being caught in a 'vicious circle of poverty', 'a low level equilibrium trap', 'a set of interlocking vicious circles' and so on. Indeed, Hirschman (1958) argued that 'once development has started, the circle is likely to become an upward spiral – [and that] development depends not so much on finding optimal combination for given resources and factors of production as on calling forth and enlisting for development purposes resources and abilities that are hidden, scattered or badly utilized' (p. 5) and that 'Development presumably means the process of *change* of one type of economy *into* another more advanced type' (p. 52, emphasis in the original).

The economists' view of the development process as breaking out of a pre-existing equilibrium has its parallels in the view of policymakers that development involves a break from tradition towards modernity. Prime Minister J. Nehru of India put it thus: 'But we have to deal with age-old practices, ways of thought, ways of action. We have to get out of many of these traditional ways of production, traditional ways of distribution and traditional ways of consumption. We have to get out of all that into what might be called modern ways of doing so ... The test of a country's advance is how far it is utilizing modern

111

techniques . . . Modern technique is not just getting a tool and using it. Modern technique follows modern thinking. You can't get hold of a modern tool and have an ancient mind. It won't work' (Nehru, 1961).

Briefly stated, the development process involves a structural transformation of a technologically-backward economy with a subsistence sector (agriculture) that has a large share (exceeding half) in output and an even larger share (exceeding two-thirds) in employment; a population experiencing high fertility *and* mortality; a workforce with low literacy and skills; with its exports concentrated in a few primary products; with many markets (for example, for risk bearing and sharing) missing or imperfectly functioning (for example, capital and credit markets) or segmented (for example, labour markets); and above all poorly endowed with economic (power, transport and communications), social and administrative infrastructure. Once the transformation is completed, it becomes a technologically modern economy experiencing self-sustained growth, low fertility *and* mortality, with a literate and skilled labour force, a diversified production, employment and foreign trade structures, well-functioning markets for goods and services (including insurance and credit), and well-endowed with an efficiently operating economic infrastructure.

Four processes were emphasised by early development economists as being central to development: accumulation of physical and human capital; technical change; demographic transition; and foreign trade and investment. The respective roles of the state and the market in the development process were also matters of much debate among them. Interestingly, recent contributions to growth theory involve the very same processes, except demographic transition. Development economists were acutely aware of the pervasiveness of externalities (particularly with respect to human capital) and scale economies at early stages of development. For example, Mandelbaum (1945) argued that although

social and political factors determine the sequence in which different areas enter into the process of industrial advance – in an open international system, advantages once gained tend to become cumulative and handicaps to be perpetuated so that in the end poor countries may remain poor just because they were poor to begin with . . . In highly developed countries a new firm or industry will benefit from those cost-reducing services which an established industrial system supplies in the form of better transport facilities, training of workers, more highly organized labor and capital markets, and so forth. It is different in less advanced areas, where new enterprises, while conferring advantages on those to follow, have to increase costs and risks for which they are not compensated by external economies already in existence . . . Moreover, where the established producers of the leading industrial countries have built up monopolistic positions and exercise price discrimination in international markets, newcomers are at an additional disadvantage. Stronger and more permanent measures of state assistance than are visualized by the classical infant industry argument will then be required to provide an effective shelter against the monopolistic competitor.

At any rate, there is no reason why poor countries should accept as a datum a specialisation among regions which, since it is based on existing cost relationships, is rational only with regard to given conditions of underdevelopment. These conditions may be summarised under the headings 'Lack of Demand and Lack of Capital' (Mandelbaum, 1945, p. 4). These very same arguments of cumulative causation, path dependence and hysteresis (that is, the influence of initial conditions and the long lasting effects of 'small' and temporary shocks) reappear in endogenous growth theory.

The scarcity of physical capital and the paucity of savings were viewed as being critical bottlenecks. Mandelbaum (1945) is typical: 'in poor peasant countries average incomes are so low and the propensity to consume is so high that little is saved and left own for investment'. While noting that 'development would proceed more quickly, if the home savings . . . were supplemented by foreign loans on reasonable terms', Mandelbaum anticipated the problems that might arise if foreign loans were used to augment domestic *consumption* instead of *investment*, if only partially. The reason was that such diversion would result in default of such loans and 'even *if* their servicing is possible, it causes a fall in the real income of the borrowing country whose capacity to produce has not increased *pari passu* with loans received' (p. 9). Arthur Lewis (1954) was emphatic that the

central problem of economic development is to understand the process by which a community which was previously saving and investing 4 or 5 percent of its national income or less converts itself into an economy where voluntary saving is running at about 12 to 15 percent of national income or more. This is the central problem because the central fact of economic development is rapid capital accumulation (including knowledge and skills with capital). (p. 155)

Unfortunately, Arthur Lewis did not anticipate that unless capital was used efficiently, increasing rates of investment need not result accelerated rates of growth of GDP. According to the World Bank (1993, tables 2 and 9), while the weighted average of gross domestic investment as a proportion of GDP (with each country's share in World GDP in 1987 as its weight) in low- and middle-income developing countries had risen to 23 per cent by 1970 and was 24 per cent in 1991, the weighted average of annual growth rates of GDP *declined* from 5.3 per cent during 1970–80 to 3.3 per cent in 1980–91. Be that as it may, the view that physical capital was the most critical bottleneck and, hence, its accumulation has to be speeded up, augmenting domestic savings as well as by actively seeking external capital, motivated the choice of particular growth models in policy-making in developing countries in the 1950s and 1960s (see below).

The importance of human capital accumulation in the development process was stressed early, notably by T. W. Schultz (1961). However, even Schultz viewed human capital as being complementary to physical capital in the development process by stressing the low rate at which poor countries can absorb additional physical capital. He argued that

The new capital available to these countries from outside as a rule goes into the formation of structures, equipment and sometimes also into inventories. But it is generally not available for additional investment in man. Consequently, human capabilities do not stay abreast of physical capital, and they do become limiting factors in economic growth. It should come as no surprise, therefore, that the absorption rate of capital to augment only particular nonhuman resources is necessarily low. (p. 7)

The role played by human capital in many, though not all, of the recent models of growth is different: it is not just another input into the production process (albeit complementary to other inputs such as physical capital) with diminishing marginal returns, but one (particularly in the form of knowledge capital) with the characteristics of a non-rival public good and whose accumulation can make marginal returns to other inputs, particularly physical capital, increasing rather than diminishing.

It should also be pointed out that while there was an extensive debate in the early development literature about the choice among techniques of production that differed in their labour intensity from short-run employment-maximising versus long-run growth-maximising perspectives, and the production-enhancing effffect of sectoral shift in resources in the process of development was recognised, the role of technical progress (that is, expansion of the set of available techniques) was not that much emphasised. Once again, the emphasis on the latter, in particular the endogenisation of the process of technical change, distinguishes the recent growth literature from earlier literature on growth and development. It will now turn to the growth models used in development analysis.

II EARLY MODELS OF GROWTH AND DEVELOPMENT

One could distinguish three strands in the growth theoretic literature of the 1960s and earlier. The first strand is *positive* or, better still, *descriptive*, theory aimed at explaining the stylised facts of long-run growth in industrialised countries (particularly in the United States of America) such as a steady secular growth of aggregate output, and relative constancy of the share of savings, investment, labour and capital income in aggregate output. These stylised facts themselves had been established by the works of empirically oriented economists, such as Abramovitz (1956), Denison (1962) and Kuznets (1966), who were mainly interested in accounting for observed growth. Solow's (1956, 1957) celebrated articles and later work by Jorgenson and Griliches (1966) and others are examples of descriptive growth theory and related empirical analysis. Uzawa (1961, 1963) extended Solow's descriptive one-sector model into a two-sector model. As Stiglitz (1990) remarked, by showing that the long-run steady state growth rate could be unaffected by the rate of savings (and investment), even in the short run, the rate of growth was mainly accounted for by the rate of labour augmenting technical progress, Solow challenged then conventional wisdom.

The second strand is *normative* theory, which drew its inspiration from Ramsey's (1928) classic paper on optimal saving. In contrast to the descriptive models in which the aggregate savings rate was exogenously specified (usually as a constant over time), the normative models derived time-varying savings rates from the optimisation of an intertemporal social welfare function. There were mainly two variants of such normative models: one-sector models (for example, Koopmans (1965) and Cass (1965)), and two-sector models (Srinivasan (1962, 1964) and Uzawa (1964)). The contribution of Phelps (1961) is also normative, but it focused only on the steady-state level of consumption per worker rather on the entire transitional time path to the steady state, and solved for that savings rate which maximised the steady-state level of consumption per worker.

The third strand of theory is primarily neither descriptive nor normative, though it is related to both. Harrod's dynamic extension of the Keynesian model (with its constant marginal propensity to save) raised the issue of stability of the growth path by contrasting two growth rates: the *warranted* rate of growth that would be consistent with maintaining the savings–investment equilibrium, and the *natural* growth rate as determined by the growth of labour force and technical change. In this model, unless the economy's behavioural and technical parameters keep it on the knife edge of equality between warranted and natural growth rates, there would be either growing underutilisation of capacity if the warranted rate exceeds the natural rate, or growing unemployment if the natural rate exceeds the warranted rate. Indeed, this knife-edge property was viewed by Solow (1956) as resulting from the assumption that capital and labour are used in fixed proportions, and led him to look for growth paths converging to a steady state by replacing Harrod's technology with a neoclassical technology of positive elasticity of substitution between labour and capital. However, Harrod disclaimed ever having made such an assumption!

J. von Neumann's (1945) model is also part of the third strand. In this model, production technology is characterised by a finite set of constant return-to-scale activities, with inputs being committed at the beginning and outputs emerging at the end of each discrete production period. There are no non-produced factors of production such as labour or exhaustible natural resources. In the 'primal' version, von Neumann characterised the vector of activity levels that permitted the maximal rate of *balanced growth* (that is, growth in which outputs of all commodities grew at the same rate) given that the outputs of each period were to be ploughed back as inputs in the next period. In the 'dual' version, a vector of commodity prices and an interest rate were derived which had the properties that the value of output of each activity was no higher than the value of inputs inclusive of interest and that the interest rate was the lowest possible. Under certain assumptions about the technology, von Neumann showed that, first, the maximal growth rate of output of the primal was equal to the (minimal) interest rate associated with the dual; and second, the usual complementary slackness relations obtained between the vector of activity levels, prices, growth and interest rates.

Although *prima facie* there is no normative rationale for balanced growth and the maximisation of the growth rate, particularly in a setup with no final consumption of any good, it turned out that the von Neumann path of balanced growth at the maximal rate has a 'normative' property. As Dorfman *et al.* (1958) conjectured, and Radner (1961) later rigorously proved, given an objective that is a function only of the terminal stocks of commodities, the path starting from a given initial vector of stocks that maximises this objective would be 'close' to the von Neumann path for 'most' of the time, as long as the terminal date is sufficiently distant from the initial date regardless of the initial stocks and of the form of the objective function. This so-called 'turnpike' feature was later seen in other growth models in which final consumption is allowed and production involves the use of non-produced factors. For example, in the Koopmans–Cass model, in which the objective is to maximise the discounted sum of the stream of utility of per capita consumption over time, a unique steady-state exists which is defined by the discount rate, the rate of growth of the labour force and technology of production. *All* optimal paths, that is, paths that maximise the objective function and start from different initial conditions, converge to this steady state regardless of the functional form of the utility function. As such, all optimal paths stay 'close' to the steady state path for 'most' of the time. Models from each of these strands were used in early development analysis.

With the scarcity of physical capital seen as being the major cause of low incomes in developing countries, and the propensity to save and invest as the constraints on its accumulation, and hence, on the growth of income, the Harrod–Domar closed economy model came in handy for a variety of development planning exercises. It combined a very simple Keynesian model of savings with an equally simple model of production, in which physical capital was the only input (or equivalently, all other inputs including labour are assumed to be in excess supply for ever). Thus, with a constant average propensity s to save out of income Y, the total savings $S - sY$. With savings assumed to equal investment (that is, in the absence of a Keynesian effective demand constraint) and with a constant incremental capital output ratio k the change in income, ΔY, would equal sY/k (assuming for simplicity that capital does not depreciate). This in turn meant that the *growth rate* $\Delta Y/Y = g$ of income would equal s/k or $g = s/k$. This simple growth equation was used to solve for any one of the three variables g, s and k, given the other two. Thus, given a *target* rate of growth g_T and the value of k, the *required* savings ratio would be kg_T, so that domestic resource mobilisation effort could be geared to achieving these savings. This was a *planning or normative* use of the model. Used in a *positive* mode, one derived the growth rate g as the outcome of the given savings rate and capital–output ratio. A somewhat unconventional normative use was to infer the required capital–output ratio to achieve a growth target g_T, given the savings rate s as $k = s/g_T$. Efforts to improve the efficiency of capital use could then be devoted to achieving this required k. An early use of the Harrod–Domar model in a development plan was in India's First Five-Year Plan.

It was also obvious that by augmenting domestic savings S by foreign capital inflow F, investment could be raised to $S + F$, so that the Harrod–Domar equation became modified to $g = (s + f)/R$, where f was the foreign capital inflow as a proportion of income or GDP. In a typical normative use, given a growth target g_T, savings rate s and capital–output ratio k, the required foreign capital inflow or foreign aid as a proportion of GDP became $(kg_T - s)$. The other normative as well as positive uses of this augmented growth equation are straightforward.

The next step, following Chenery and Bruno, was to introduce another constraint on development identified in the early writings; namely, the capacity to import as determined by foreign capital inflow and export earnings (assumed fixed exogenously in keeping with export pessimism in its extreme form). Thus, if to operate a unit of capacity one needed m units of imports of intermediaries and if each unit of investment required d units of domestic input and x units of imported input, choosing units of measurement such that all prices are unity, and assuming for simplicity that there are no imports of consumer goods, one can write the domestic savings constraint on investment as $dI \leq X - C - E$. This expresses the fact that the domestic input requirement of investment cannot exceed what is available, that is, gross output X net of domestic consumption C and exports E. Assume for a moment that E is set at some level below the exogenous upper limit $\overline{E}$. The capacity to import constraint can then be written as $xI + mX \leq E + F$, where the left-hand side represents the demand for imports for investment (xI) and maintenance (mX) and the right-hand side represents the capacity to import – that is, the sum of exports E and foreign inflow F. By adding the two constraints one gets $(x + d)I + mX \leq X - C + F$, or $(x + d)I \leq (1 - m)X - C + F$. By the choice of units and price normalisation $(x + d) = 1$ and $(1 - m)X$ represents value added or income. Thus $(1 - m)X - C$ is income minus consumption; that is, domestic savings S. Thus $I \leq S + F$, or the value of investment, cannot exceed the sum of domestic savings and foreign capital inflow. Denoting $(1 - m)X$ as Y, assuming that consumption C equals $(1 - s)Y$, one can rewrite the two constraints as:

$$d\,I \leq X - (1 - m)(1 - s)X - E = [1 - (1 - m)(1 - s)]\,X - E$$

and

$$x\,I \leq -mX + E + F.$$

Given a capacity constraint $\bar{X}$ on output, the maximum feasible investment in the economy is constrained by domestic savings and equals.

$$[(1 - (1 - m)(1 - s))\,\bar{X} - E]/d, \text{ if } \bar{X} \leq (E + dF)/[m + s$$
$$(1 - m)(1 - d)]$$

(the fact that $d + x = 1$ has been used in deriving this inequality). If $\bar{X}$ exceeds this limit, the maximum feasible investment is constrained by the capacity to import and equals $(E + F - m\bar{X})/x$.

I have not so far brought in the exogenous limit $\bar{E}$ on exports. It is clear from the above that when the domestic savings constraint is binding at some $E \leq \bar{E}$ it will be binding even if E is set at $E = \bar{E}$. Thus, with surplus capacity to import, investment is a decreasing function of exports E. Hence it is possible to increase investment by reducing exports to a level E' that will exhaust the surplus import capacity. It is easy to show that $E' = \bar{X}[m + s(1 - m)(1 - d)] - dF$, and the resulting investment $I = s(1 - m)X + F$. This is nothing but the equation that investment equals the sum of savings at full capacity income $(1 - m)X$ and foreign capital inflow F.

If, given $E = \bar{E}$, the capacity to import is binding (so that there is surplus domestic savings) investment *increases* with E at any $E \leq \bar{E}$, and hence by setting $E = \bar{E}$ one can raise investment to $(\bar{E} + F - mX)/x$. Thus the model yields:

Situation A

$X = \bar{X}, I = s(1 - m)\,\bar{X} + F, E = E' = \bar{X}\{m + s(1 - m)(1 - d)\} - dF$
if $\bar{X} \leq (E + dF)/[m + s(1 - m)(1 - d)]$

Situation B

$X = \bar{X}, I = (E - m\bar{X} + F)/x, E = \bar{E}$
if $\bar{X} > (E + dF)/[m + s(1 - m)(1 - d)]$.

An important inference drawn from the above model is that when the economy is import constrained (Situation B), an extra unit of foreign aid increases investment by $1/x > 1$ units (as long as domestic savings still does not bind), whereas if it is savings constrained (Situation A), it yields only one unit of additional investment. The case for external aid is much strengthened in the first case. Of course, the extreme rigidities about input use and the pessimism about exports heavily influence the results.

The analytics of the case for investment in heavy industry can be seen from the two-sector Mahalanobis–Fel'dman model, which by assuming a closed economy, excluded foreign trade altogether. In the simple discrete time version, with all inputs other than capital assumed to be in surplus for ever, the output of consumer goods C_t in period t equals $B^c K_t^c$, where K_t^c is the capital stock, and B^c the output–capital ratio, in the consumer goods sector. Total investment I_t equals the output $B^i K_t^i$ of the capital goods, where K_t^i is the capital stock, and B^c the output–capital ratio in the capital goods or the heavy industry sector. Assuming that, once installed, capital lasts for ever, and cannot be shifted from one sector to the other, and there is a one period lag between investment and capacity creation, one obtains $K_{t+1}^i - K_t^i = r I_t$ and $K_{t+1}^c - K_t^c = (1 - r)I_t$ where r is the proportion of total investment I_t that is invested in heavy industries. It is straightforward to solve this system to yield:

$$K_t^i = K_0^i (1 + rB^i)^t \text{ and } K_t^c = K_0^c + (1 - r)K_0^i [(1 + rB^i)^t - 1]$$

Several conclusions follow from the model. First, the long-run growth rate of consumption and investment is *the same* – it equals rB^i, which is an *increasing* function of the productivity B^i of capital in the capital goods industry and the proportion r of investment devoted to heavy industry. Thus from a *growth* perspective, the consumption goods industry is utterly irrelevant. Second, at one extreme if $r = 0$ so that the entire output of the capital goods sector is invested in the consumptions goods industry, the output of consumer goods will grow *linearly* over time at the rate $B^i K_0^i$. Third, at the other extreme, if $r = 1$ so that the entire output of the capital goods output sector is invested in heavy industry, there is no growth of consumer goods but capital goods industry grows for ever at the rate of rB_i. This is the Stalinist strategy taken to its extreme limit. Fourth, and more generally, the path of output of *consumption goods* associated with some r in the open interval $(0, 1)$ will cross from below at some finite time and remain above *for ever thereafter*, any path associated with a lower value of r. Thus, higher *consumption* in the long run is achieved by greater investment in heavy industry.

Mahalanobis used this model essentially to draw attention to the point that current sacrifices in the sense of slower growth of the consumption goods sector will have a long-term payoff. However, he did not bring in time-preference explicitly into the analysis to evaluate this tradeoff. Also, introducing an additional labour-intensive technique of production of consumer goods and a service sector, he put together a four-sector model. This was the framework for India's Second Five-Year Plan (1956–61). It articulated a development strategy in which a significant part of aggregate investment was devoted to heavy industries, and the problem of consumption (as well as employment) was to be tackled through expanding small-scale and cottage industries which Mahalanobis believed were efficient though labour-intensive. It is no exaggeration to say that the Mahalanobis strategy has continued to underpin all subsequent five-year plans in India.

The multisector planning models drew their analytical tools from the Leontief Input–Output System. In its static version, given the $n \times n$ matrix $A \equiv (a_{ij})$ of input coefficients, where a_{ij} is the amount of sector i's output required as input for producing a unit of output of sector j, $(i, j = 1, 2, \ldots n)$ the material balance equations for the economy could be written as $X = AX + D$, where $\mathbf{X}$ is the column vector of gross outputs and $\mathbf{D}$ is the column vector of final demands. Formally, one can solve for the gross output vector X as $(I - A)^{-1}D$. If the economy is viable then the solution of X given *any* non-negative D must be non-negative. This, in essence, means that the inverse matrix $(I - A)^{-1}$ will consist of non−negative elements. If A satisfies the so-called Simon–Hawkins conditions, then $(I - A)^{-1}$ will be non-negative and the technology will be viable. Besides the intermediate input requirements (a_{ij}), the k primary-factor requirements can be represented by a $k \times n$ matrix $F \equiv = ((f_{ij}))$ where f_{ij} represents the amount of lth primary factor required per unit of output of sector j, $l=1, \ldots k, j=1, \ldots n$. Thus the primary factor requirements for meeting final demand D is equal the column vector $\mathbf{F} (I - A)^{-1}D$.

The development planning uses of the model are straightforward. As above, given a target final demand vector D_T (which in turn is the sum of consumption demand vector $\mathbf{C}$, investment demand (by sector of origin) vector I and the *net* export demand vector $\mathbf{E} - \mathbf{M}$, (that is, the difference between $\mathbf{E}$, the gross export vector, and $\mathbf{M}$, the gross import vector), one solves for a consistent gross output vector $\mathbf{X}_T = (I - A)^{-1}\mathbf{D}_T$ and primary factor requirement vector $\mathbf{F}(I - A)^{-1}\mathbf{D}_T$. The feasibility of the planned target D_T can be judged by comparing the required vector of primary factors with the vector of their availabilities.

Given the emphasis on import substitution, one particular use of the input–output model was of interest then. Imports were divided into two categories; those that competed with domestic production, called *competitive imports*, and those imports for which there was no potentially substitutable domestic production, called *non-competitive imports*. The final demand component of the latter was set exogenously and the intermediate demand could be calculated once the gross output vector was determined, as in the case of primary factor requirements. The strategy of import substitution was obviously related to competitive imports. A target for import substitution in each sector was often defined in terms of a target for the share of imports in total domestic use. For example, in sector i, if this target share was m_i^T, then the level of competitive imports was $M^{Ti} = m_i^T(X_i^T + M_i^T)$ or $M_i^T = m_i^T X_i^T/(1 - m_i^T)$. Thus the vector of competitive imports could be solved as $\mathbf{M}\mathbf{X}^T$ where M is a diagonal matrix with $m_i^T/(1 - m_i^T)$ as the ith diagonal element. Given other elements of final demand and exogenously set export target E^T one could solve for the gross output target vector $\mathbf{X}^T$ that will achieve the desired import substitution targets. Numerous other planning exercises were done with the static input–output model.

A dynamic model, with an input–output matrix and an associated capital coefficients matrix was often used to determine not only gross output targets but the associated investment both in terms of sectors of origin and of destination. This is not the occasion to elaborate the development use of various input–output matrix-based, and more generally, activity-analysis-based, dynamic models, except to point out that the usually unique von Neumann type balanced growth path of such models was used as the 'terminal' path to be reached at the end of the plan period from given initial conditions (see Eckaus and Parikh (1968) for one such use for India). However, it should be emphasised that the assumption of fixed technical coefficients (that is, the absence of substitution possibilities in production among material inputs and factors) was natural given the structuralist predilections of planners and their total disregard for prices and markets.

The dual economy models, as their name indicates, were based on the view that the economy was 'dualistic'. It consisted of two sectors. The larger of the two was the traditional rural–agricultural sector, in which market penetration was assumed to be insignificant. Production, mainly for subsistence, was organised in household-based units (farms), land and labour were the chief inputs, and work and output sharing was the rule. The smaller sector was the modern urban-manufacturing sector which produced for the market and in which inputs of capital and labour were used in a constant-returns-to-scale production function by firms that maximised profits through appropriate choice of inputs. The assumed organisational and behavioural differences between the sectors were the reasons for the model to be termed 'dualistic'!

In the Lewis (1954) version of the model, the urban wage was fixed so that profit maximising firms, given their capital stock, employed labour up to the level at which the marginal product of labour equalled the fixed product wage. Given constant returns to scale, the distribution of capital stock among firms was irrelevant, so that total capital stock determined urban employment. As long as the marginal product of labour in the traditional sector was less than that of labour in the modern sector (given fixed terms of trade between the two sectors) there was surplus labour in the traditional sector. The rate of accumulation of capital followed from Lewis's classical assumption that firms invested all their profits. The simple dynamics of the model continued to hold as long as there was a labour surplus that could be drawn from the traditional sector. A formal analysis of the dynamics and the determination of the turning point at which the labour surplus is exhausted, and so on can be found in Fei and Ranis (1964), who also allow for the terms of trade to be determined by the market.

Another strand of the literature on dual economy models is the one that originated with a seminal article by Harris and Todaro (1970), in which, given a non-market-clearing modern sector real wage, which is higher than the traditional sector real wage, workers migrate from the latter to the former sector until the *expected* real wage in the modern sector that takes into account the positive probability unemployment equals the traditional sector wage. Subsequent writers have analysed the implications of this model for policy intervention, protection and shadow pricing. A large number of increasingly complex and mainly irrelevant models have appeared in the literature, taking off from the simple Harris–Todaro model which at least had a germ of empirical truth in it.

A brief mention should also be made of the debates (and the vast literature they spawned) on investment criteria and choice of techniques of production. Once it is admitted that for various reasons the market wage in the modern sector was higher than social opportunity cost of labour to that sector, it is clear that the technique associated with the profit-maximising calculus of firms would be more capital intensive. It would generate less employment than the technique at which marginal product of labour equalled its social opportunity cost. But, given that only profits generated investment, and hence the future capital stock as well as employment, by using the latter rather than the former technique, more employment would be generated in the present at the cost of less employment in the future. If externalities in the future were pervasive, then the private market rate of return to investment would differ from its social rate of turn, and a conflict between private and social considerations in investment decisions would arise. These issues discussed in the 1950s and 1960s were reflected also in the literature on optimising planning models and in the debates about policy use of 'shadow' prices of goods and factors. These models were precursors of the later literature on social cost–benefit analysis and project evaluation, which was also concerned with the same set of issues. In many ways, some of the simple rules of project evaluation emerging from this literature are successful attempts to derive robust general equilibrium shadow prices. This is achieved without either having it build general equilibrium models or lapse into using simplistic partial equilibrium models that most, though not all, early writers on choice of techniques and investment criteria often used.

The one-sector descriptive growth models in which the savings rate was exogenously specified (and the two-sector models in which the share of investment devoted to the capital goods sector was exogenous) soon led to models in which the savings rate (or the investment share) was endogenous and determined through the maximisation of an intertemporal welfare function. This literature was not exclusively development-oriented and although the debates in it about how this function should be defined: for example, whether the welfare of future generations should be accorded a lower weight than that of the present generation and so on, were important, it is fair to say that it did not influence policy thinking, let alone policy-making directly. Somewhat more influential were the multisector static and dynamic linear optimising models, in part because they were flexible enough to incorporate several *ad hoc* constraints that policy-makers believed were relevant. For example, in the 1960s and 1970s, when foreign aid donors tied their aid to purchases in their own countries and often to the purchase of specific commodities, these models allowed separate constraints to be introduced for the earning and use of 'free' or untied foreign exchange and for the use of tied aid. Even the perception that the world demand for and marginal revenue from exports of particular commodities from a country were downward-sloping can easily be accommodated in such linear models. Capacity and location constraints, import substitution targets, gestation lags in investment, anticipated productivity increases and so on could all be modelled.

It is worth emphasising that, in keeping with the temper of the times, real-life markets and prices played essentially no role in the optimising planning models. The only prices were those churned out by the model itself: namely, the 'shadow' prices or marginal values in units of the chosen objective function of a small change in the level of each constraint. The interpretation of these shadow prices (and their derivation from market prices as the needed taxes or subsidies) was straightforward if the constraint happened to relate to a commodity or service traded in a market. The shadow prices of *ad hoc* constraints not of this nature were often hard to interpret. Worst of all, the shadow prices, because of the linear character of the models, were not robust – a small perturbation of one constraint could make the shadow price of that or some other constraint change from being positive to zero. Further, few (if any) of these models had any meaningful macroeconomic features, so that issues relating to nominal price inflation and so on were incapable of being handled. Thus the belief that such a model will generate an 'optimal' plan that could be implemented through an appropriate set of taxes, subsidies, and credit policies was naïve.

It is fair to say, however, that the more knowledgeable policy-makers were not only not naïve but were also clear in their minds as to the utility of plan models as a fairly inexpensive way of generating *consistent and efficient* alternative plan scenarios. And these scenarios (particularly those that varied aid patterns and levels) came in handy in negotiations with aid donors, including multilateral agencies such as the World Bank. These agencies, and particularly private foundations, often financed modelling exercises and research at foreign universities and also helped by enabling countries to acquire modelling capabilities. Occasionally, clumsy attempts were made by those (without a full understanding of the limitations of such models) to make political use of model results to modify policies of the developing country that was modelled.

A celebrated case of such an attempt was by some at the Centre for International Affairs at Massachusetts Institute of Technology (MIT). Based on results from a model, they commented critically on India's Third Five-Year Plan and tried to persuade the Planning Commission to modify it through their discussions with the Indian Ambassador in Washington without first presenting the results to those economists in India at the Planning Commission and outside who knew the limitations of the MIT model for their critical evaluation. Rosen (1985) presents a fascinating description of this unfortunate episode. Be that as it may, the World Bank itself devoted a significant amount of its resources in building models for both internal use and for some developing countries.

The volume Blitzer *et al.* (1974), sponsored by the World Bank and appropriately entitled *Economy-wide Models for Development Planning* surveyed the then state-of-the-art of such modelling. This volume continues to be a good guide to the models' extent as of that time. A more recent survey is by Robinson (1989), which also covers the literature on Applied General Equilibrium Models.

III   RECENT MODELS

Barring a few exceptions to be noted below, in the neoclassical growth models production technology was assumed to exhibit constant returns to scale and in many, though not all models, smooth substitution among inputs with strictly diminishing marginal rates of substitution between any two inputs along an isoquant was also posited. Analytical attention was focused on conditions ensuring the existence and uniqueness of steady-state growth paths along which all inputs and outputs grew at the same rate – the steady state being the path to which all transitional paths, starting from any given initial conditions and satisfying the requirements of specified descriptive rates of accumulation or of intertemporal welfare optimality, converged. The steady-state growth rate was the *exogenous* rate of growth of labour force in efficiency units, so that in the absence of (exogenous) labour-augmenting technical progress, output per worker was constant along the steady state.

Turning to the exceptions, Solow (1956) himself drew attention to the possibility that a steady state need not even exist, and even if one existed it need not be unique. Indeed, output per worker could grow indefinitely, even in the absence of labour-augmenting technical progress, if the marginal product of capital was bounded below by a sufficiently high positive number. Helpman (1992) also draws attention to this. In addition, there could be multiple steady states, some of which were unstable if the production technology exhibited non-convexities. We return to these issues below.

There were also exceptions to the exogeneity of technical progress and of the rate of growth of output along a steady state. In the one-sector, one-factor models of Harrod and Domar and the two-sector models of Fel'dman (1928, as described in Domar (1957)) and Mahalanobis (1955), marginal capital–output ratios were assumed to be constant so that, by definition, marginal product of capital did not decline. Growth rate was *endogenous* and depended on the rate of savings (investment) in such one-sector models, and on the aggregate rate of investment and its allocation between sectors producing capital and consumer goods in the two-sector models. Kaldor and Mirrlees (1962) endogenised technical progress (and hence the rate of growth of output) by relating productivity of workers operating newly-produced equipment to the rate of growth of investment per worker. And there was the celebrated model of Arrow (1962) of 'learning by doing', in which factor productivity was an increasing function of cumulated output or investment. Uzawa (1965) also endogenised technical progress by postulating that the rate of growth of labour-augmenting technical progress was a concave function of the ratio of labour employed in the education sector to total employment. The education sector was assumed to use labour as the only input. Uzawa's model has influenced recent contributions to growth theory. Besides, in the literature on induced innovation (Ahmad (1966), Boserup (1965), Kennedy (1964)) technical change was, by definition, endogenous.

The recent revival of growth theory started with the influential papers of Lucas (1988) and Romer (1986). Lucas motivated his approach by arguing that neoclassical growth theory cannot account for observed differences in growth across countries and over time and its evidently counter-factual prediction that international trade should induce rapid movements toward equality in capital–labour ratios and factor prices.[1] He argued that 'In the absence of differences in pure technology then, and under the assumption of no factor mobility, the neoclassical model predicts a strong tendency to income equality and equality in growth rates, tendencies we can observe within countries and, perhaps, within the wealthiest countries taken as a group, but which simply cannot be seen in the world at large. When factor mobility is permitted, this prediction is powerfully reinforced' (Lucas (1988), pp. 15–16). He then goes on to suggest that the one factor isolated by the neoclassical model, namely, variation across countries in technology:

has the potential to account for wide differences in income levels and growth rates ... when we talk about differences in 'technology' across countries we are not talking about knowledge in general, but about the knowledge of particular people, or particular subcultures of people. If so, then while it is not exactly wrong to describe these differences [as] exogenous ... neither is it useful to do so. We want a formalism that leads us to think about individual decisions to acquire knowledge, and about the consequences of these decisions for productivity.

He draws on the theory of 'human capital' to provide such a formalism: each individual acquires productivity-enhancing skills by devoting time to such acquisition and away from paying work. The acquisition of skills by a worker not only increases his or her productivity, but by increasing the average level of skills in the economy as a whole, it has a spillover effect on the productivity of all workers.

Romer also looked for an alternative to the neoclassical model of long-run growth to escape from its implications that 'initial conditions or current disturbances have no long-run effect on the level of output and consumption ... in the absence of technical change, per capita output should converge to a steady-state value with no per capita growth' (Romer, 1986, pp. 1002–3). His is 'an equilibrium model of endogenous technological change in which long-run growth is driven primarily by the accumulation of knowledge by forward-looking, profit-maximizing agents' (p. 1003). While the production of new knowledge is through a technology that exhibits diminishing returns, 'the creation of new knowledge by one firm is assumed to have a positive external effect on the production possibilities of other firms ... [so that] production of consumption goods as a function of stock of knowledge exhibits increasing returns; more precisely, knowledge may have an increasing marginal product' (p. 1003).

It should be noted that the spillover effect of the average stock of human capital per worker in the Lucas model and of knowledge in the Romer model are externalities unperceived (and hence not internalised) by individual agents. However, for the economy *as a whole* they generate increasing scale economies even though the perceived production function of each agent exhibits constant returns to scale. Thus by introducing non-convexities through the device of a Marshallian externality, Lucas and Romer were able to work with an intertemporal competitive (albeit a socially non-optimal) equilibrium. Thus both avoid facing the problem[2] that R&D that leads to technical progress is 'naturally associated with imperfectly competitive markets, as Schumpeter (1942) had forcefully argued ...' (Stiglitz, 1990, p. 25). Later work by others (for example, Grossman and Helpman, 1991) formulated models in which firms operating in an imperfectly competitive markets undertook R&D.

In sorting out the differences between neoclassical and recent growth models it is useful to start with Solow's growth model. Solow assumes an aggregate production function,

$$Y_t = A_t F(K_t, b_t L_t), \tag{6.1}$$

where Y_t is aggregate output at time t; K_t is the stock of capital; L_t is labour hours at time t; A_t ($A_0 \equiv 1$) is the disembodied technology factor (that is, index of total factor productivity), so that output at time t associated with any combination of capital stock and labour input in efficiency units is A_t multiplied by that at time zero with the same combination. Analogously, b_t (with $b_0 \equiv 1$) is the efficiency level of a unit of labour in period t, so that a unit of labour at time t is equivalent to b_t units of labour at time zero. Thus the technical progress induced by increases in b_t is *labour augmenting*. It is easily seen that technical progress through A_t is Hicks neutral, and that through b_t is Harrod neutral.

Let us denote by $\bar{k}_t \equiv \dfrac{K_t}{b_t L_t}$, the ratio of capital to labour in efficiency units in period t, and by $k_t = \dfrac{K_t}{L_t}$, the ratio of capital to labour in natural units, $y_t \equiv \dfrac{Y_t}{b_t L_t}$, the level of output or income per unit of labour in efficiency units. Solow made the following crucial assumptions:

Assumption 1 (Neoclassical)
F is homogeneous of degree 1 in its arguments and concave.

Given Assumption 1, the average product of an efficiency unit of labour, that is, $\dfrac{1}{b_t L_t} F(k_t, b_t L_t)$ equals $F(\bar{k}_t, 1)$. Let $f(\bar{k}t) = F(\bar{k}t, 1)$. Clearly, concavity of F implies concavity of f as a function of $\bar{k}_t$. In fact, f is assumed to be strictly concave with $f(0) = 0$.

Assumption 2 (Inada)

$$\lim_{k \to 0} f'(\bar{k}) = \infty \quad \text{and} \quad \lim_{k \to \infty} f'(\bar{k}) = 0.$$

In a closed economy, assuming that labour is growing exogenously as $L_t = (1 + n)^t L_0$, human capital or skill level is growing exogenously as $b_t = (1 + b)^t$, capital depreciates at the rate δ per period, and denoting by c_t the level of consumption per efficiency unit of labour, we have:

$$\bar{k}_{t+1} = \frac{A_t f(\bar{k}_t) + (1 - \delta)\bar{k}_t - c_t}{(1 + n)(1 + b)}. \tag{6.2}$$

Solow further assumed that the savings rate is constant, that is, $c_t = (1 - s)y_t$. Then Equation (6.2) becomes:

$$\bar{k}_{t+1} = \frac{sA_t f(\bar{k}_t) + (1 - \delta)\bar{k}_t}{(1 + n)(1 + b)} \qquad (6.3)$$

Equation (6.3) is the fundamental difference equation of the Solow model. If there is no disembodied technical progress so that $A_t = 1$ for all t, then the phase diagram of the dynamic system can be represented as in Figure 6.1. It is clear from Figure 6.1 that starting from any arbitrary initial capital labour ratio $\bar{k}^*$, the economy will converge (ignoring the inessential problem caused by discreteness of time) to the steady-state $\bar{k}^*$ in which all the per capita variables, including per capita income, will grow at the rate b. Thus if $b = 0$ per capita income, consumption and savings do not grow along the steady state. Further, policies that permanently affect savings rate or fertility rate will have no long-run growth effects.

It is clear from Figure 6.1, however, that out of the steady state (that is, along the transition to it), economies will exhibit growth in per capita income even without technological change. The rate of growth will depend on the initial capital–labour ratio and the time period over which the average growth rate is calculated. It can be shown that the average growth rate *decreases* as the initial capital–labour ratio $\bar{k}_0$ (and hence initial income per head) *increases*. As the initial capital–labour ratio tends to $\bar{k}^*$, the average growth rate of per capita income converges to b, the exogenously given rate of labour-augmenting technical progress. This is indeed one of the convergence hypotheses that are tested in the recent empirical literature on growth. Policies that affect s and n clearly affect them outside steady-state growth rates. However, the effect of changes in s and n on the growth rate of per capita income are only temporary and the marginal product of capital will be declining over time. It should be noted that this predicted fall in the marginal product of capital is not, however, observed, for example, in US historical data.

It is also clear that per capita output can grow indefinitely even in traditional growth models if the marginal product of capital is bounded away from zero as the capital–labour ratio grows indefinitely. Thus the standard neoclassical assumption that the marginal product of capital is a strictly decreasing function of the capital–labour ratio is not inconsistent with indefinite growth of per capita output. It has to diminish to zero as the capital–labour ratio increases indefinitely to preclude

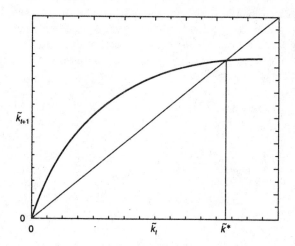

Figure 6.1   Phase diagram of Solow model $g(\bar{k}_t)$

such growth. This is easily seen from Equation (6.3)

Consider the simplest version of the neoclassical growth model with $b_t = 1$, and $A_t = 1$ for all t, so that $\bar{k}_t = k_t$. Let $f(0) = 0$ and let the marginal product of capital, that is, $f'(k)$, be bounded away from $(n + \delta)/s$ (that is, $f'(k) > (n + \delta)/s$ for all k). Strict concavity of $f(k)$ together with $f(0) = 0$ implies $f(k) > kf'(k) > [k(n + \delta)]/s$ so that from Equation (6.3) it follows that $k_{t+1} > k_t$. This in turn implies that output per worker $f(k_t)$ grows at a positive rate at all t. Moreover, given strict concavity of $f(k)$ it follows that $f'(k)$ is monotonically decreasing, and hence has a limiting value as $k \to \infty$, say γ_y, that is at least as large as $(n + \delta)/s$. As such it can be verified that the asymptotic growth rate of output and consumption will be at least as large as $[s\gamma_y - (n + \delta)]$ $(1 + n) \geq 0$. The savings rate, s, can be made endogenous, thus leading to a theory of endogenous and sustained long-run growth in per capita income. Thus the neoclassical framework can generate long-run growth in per capita income endogenously. However, the assumption that the marginal product has a positive lower bound is not particularly attractive, since it implies that labour is not essential for production.[3]

A primary goal of the recently revived growth theory is to build models that can generate sustained long-run growth in per capita income. A related objective is to ensure that the long-run growth rate of income (and, in fact, the entire time path of income) not only depends on the parameters of the production and utility functions, but also on fiscal policies, foreign trade policies and population policies. In most models of 'new' theory, the primary goal is accomplished through increasing scale economies in the aggregate production. The resulting non-convexities lead to multiple equilibria and hysteresis in some models, so that history (that is, initial conditions as well as any past shocks experienced by the economy) and policies could have long-term effects (see Matsuyama, 1991) for a criticism of this interpretation and an analysis of local and global dynamics of multiple equilibria.

In assessing the role of increasing scale economies in growth, it is useful to distinguish between generating *sustained growth* in output per head and *endogenising* the rate of growth. For example, with the production function $Y = K^a L^b$, where $0 < a, b < 1$ and $a + b > 1$ and the labour force growing *exogenously* at rate n there exists a unique steady state regardless of the savings rate in which output grows at the exogenous rate of $n(a + b - 1)/1 - a > 0$. Thus *increasing scale economies together with marginal product of capital strictly diminishing to zero* (that is, $0 < a < 1$) leads to *sustained* but *exogenous* growth. On the other hand, *constant returns to scale with marginal product of capital bounded away from zero* at a sufficiently high positive number leads to *endogenous* and *sustained* growth. Thus increasing scale economies *by themselves* need not generate endogenous growth. It is also important to distinguish how different types of increasing returns to scale in aggregate production arise in various growth models. I consider here only two types: locally increasing marginal product of capital, and scale economies caused by spillover effects. For simplicity, assume that in Equation (6.1) $L_t \equiv 1$, $A_t = 1$, $b_t = 1 \; \forall \; t \geq 0$. The first type arises when the marginal product of capital $f'(k)$ first increases with k and then decreases, or more generally when $f''(k) = 0$ has more than one but a finite number of solutions.

The second type arises in the models of Lucas and Romer. Building upon the works of Arrow (1962) and Sheshinski (1967), Romer (1986) considers an economy in which there are n identical firms, each has a production function of the form $Y_i = G(K_i, L_i, K)$, where K_i is the stock of knowledge capital or R&D capital employed by firm i, and $K = \Sigma_{i=1}^{n} K_i$, the industry level aggregate stock of knowledge, and L_i is the labour or any other inputs. K is assumed to have positive spillover effect on output of each firm, although the choice of K is external to the firm. Romer assumes that for fixed K, G is homogeneous of degree one in other inputs. Supposing that all identical firms choose identical inputs, we can write $Y_i = G(K_i, L_i, nK_i)$. Define $F(K_i, L_i) \equiv G(K_i, L_i, nK_i)$. It is obvious that F exhibits increasing returns to scale in the inputs K_i, and L_i. Again, besides those scale economies one needs to assume that the asymptotic marginal product of aggregate capital is positive to generate endogenous growth. Empirical support for the spillover effect of R&D capital is found in several empirical investigations (see Bernstein and Nadiri, 1989) on Canadian industry data, Jaffé (1986) on the US manufacturing firm level data, and Raut (1991a) on Indian manufacturing firm level data).[4]

Following Uzawa (1965), Lucas (1988) endogenises Harrod neutral (that is, labour augmenting) technological change through a mechanism of human capital accumulation. Suppose a worker of period t is endowed with b_t units of human capital or skill and one unit of labour. S/he has to allocate his or her labour endowment between accumulating skills and earning wage income. If s/he devotes the fraction, ϕ_t, of his or her time in the current production sector, and $1 - \phi_t$ (where $0 \leq \phi_t \leq 1$) in the learning sector (such as schooling or some vocational training programme), s/he can increase his or her human capital in the next period by

$$\dot{b}_t = b_t \delta(1 - \phi_t). \tag{6.4}$$

The budget constraint for the representative agent is given by:

$$c_t + \dot{k}_t = F(k_t, \phi_t b_t) - (n + \delta)k_t. \tag{6.5}$$

From Equation (6.5) it is clear that for given c_t, and k_t, the agent faces a tradeoff. S/he can spend more time currently (that is, choose a larger ϕ_t) in the production sector and thus have a larger *current consumption* or *future physical capital*, or have a lower ϕ_t and thus have *larger future human capital* (that is, higher $\dot{b}_t$) and hence a *larger future stream of output*. It is clear that s/he would divide his or her savings between human capital and physical capital in a balanced way so that the marginal product of capital does not fall to zero. Under the further assumption that the production function is of the Cobb–Douglas form:

$$F(K, L) = A(b_t)K_t^\alpha(b_t L_t)^\beta, \; \alpha + \beta = 1, \; \alpha, \beta > 0 \tag{6.6}$$

where the spillover effect is given by $A(b_t) = Ab_t^\mu$, $0 < \mu$, it can be shown that along the balanced growth path, the capital–labour ratio, and hence per capita income and consumption, will be growing at the rate where ϕ_t is a constant equal to ϕ. Since γ_y is a function of ϕ, which is:

$$\gamma_y = \left(\frac{1 - \beta + \mu}{1 - \beta}\right)(1 - \phi)\delta \qquad (6.7)$$

endogenously determined, the growth rate of per capita income is endogenously determined.

It should be noted that even if there is no spillover effect, that is, $\mu = 0$, γ_y is positive, and this, of course, is the consequence of the crucial assumption that the marginal return to time devoted to skill accumulation is constant and not diminishing. As Lucas himself points out, this is crucial for generating sustained growth per capita consumption in the long run. Since the opportunity cost of time spent on skill acquisition is forgone income that could have been used for consumption or accumulation of physical capital, this crucial assumption should be viewed as the equivalent of assuming that the marginal product of physical capital is constant, as in the Harrod–Domar model.

The Lucas model is essentially a two-sector growth model. Human capital and the process of its accumulation play essentially the same role as the capital goods sector in the two-sector model of Mahalanobis (1955). In this model, marginal product of capital in the capital goods sector is constant – an assumption that is the equivalent of Lucas's crucial assumption about the process of human capital accumulation (Srinivasan, 1993).[5] The rate of growth of income and consumption was determined endogenously in the Mahalanobis model by the share of investment devoted to the accumulation of capacity to produce capital goods. The share $(1 - \phi_t)$ of time devoted to skill acquisition plays an analogous role in the Lucas model.

Linearity of the technology of skill acquisition in the Lucas model is restrictive. It leads to a unique balanced growth solution. However, if a non-linear (convex) technology is assumed, there could be multiple optimal balanced growth paths that are locally stable, as has been shown by Azariadis and Drazen (1990).

Raut and Srinivasan (1991) present a model that not only endogenises growth and the process of shifts in production possibilities over time (that is, technical change) but also generates richer dynamics than the models of recent growth theory. First, by assuming fertility to be endogenous,[6] they preclude the possibility of aggregate growth being driven solely by exogenous labour force growth in the absence of technical change. Second, by assuming that population density has an external effect (not perceived by individual agents) on the production process, either through its negative congestion effect or through its positive effect in stimulating innovation and technical change, they make the change in production possibilities to be endogenously determined by fertility decisions of individual agents. However, unlike the new growth literature, their model, which is an extension of Raut (1985, 1991b), is not necessarily geared to generating steady states. In fact, the non-linear dynamics of the model generates a plethora of outcomes (depending on the functional forms, parameters and initial conditions) that include not only the neoclassical steady state with exponential growth of population with constant per capita income and consumption, but also growth paths that do not converge to a steady state and are even chaotic. Per capita output grows exponentially (and superexponentially) in some of the examples.

The model draws on the insights of E. Boserup (1981) and J. Simon (1981) who, among others, have argued that the growth of population could itself induce technical change. In the Boserup model, increasing population pressure on a fixed or very slowly growing supply of arable land induces changes in methods of cultivation, not simply through substitution of labour for land by choice of techniques within a known set of techniques but, more importantly, through the invention of new techniques. Simon also attributes a positive role for increases in population density in inducing technical progress. Since having a large population is not sufficient to generate growth (Romer, 1990), it is important to examine the mechanism by which population density influences innovation. However, neither of the two authors provides a complete theory of induced innovation. Raut and Srinivasan do not provide one either, and point out that the inducement to innovate will depend largely on the returns and risks to resources devoted to innovative activity, and there is no particular reason to suggest that pre-existing relative factor prices or endowments will necessarily tilt these returns towards a search for technologies that save particular factors. They simply analyse the implications of assuming that technical change is influenced by population density (strictly speaking, population size) in a world where fertility is endogenous.

More precisely, they assume that technical change in our model economy is Hicks neutral and its rate is determined by the change in the size of the working population. Thus, instead of the aggregate production function given in Equation (6.1), they use the following:

$$Y_t = A(L_t)F(K_t, L_t). \qquad (6.8)$$

However, for both consumers and firms in this economy $A(L_t)$ is an externality. We introduce this externality in a model of overlapping generations in which a member of each generation lives for three periods, the first of which is spent as a child in the parents' household. The second period is spent as a young person working, producing and raising children, and accumulating capital. The third and last period of life is spent as an old person in retirement living off support received from offspring and from the sale of accumulated capital. Members of each generation are identical in their preferences defined over their consumption during their working and retired periods. Thus, in this model, the only reason that an individual would want to have a child is for the support the child would provide during the parent's retired life. Production (of a single commodity which can be consumed or accumulated) is organised in firms which buy capital from the retired and hire the young as workers. Markets for product, labour and capital are assumed to be competitive.

Formally, a typical individual of the generation that is young in period t has n_t children (reproduction is by parthenogenesis!), consumes c_t^t, c_{t+1}^t in periods t and $t + 1$, and saves s_t in period t. S/he supplies one unit of labour for wage employment. His or her income from wage labour while young in period t is w_t, and that is the only income in that period. A proportion a of this wage income is given to parents as old-age support. While old in period $t + 1$, s/he sells his or her accumulated saving to firms and receives from each of his or her offspring the proportion α of his/her wage income. S/he enjoys a utility $U(c_t^t, c_{t+1}^t)$ from consumption. Thus her choice problem can be stated as:

$$\max_{s_t, \, n_t \, > \, 0} U(c_t^t, c_{t+1}^t) \tag{6.9}$$

subject to

$$c_t^t + \theta_t n_t + s_t = (1 - \alpha)w_t \tag{6.10}$$

$$c_{t+1}^t = (1 + r_{t+1})s_t + \alpha w_{t+1} n_t \tag{6.11}$$

where θ_t is the output cost of rearing a child until adult.

Profit maximisation of the producer yields (using the notation of Section 2.3):

$$w_{t+1} = A(L_{t+1})(f(k_{t+1}) - k_{t+1}f'(k_{t+1})) \tag{6.12}$$

$$1 + r_{t+1} = A(L_{t+1})f'(k_{t+1}). \tag{6.13}$$

In equilibrium, the private rates of return from investing in children and physical capital are equal, so arbitrage opportunities are ruled out. This implies that:

$$\frac{\alpha w_{t+1}}{\theta_t} = 1 + r_{t+1}. \tag{6.14}$$

Plugging Equations (6.12) and (6.13) into Equation (6.14), we get an implicit equation linking k_{t+1}, θ_t and α. It can be shown that under standard neoclassical assumptions on the production function, we can solve for k_{t+1} as a function $\Psi(\theta_t/\alpha)$. Since $k_{t+1} = s_t/n_t$ (given the assumption that capital depreciates fully in one generation), the budget constraints in Equations (6.10) and (6.11) become respectively $c_t^t = (1 - \alpha)w_t - S_t$ and $c_{t+1}^t = (1 + r_{t+1})S_t$, where $S_t = [\theta_t + \Psi(\theta_t/\alpha)]$. n_t. S_t could be thought of as total savings.

Let us denote the solution of the above utility maximisation problem as before by $S_t = H(w_t, 1 + r_{t+1})$. We can now express the solutions for n_t and s_t, as:

$$n_t = \frac{H(w_t, 1 + r_{t+1})}{\theta_t + \Psi(\theta_t/\alpha)} \text{ and } s_t = \frac{H(w_t, 1 + r_{t+1})}{\Psi(\theta_t/\alpha) [\theta_t + \Psi(\theta_t/\alpha)]} \tag{6.15}$$

Equation (6.15) determines the dynamics of the system. Let us first consider the simplest case, in which child-rearing cost $\theta_t = \theta$, for all $t \geq 0$. It is clear that $k_{t+1} = k^*$ for all $t \geq 1$ in this case. Assuming further that utility function is Cobb–Douglas, that is, $U = a \log c_t^t + (1 - a)\log c_{t+1}^t$, we have $H(w_t, 1 + r_{t+1}) = (1 - a)w_t$. Equation (6.15) now yields:

$$n_t = \frac{L_{t+1}}{L_t} = \frac{(1 - \alpha)(1 - a)}{(\theta + k^*)} w^* A(L_t)$$

or

$$L_{t+1} = \lambda L_t A(L_t) = G(L_t) \quad \text{say} \tag{6.16}$$

where $\lambda = \dfrac{(1 - \alpha)(1 - a)w^*}{\theta + k^*}$.

From Equation (6.8), one notes that per capita income is given by $y_t = A(L_t)f(k^*)$. Thus the dynamics of population long-run behaviour of per capita income hinge on the form $A(L_t)$. It should be recalled that although the fertility decisions of individuals determine L_t and hence $A(L_t)$, this is an unperceived externality. A few possibilities are depicted in Figures 6.2a–6.2c.

Suppose $A(L_t)$ is such that $G(L_t)$ is a concave function, which is zero at $L_t = 0$, and satisfies the Inada condition. Then, in the long run, population will be stationary and per capita income will be constant, as in the standard neoclassical growth model. This is shown in Figure 6.2a. Now suppose $A(L_t)$ is such that $G(L_t)$ is concave and $G'(L_t)$ is bounded away from 1. In this case, we have long-run growth in L_t and hence in per capita income. This is shown in Figure 6.2b.

Suppose now that $A(L_t)$ is a logistic function with a positive asymptote, such as $A(L) = \gamma e^{-(L - \bar{L})^2}$, for $L \geq 0$. It could be shown (Raut and Srinivasan, 1991; also see Figure 6.2c) that there are multiple steady states. The properties of these steady states depend on the parameter values. If the maximum $\bar{L}$ is to the right of L^{**}, then L^{**} is locally stable and there exists a neighbourhood around L^{**} within which the system is monotonic. On the other hand, if $\bar{L}$ is to the left of L^{**}, there can be a non-generic set of parameter values for which the system will exhibit endogenous fluctuations that can be damped, exploding or even chaotic. However, if α is partly influenced by the government through social security schemes, since α can affect λ, by influencing α

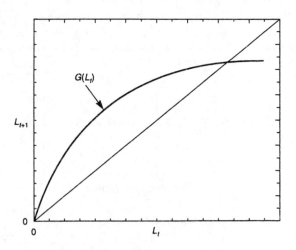

Figure 6.2a   Stationary population and income

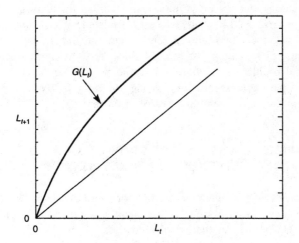

Figure 6.2b Sustained growth in population and income

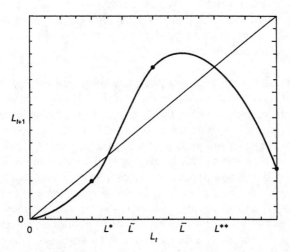

Figure 6.2c Phase diagram of $G(L_t)$

the government can shift $\bar{L}$ to the right of L^{**} and thus, locally at least, a social security programme can stabilise fluctuations.

More general child-bearing costs are considered by Raut and Srinivasan (1991, section 4a) involving parents' time and depending on the rate of technological change. Naturally these lead to more complicated dynamical problems. They show that there could be superexponential growth in per capita income in the long run in the case of some specific functional forms for general costs of child-rearing.

IV EMPIRICAL ANALYSIS OF GROWTH: GROWTH ACCOUNTING AND GROWTH REGRESSIONS

Jorgenson (1990) commemorated fifty years of research on economic measurement by contributing to the theme of economic growth and its sources. He points out that, until recently,

> the study of sources of economic growth has been based on the notion of an aggregate production function [which makes] it possible to summarize a welter of detailed information within a single overarching framework . . . At the same time the concept of an aggregate production function is highly problematical, requiring very stringent assumptions on production patterns at the level of individual sectors of the economy. (p. 19)

In contrast to the findings of others, and following the approach outlined in the justly celebrated article of Solow (1957), Jorgenson finds that growth of inputs, rather than growth in total factor productivity, is the driving force behind the expansion of the US economy between 1947 and 1985. To the growth of valued added at 3.28 per cent per year on average during this period, growth capital inputs accounted for 44 per cent, labour inputs 34 per cent and productivity accounted for the least, namely, 22 per cent. The difference between followers of Solow (1957) and Jorgenson arise from the fact that Jorgenson distinguishes carefully between the separate contributions of capital and labour quality from the contributions of capital stock and hours worked. This distinction is extremely important, since both capital and labour inputs are very heterogeneous. Solow (1957) and others following him do not allow for quality differences in their measurement of quantity of inputs. Since Jorgenson's assumptions about the aggregate production function are strictly neoclassical (in particular, returns-to-scale are assumed to be constant and externalities virtually absent), the fact that he is able to explain most of the observed growth in the USA by growth of inputs appropriately measured suggests that, if his framework is accepted, then the analytical innovations of recent growth theory need not be invoked to explain growth performance!

Unfortunately, it is not simple to decide whether frameworks that maintain neoclassical assumptions are indeed the appropriate ones. After reviewing the conventional methodology of the measurement of technical progress and growth accounting, and the results of the growth accounting exercises of various authors, Boskin and Lau point to two major

> pitfalls of maintaining the traditional assumptions of constant returns to scale, neutrality of technical progress and profit maximization with competitive output and input markets in the measurement of technical progress and growth accounting. First, ... for an economy in which aggregate real output and inputs are all growing over time, it is in general difficult to identify separately the effects of returns to scale and technical progress – either one can be used as a substitute explanation for the other. Thus, to the extent that there are increasing returns to scale, maintaining the hypothesis of constant returns to scale results in an over estimate of technical progress; and to the extent there are decreasing returns to scale, maintaining the hypothesis results in an underestimate ... A further implication (of maintaining constant returns to scale when there are increasing returns to scale) is that the contributions of the capital and labor inputs to economic growth will also be underestimated. The reverse is true if there are decreasing returns to scale.
>
> Second ... if technical progress is non-neutral, then the rate of technical progress at time t will vary depending on the quantities of capital and labor inputs at time t. Moreover, technical progress by many periods cannot be expressed simply as a cumulative sum of the technical progress that has occurred over the individual periods, nor can it be expressed simply as an average. (Boskin and Lau, 1992a, p. 24)

In a series of papers, Boskin and Lau (1992a, 1992b) and Kim and Lau (1992a, 1992b, 1992c) apply 'a new framework for analysis of productivity and technical progress, based on the direct econometric estimation of an aggregate meta-production function, that does not require the traditionally maintained assumption ... This new approach enables the separate identification of not only the degree of returns to scale and the rate of technical progress . . . but also their biases, if any' (Boskin and Lau, 1992a, p. 33).

Their application (Boskin and Lau, 1992b) to Group of Five countries (France, West Germany, Japan, the United Kingdom and the United States) shows that while the assumption that all countries have the same underlying metaproduction function of the transcendental logarithmic form cannot be rejected, traditional growth accounting assumptions are all rejected. Returns to scale are found to be diminishing sharply, and technical progress may be represented as purely capital-augmenting, and capital-saving rather than labour-saving. Their growth accounting exercise leads them to conclude that technical progress is the most important source of growth, accounting for more than 45 per cent, followed by growth of capital input. Yet since apparently they do not allow for changes in the quality of inputs as Jorgenson does, it is possible that their results would be dramatically altered were they to redo their analysis with proper allowance of quality changes.

Kim and Lau (1992a) apply the same approach (once again without allowing for changes in quality of inputs) to nine countries including the Group of Five and four East Asian Newly Industrialised Countries (NICs) (Hong Kong, Singapore, South Korea and Taiwan). Interestingly, they find that the hypothesis of a single metaproduction function applying to all nine countries cannot be rejected. While they reaffirm the findings of Boskin and Lau that technical progress can be represented as purely capital augmenting, they cannot reject the hypothesis that there has been no technical progress in the NICs with more than 80 per cent of their economic growth being explained by capital accumulation. Young (1993) reaches similar conclusions using what he calls 'simple back of the envelope calculations'. The NICs have experienced an unusually rapid growth of output per worker. This output growth, however, 'is not substantially greater than what one would have predicted, given the doubling, tripling and quadrupling of the investment to GDP ratios in these economies' (p. 12).

It has long been argued (Mahalanobis, 1995; Rosenberg, 1963) that the cost of equipment (and, alternatively, investment in equipment) might have an important role to play in the growth process. Indeed, in arguing for the establishment of a domestic heavy machinery industry, Mahalanobis insisted that

For rapid industrialization of an under-developed country it would be desirable to keep the cost of capital goods as low as possible.

The further removed the type of capital goods under consideration is from the production of final consumer goods the greater is the need of keeping the price low. Heavy machinery which would manufacture machinery to produce investment goods is the furthest removed from the consumption end. (Mahalanobis, 1955, p. 51)

Interestingly enough, some economic historians have attributed the Western success in industrialisation to the development of heavy industries, particularly those producing machine tools and capital goods. In words that echo Mahalanobis's quoted above, Nathan Rosenberg asserts that

a major handicap of underdeveloped countries, then, is located in their inability to produce investment goods at prices sufficiently low to assure a reasonable rate of return on prospective investments. Reasoning symmetrically, of the most significant propelling forces in the growth of currently high-income countries has been the technological dynamism of their capital goods industries which has maintained the marginal efficiency of capital at a high level. (Rosenberg, 1963, p. 226)

More recently, DeLong and Summers (1991) found that variations in investment in equipment explained a significant part of the variations in economic growth in countries. Kim and Lau (1992c) test a version of a related hypothesis, namely that technical progress is embodied in new investments so that it can affect the output of an economy only through the form of new capital goods. They found, using an aggregate metaproduction model incorporating vintage effects, that the hypothesis of no embodied technical progress can be rejected for the Group of Five countries, with the vintage effect, namely the productivity of new equipment relative to that in the preceding period is higher by 4–5 per cent. The contribution of embodied technical progress to growth was found to range from 55 per cent for Japan to 70 per cent for the other four countries.

The studies by Lau and his co-authors, on the one hand, apparently restore (provided the results are not overturned, once changes in the quality of inputs are allowed for) a significant role for productivity growth in explaining aggregate growth, but on the other, find little productivity growth in NICs. This creates a problem for those who attribute the spectacular growth of NICs to the dynamic productivity gains arising from their outward orientation! As Young (1993) puts it,

'In general, rapid factor accumulation of both capital and labour, explains the lion's share of the East Asian growth miracle . . . Consequently, it would be a mistake to conclude that East Asian NICs are a prime example of potential dynamic gains from outward oriented policies' (p. 15).

The time-series-cum-cross-section analysis of growth by Jorgenson as well as Lau and his co-authors have the virtue that the econometric model they estimate is derived from a well-specified theory, and further, the possibility of testing the specification is also present. Unfortunately, many recent cross-section analyses of growth using 'data' literally from a hundred or more countries (for example, Barro and Lee (1994) include 133 countries in growth-rate regressions) are rarely based on well-specified microeconomic foundations. For example, inclusion of variables such as school attainment of the population, or some measure of educational stocks, is motivated merely by appeals to the role of human capital in growth. However, without an analytical framework that formalises the process of human capital accumulation (for example, learning by doing) and how it relates to *aggregate* growth in different economies, it is impossible to infer anything meaningful from the significant statistical significance (or lack thereof) of the estimated parameter associated with the human capital variable.

Indeed, as Lucas (1993) points out in his extremely stimulating lecture, 'establishing the importance of learning by doing for productivity growth on a specific production process is very different from establishing its importance for one entire economy as a whole, or even an entire sector' (pp. 252–3). In attempting to explain episodes of sustained and rapid growth over nearly three decades, as in East Asian economies, Lucas correctly suggests that one needs a theory that incorporates the *possibility* of rapid-growth episodes, but at the same time does not imply their occurrence as a simple consequence of relative backwardness of the countries experiencing them. In his view, a successful theory should be as consistent with the experience of Korea with its rapid growth since the mid-1960s as of the Philippines which experienced no such growth, although both economies started from roughly similar situations. Lucas finds that models of technical learning with spillover such as those of Stokey (1988), Young (1991) and Grossman and Helpman (1991) constitute such a theory. Whether or not this is the case, the cross-section growth analysts, by the very fact of their estimating the same model using data from many countries, *assume* that the theory, if any, that is implicit in the estimated model is applicable to all of them!

In a series of papers, Levine and Renelt (1991, 1992) and Levine and Zervos (1993a, 1993b) have thoroughly reviewed the methodological, conceptual and statistical problems of cross-country studies, as well as isolated what they deem to be 'robust' findings in these studies. The data and measurement problems are far more serious than they realise. For example, in the cross-country study of growth by Barro and Lee (1994) the variables considered include school attainment, life expectancy at birth, and infant mortality in 1965, 1975 and 1985. In Sen's (1994) study of 'regress', the change in the rate of mortality of children under five during 1965–91 is an important indicator. Unfortunately, the authors do not recognise that the data they use for many developing countries are at best projections and certainly not actual observations. According to United Nations (1991), relatively reliable and recent (that is, a reference period of 1980 or later) data for estimating life expectancy at birth (respectively, infant mortality) are not available for as many as 87 (respectively, 65) out of 177 less-developed countries, many of which are included in the Barro and Lee (1993) study! The same source points out that reliable data on levels of under-fives mortality are not available for 29 and available data related to a period prior to 1980 for as many as 54 out of the same 117 countries. UNESCO (1991) finds that out of a total of 145 countries (including developed countries), for 19 no data exist on adult literacy since 1970, and for 41 the latest data relate to a year in the decade 1970–9!

Many of the cross-country studies use the purchasing policy parity exchange rate based data on GDP put together by Summers and Heston (1988, 1991). Although Summers and Heston are careful to list the problems with their data, including in particular in identifying commodities that are close to being identical in different countries so they can be priced out using a common set of prices, the users pay scant attention to their cautionary warnings.[7] It is one thing to adjust for international differences in *price* structures as Summers and Heston do. But what they do not adjust for, and what in many cases is more serious, are *biases* in measurement of quantities (Srinivasan, 1994). Indeed, Summers and Heston (1991) themselves assign a quality rating of D+ or D to the data of 66 out of their 138 countries, most of which are less-developed countries, 37 of them being African countries. Data on investment are particularly unreliable. Biases as well as measurement errors might vary in an unknown fashion over time and across countries, and obviously such variations have implications for growth regressions.

Levine and Renelt (1992) and Levine and Zervos (1993a) use the methodology of extreme-bound analysis pioneered by Edward Leamer for distinguishing 'robust' from 'fragile' relationships. In this methodology, a cross-country regression, a set of basic explanatory variables, I is always included and Z is a set of up to three explanatory variables chosen from a pool of policy indicators. M is the policy indicator of particular interest. If the coefficient of M in the regression is consistently significant and of the same sign as the set of Z variables is varied over the pool of policy indicators, then the relationship between the dependent variable and policy indicator M is deemed to be 'robust'; otherwise 'fragile'. The motivation for this is the finding in Levine and Renelt (1992) that small changes in the right-hand side variable produce different conclusions between individual policies and growth in cross-country studies. While the motivation is admirable and the procedure certainly interesting, there are conceptual problems with the procedure. In principle, these different sets of right-hand-side variables in explaining the same dependent variable imply different 'models' of growth. As such, the sign, as well as the statistical significance of the coefficient of a given variable M is thus model-specific. Should the sign or significance change as 'models' are changed, does it imply the relationship between M and the dependent variable be viewed as being fragile? I should think not: the reason the sign itself may be specific to the model, and certainly the test of significance, is model specific. For example, the same policy variable M may be positively related to growth in one model or theory of growth as represented by the other variables included and negatively related in another. This problem does not disappear, even if the policy variables included in the pool are of the same 'genre' (that is, trade policy, financial policy and so on) as M.

It is worth recognising that policy indicators as well as some of the other variables often included in cross-country regressions are *endogenous*. In studies involving cross-sections repeated over time, sometimes country-specific effects (fixed or random) are included. Since the other explanatory variables (particularly policy variables) might plausibly correlate with country-specific effects, as Deaton (1993) points out, the random effects estimator will be inconsistent. On the other hand, if these effects are treated as *fixed*, removing fixed effects by differencing introduces a correlation between the disturbance term in the differenced regression and its explanatory variables, if the latter include lagged values of the dependent variable. If the number of time periods over which the cross-sections are repeated is small relative to the number of countries included in each cross-section, the fixed effect estimate will also be inconsistent. Not all analysts address such problems by the use of appropriate econometric techniques, such as the use of instrumental variables. Even those who do rarely report how good the instruments they used were, and how robust the results were to changes in the instruments.

V CONCLUDING REMARKS

The purpose of the cross-country regression analysis is not only to 'explain' the growth process and its determinants but also presumably to derive policy lessons. In an earlier set of studies, Chenery (1960) and Chenery and Syrquin (1975, 1989) suggested that their cross-country regression 'can be thought of as reduced forms of a more detailed general equilibrium system' (Chenery and Syrquin, 1975, p. 10) and viewed their analysis as leading 'to the identification of three main patterns of resource allocation identified . . . as: large country, balanced allocation, small country, primary specialization; small country, industry specialization' (ibid., p. 4). In inferring a typology of development patterns from a policy perspective, these authors were eclectic, since they were aware that causal interpretation of reduced form relationships is hazardous. Their inferences were based on comparing countries that are following similar development patterns and the policies chosen by countries under similar conditions.

There can be no doubt that the recent contributions to the theory and empirical analysis of the process of growth have increased substantially our knowledge about the analytics of growth and the potential role of human capital accumulation, investment in research and development, international trade, and externalities and scale economies (arising in part from non-rivalry and non-excludability in use of knowledge) in the growth process. On the issue of whether public policy intervention in the economy is called for from the perspective of influencing the growth process and, if so, what the character of such intervention should be, are issues on which recent work has provided some valuable insights; but, understandably, no conclusive answers have yet emerged. For example, if the contribution of *endogenous* factor accumulation is *small* and an overwhelming share of observed growth is due to *exogenous* technical progress, as in the Solow (1957) story of US growth, there is little that public policy could do to affect the growth process significantly. In contrast, if most of the growth could be attributed to factor accumulation (physical and human), as in Jorgenson (1990), then public policy intervention could influence growth. This is not to say either that the US experience is likely to be repeated in the developing world, or that public policy intervention is desirable from a welfare perspective.

To take another example, it is undeniable that the East Asian economies of Hong Kong, Korea, Singapore and Taiwan have grown, not only substantially faster than almost all other developing countries since 1960, also that such rapid and sustained growth is historically unprecedented. Whether it is a miracle, as a recent study (World Bank, 1993) and Lucas (1993) deem it, is arguable. They all had two things in common in their policies, namely their emphasis on human capital and on outward orientation, while they differed in the extent of government intervention in markets ranging from no intervention in Hong Kong to extensive intervention in Korea. The nature of their regimes differed as well, although all were authoritarian to a considerable extent. Analogous to the Solow–Jorgenson differences in accounting for US growth, in the case of East Asia, some find substantial contributions of total factor productivity growth to total growth, whereas Kim and Lau (1992a) and Young (1993) find factor accumulation (human and physical capital) accounting for most of their growth. To what extent their outward orientation and public policy interventions contributed to their unprecedented growth is a matter of intensive debate as well, with some (for example, Anderson, 1989) emphasising that interventions in the economy succeeded only where they met the test of competitiveness in world markets, with World Bank (1993) being in the middle!

Cross-country regressions testing some version or other of the convergence hypothesis relating to *aggregate* growth (whatever other insights they have yielded about the growth process) by their very nature have little to say about the microeconomic forces that together generate the aggregate outcome. Here, again, the observations of Lucas are pertinent:

> I do not intend these conjectures about the implications of a learning spillover technology for small countries facing given world prices to be a substitute for the actual construction of such a theory... What is the nature of human capital accumulation decision problems faced by workers, capitalists and managers? What are the external consequences of the decisions they take? The purpose cited here considers a variety of possible assumptions on these economic issues, but it must be said that little is known, and without such

knowledge there is little we can say about the way policies that affect incentives can be expected to influence economic growth. (Lucas, 1993, p. 270)

Even if one were to ignore their lack of solid microeconomic foundations and their uncritical use of aggregate data with serious measurement errors and biases, the inference drawn from many convergence regressions could be questioned on econometric grounds, as Quah (1993a, 1993b and 1994) has done. He suggests that these studies 'do not at all shed light on the important, original question: Are poor economies catching up with those richer' (Quah 1994, p. 52). This is indeed the fundamental question of development and it is yet to be answered satisfactorily.

Notes

* This chapter is the revised and expanded text of a lecture delivered on 7 July 1994 at the Workshop on 'Endogenous Growth and Development' held at the International School of Economic Research, University of Siena, Italy. Sections I–III draw extensivey from my unpublished background paper, 'Development Thought, Strategy and Policy: Then and Now', for the *World Development Report 1991* of the World Bank. Sections III–V reproduce most of my forthcoming paper, 'Long-Run Growth Theories and Empirics: Anything New?', in Takatoshi Ito and Anne Krueger (eds) *Lessons from East Asian Growth* (Chicago: University of Chicago Press).

1. In fact, besides introducing the constant elasticity of substitution production function, Arrow *et al.* (1961) and, in his dissertation, Minhas (1963), were concerned with precisely this issue.
2. However, in Romer (1990) innovation is driven by profit-maximising entrepreneurs.
3. One can easily prove it as follows: Suppose $\inf_{(K,L)>0}(\partial F/\partial K) = \gamma > 0$. Since F is homogeneous of degree one, $F(1, L/K) = \partial F/\partial K + (L/K)(\partial F/\partial L) \geq \partial F/\partial K > \gamma > 0$. Now suppose $L \to 0$, then it follows that $F(1, 0) > 0$.
4. However, Benhabib and Jovanovic (1991) do not find any evidence for spillover using the US macro data.
5. It is also evident that the absence of long-run growth effects of trade in dynamic versions of Heckscher–Ohlin–Samuelson-type modells of international trade is again because of their implicitly or explicitly precluding the marginal product of capital being bounded away from zero.
6. There are a number of models in the literature in which the interaction of endogenous fertility and productive investment in human capital are analysed in a growth context. My purpose here is not to survey this literature. I refer the interested reader to one of the very interesting models by Becker *et al.* (1990).

7. There are two extrapolations involved in the Summers-Heston data: the first from *benchmark countries* (which varied from 16 in 1970 to 56 in 1985) to *other countries* for the benchmark year; and the second, from *benchmark years* (1970, 1975, 1980 and 1985) to *other years* in the period 1960–85 (Summers and Heston (1991) appendix A-2).

For the first, they use 'capital city price surveys conducted around the world by the United Nations International Civil Service Commission, a British firm serving an association of international businesses, and the U.S. State Department' (ibid., p. 341). While recognising 'The price indexes appropriate for this very special population – high-income non-nationals, living usually in capital cities – does not properly reflect all the prices in the country, of course, nor do the individual price weights reflect the relative importance of the individual goods in the countries for the nationals' (ibid., p. 341), they none the less found a structural relationship 'in the benchmark country's PPP and its postallowance PPP' and exploited it 'to estimate for the non-benchmark countries missing PPP's from their post allowance PPP's' (ibid., p. 342). For the second, they go from a benchmark year, say 1985, to other years 'by applying the relevant growth rates from the constant-price national accounts series – the values for the year of interest divided by the corresponding 1985 ones – to the 1985 number' (ibid., p. 343). As is well known, the arguments in favour of using one set of prices as opposed to another in appraising growth performance are not often strong. In any case, Summers and Heston correctly caution that 'Growth rates based on international prices can differ significantly from those based on national prices, but when they do, it is nearly always the case that relative prices within the countries have changed substantially over the period' (ibid., p. 361). I might add that rapid development over an extended period will almost always involve substantial changes in relative prices, particularly of the basket of international traded goods relative to non-traded goods.

References

Abramovitz, M. (1956) 'Resource and Output Trends in the United States Since 1870', *American Economic Review, Papers and Proceedings*, vol. 46, pp. 5–23.

Ahmad, Syed (1966) 'On the Theory of Induced Innovation', *Economic Journal*, vol. 76, pp. 344–57.

Anderson, A. (1989) *Asia's Next Giant: South Korea and Late Industrialization* (New York, Oxford University Press).

Arrow, K. J. (1962) 'The Economic Implications of Learning by Doing', *Review of Economic Studies*, vol. 29, pp. 155–73.

Azariadis, C. and Drazen, A. (1990) 'Threshold Externalities in Economic Development', *Quarterly Journal of Economics*, pp. 501–26.

Barro, R. J. and J. Lee (1994) 'Losers and Winners in Economic Growth', in *Proceedings of the World Bank Annual Conference on Development Economics 1993*, Supplement to the *World Bank Economic Review* and *World Bank Research Observer* (Washington DC: World Bank), pp. 267–97.

Bernstein, J. and M. Nadiri (1989) 'Research and Development and Intraindustry Spillovers: An Empirical Implication of Dynamic Duality', *Review of Economic Studies*, vol. 56, pp. 249–68.

Blitzer, C., L. Taylor and P. Clark (1974) *Economy-wide Models in Development Planning* (London: Oxford University Press).

Boserup, E. (1965) *The Conditions of Agricultural Growth* (Chicago: Aldine).

Boserup, E. (1981) *Population and Technical Change: A Study of Long-Term Trends* (Chicago University Press).

Boskin, M. J. and L. J. Lau (1992a) 'Capital, Technology, and Economic Growth', in N. Rosenberg, R. Landau and D. Mowery (eds), *Technology and Wealth of Nations* (Palo Alto, Calif.: Stanford University Press), ch. 2, pp. 17–55.

Boskin, M. J. and L. J. Lau (1992b) 'Post-war Economic Growth in the Group-of-Five Countries: A New Analysis', Department of Economics, Stanford University.

Cass, D. (1965) 'Optimum Growth in an Aggregative Model of Capital Accumulation', *Review of Economic Studies*, vol. 32, pp. 233–40.

Chenery, H. (1960) 'Patterns of Industrial Growth', *American Economic Review*, vol. 50 (September), pp. 624–54.

Chenery, H. and M. Syrquin (1975) *Patterns of Development 1950–1970* (Oxford University Press World Bank).

Chenery, H. and M. Syrquin (1989) *Patterns of Development, 1950 to 1983* (Washington, DC: World Bank).

Deaton, A. (1993) 'Data and Econometric Tools for Development Analysis', in J. Behrman and T. N. Srinivasan (eds), *Handbook of Development Economics*, vol. 3 (Amsterdam: North-Holland).

DeLong, B. J. and L. Summers (1991) 'Equipment Investment and Economic Growth', *Quarterly Journal of Economics*, vol. 106 (May), pp. 445–502.

Denison, E. F. (1962) 'Sources of Economic Growth in the United States and the Alternatives Before Us' (New York: Committee for Economic Development).

Dorfman, R., P. Samuelson and R. Solow (1958) *Linear Programming and Economic Analysis* (New York: McGraw Hill).

Domar, E. (1957) *Essays in the Theory of Economic Growth* (London, Oxford University Press).

Eckaus, R. and K. Parikh (1968) *Planning for Growth: Multi-sectoral, Intertemporal Models Applied to India* (Cambridge, Mass.: MIT Press).

Fel'dman, G. A. (1928) 'K teorii tempov narodnogo dokhoda', *Planovoe Khoziaistvo*, vol. 11, pp. 146–70; and vol. 12, pp. 152–78. Discussed in Domar 1957, ch. IX.

Fei, John and Gustav Ranis (1964) *Development of the Labor Surplus Economy*, (Homewood, Ill.: Irwin).

Grossman, G. and E. Helpman (1991) *Innovation and Growth in the Global Economy* (Cambridge, Mass.: MIT Press).

Harris, J. and M. Todaro (1970) 'Migration, Unemployment and Development: A Time Sector Analysis', *American Economic Review*, vol. 60, pp. 126–42.

Helpman, E. (1992) 'Endogenous Macroeconomic Growth Theory', *European Economic Review*, vol. 36, pp. 237–67.

Hirschman, A. (1958) *The Strategy of Economic Development* (12th edn March 1968) (New Haven, Conn.: Yale University Press).

Jaffe, A. B. (1986) 'Technological Opportunity and Spillovers of R&D: Evidence from Firms' Patents, Profits, and Market Value', *American Economic Review*, vol. 765, pp. 984–1001.

Jorgenson, D. (1990) 'Productivity and Economic Growth'. ch. 3 in Ernst R. Berndt and Jack E. Triplett (eds), *Fifty Years of Economic Measurement: The Jubilee of the Conference on Research in Income and Wealth* (University of Chicago Press).

Jorgenson, D. W. and Z. Grilliches (1966) 'Sources of Measured Productivity Change', *American Economic Review*, vol. 56, pp. 50–61.

Kaldor, N. and J. Mirrlees (1962) 'A New Model of Economic Growth', *Review of Economic Studies*, vol. 29, no. 3, pp. 174–92.

Kennedy, C. (1964) 'Induced Bias in Innovation and the Theory of Distribution', *Economic Journal*, vol. 74, no. 298, pp. 541–7.

Kim, J. and L. J. Lau (1992a) 'The Sources of Economic Growth of the Newly Industrialized Countries on the Pacific Rim', Department of Economics, Stanford University.

Kim, L. and L. J. Lau (1992b) 'Human Capital and Aggregate Productivity: Some Empirical Evidence from the Group of Five Countries', Department of Economics, Stanford University.

Kim, L. and L. J. Lau (1992c) 'The Importance of Embodied Technical Progress: Some Empirical Evidence from the Group of Five Countries', Department of Economics, Stanford University.

Koopmans, T. C. (1965) 'On the Concept of Optimal Economic Growth', in *The Econometric Approach to Development Planning* (Amsterdam: North-Holland for Pontificia Academic Science).

Kuznets, S. (1966) *Modern Economic Growth: Rate, Structure and Spread* (New Haven, Conn.: Yale University Press).

Levine, R. and D. Renelt (1991) 'Cross-Country Studies of Growth and Policy: Methodological, Conceptual and Statistical Problems', Working Paper WPS 608 (Washington DC: World Bank).

Levine, R. and D. Renelt (1992) 'A Sensitivity Analysis of Cross-Country Growth Regression', *American Economic Review*, vol. 824, pp. 942–63.

Levine, R. and S. Zervos (1993a) 'What We Have Learned About Policy and Growth from Cross-Country Regressions!', *American Economic Review, Papers and Proceedings*, vol. 84, pp. 426–30.

Levine, R. and Zervos, S. (1993b) 'Looking at the Facts: What We Know About Policy and Growth from Cross-Country Regressions', Working Paper WPS 1115 (Washington DC: World Bank).

Lewis, Arthur (1954) 'Economic Development with Unlimited Supplies of Labour', *Manchester School of Economic and Social Studies*, pp. 139–91.

Lucas, Robert (1988) 'On the Mechanics of Economic Development', *Journal of Monetary Economics*, vol. 22, pp. 3–42.

Lucas, Robert (1993) 'Making a Miracle', *Econometrica*, vol. 61, no. 2, pp. 251–72.

Mandelbaum, K. (1945) *The Industrialization of Backward Areas* (Oxford: Basil Blackwell).

Mahalanobis, P. C. (1955) 'The Approach of Operational Research to Planning in India', *Sankhya: The Indian Journal of Statistics*, vol. 16, pts 1 and 2, pp. 3–62.

Matsuyama, K. (1991) 'Increasing Returns, Industrialization, and Indeterminacy of Equilibrium', *Quarterly Journal of Economics*, vol. 106, no. 2, pp. 617–50.

Nehru, J. (1961) 'Strategy of the Third Plan', in Government of India, *Problems in the Third Plan: A Critical Miscellany* (New Delhi: Ministry of Information on Broadcasting), p. 46.

Phelps, E. S. (1961) 'The Golden Rule of Accumulation: A Fable for Growthmen', *American Economic Review*, vol. 51, pp. 638–43.

Quah, Danny (1993a) 'Empirical Cross-Section Dynamics in Economic Growth', *European Economic Review*, vol. 37, no. 2/3 (April), pp. 426–34.

Quah, Danny (1993b) 'Galton's Fallacy and Tests of the Convergence Hypothesis', *The Scandinavian Journal of Economics*, vol. 95, no. 4 (December), pp. 427–43.

Quah, Danny (1994) 'Convergence Empirics Across Economies With (Some) Capital Mobility', London School of Economics and Political Science, Suntory–Toyota International Centre for Economics and Related Disciplines, Discussion Paper No. EM/94/275.

Radner, R. (1961) 'Paths of Economic Growth That Are Optimal With Regard Only to Final States: A Turnpike Theorem', *Review of Economic Studies*, vol. 28, pp. 98–104.

Ramsey, F. P. (1928) 'A Mathematical Theory of Saving', *Economic Journal*, vol. 38, no. 152, pp. 543–59.

Raut, L. (1985) 'Three Essays on Inter-temporal Economic Development', Unpublished doctoral dissertation, Graduate School, Yale University.

Raut, L. (1991a) 'R&D Spillover and Productivity Growth: Evidence from Indian Private Firms', (University of California, San Diego).

Raut, L. (1991b) 'Capital Accumulation, Income Distribution, and Endogenous Fertility in an Overlapping Generations General Equilibrium Model', *Journal of Development Economics*, vol. 34, pp. 123–50.

Raut, L. and T. N. Srinivasan (1991) 'Endogenous Fertility, Technical Change and Growth in a Model of Overlapping Generations', Economic Growth Center Discussion Paper No. 628, Yale University.

Robinson, Sherman (1989) 'Multisectoral Models', in Hollis Chenery and T. N. Srinivasan (eds), *Handbook of Development Economics*, vol. 2 (Amsterdam: North-Holland), pp. 885–947.

Romer, P. M. (1986) 'Increasing Returns and Long-run Growth', *Journal of Political Economy*, vol. 94, no. 5, pp. 1002–37.

Romer, P. M. (1990) 'Endogenous Technological Change', *Journal of Political Economy*, vol. 98, no. 5, pt 2 (October), S71–102.

Rosenberg, N. (1963) 'Capital Goods, Technology, and Economic Growth,' *Oxford Economic Papers*, vol. 15, pp. 217–27.

Sen, A. K. (1994) 'Economic Regress: Concepts and Features', *Proceedings of the World Bank Annual Conference on Development Economics 1993*, Supplement to the *World Bank Economic Review* and *World Bank Research Observer* (Washington DC: World Bank), pp. 315–33.

Schultz, T. W. (1961) 'Investment in Human Capital', *American Economic Review*, vol. LI, no. 1, pp. 1–17.

Schumpeter, J. (1942) *Capitalism, Socialism and Democracy* (New York: Harper).

Schumpeter, J. (1961) *The Theory of Economic Development* (New York: Oxford University Press).

Sheshinski, E. (1967) 'Optimal Accumulation with Learning by Doing', in Karl Shell (ed.), *Essays on the Theory of Optimal Growth* (Cambridge, Mass.: MIT Press).

Simon, J. L. (1981) *The Ultimate Resource* (Princeton, NJ: Princeton University Press).

Solow, R. M. (1956) 'A Contribution to the Theory of Economic Growth', *Quarterly Journal of Economics*, vol. 70, pp. 65–94.

Solow, R. M. (1957) 'Technical Change and the Aggregate Production Function', *Review of Economics and Statistics*, vol. 39, pp. 312–20.

Srinivasan, T. N. (1962) 'Investment Criteria and Choice of Techniques of Production', *Yale Economic Essays*, pp. 59–115.

Srinivasan, T. N. (1964) 'Optimal Savings in a Two-Sector Model of Growth,' *Econometrica*, pp. 358–73.

Srinivasan, T. N. (1993) 'Comments on Paul Romer, "Two Strategies for Economic Development: Using Ideas vs. Producing Ideas",' *Proceedings of the World Bank Conference on Development Economics, 1992*, Supplement to the *World Bank Economic Review* and *World Bank Research Observer*, (Washington, DC: World Bank), pp. 103–9.

Srinivasan, T. N. (1994) 'Data Base for Development Analysis: An Overview', *Journal of Development Economics*.

Stiglitz, J. (1990) 'Comments: Some Retrospective Views on Growth Theory', in P. Diamond (ed.), *Growth/Productivity/Unemployment* (Cambridge, Mass.: MIT Press).

Stokey, N. (1988) 'Learning by Doing and the Introduction of New Goods', *Journal of Political Economy*, vol. 96, pp. 701–17.

Summers, R. and Heston, A. (1988) 'A New Set of International Comparisons of Real Product and Price Levels: Estimates for 130 Countries', *Review of Income and Wealth*, vol. 34, pp. 1–25.

Summers, R. and Heston, A. (1991) 'The Penn World Table (Mark 5): An Expanded Set of International Comparisons, 1950–1988', *Quarterly Journal of Economics*, vol. 106, pp. 327–68.

United Nations (1991) *World Population Monitoring 1990* (New York: United Nations).

UNESCO (1991) *Statistical Year Book, 1991* (Paris: UNESCO).

Uzawa, H. (1961) 'On a Two-Sector Model of Economic Growth', Pt I, *Review of Economic Studies*, vol. 29, pp. 40–7.

Uzawa, H. (1963) 'On a Two-Sector Model of Economic Growth', Pt II, *Review of Economic Studies*, vol. 30, pp. 105–18.

Uzawa, H. (1964) 'Optimum Growth in a Two-Sector Model of Capital Accumulation', *Review of Economic Studies*, vol. 31, pp. 1–24.

Uzawa, H. (1965) 'Optimum Technical Change in an Aggregate Model of Economic Growth', *International Economic Review*, vol. 6, pp. 18–31.

von Neumann, J. (1945) 'A Model of General Equilibrium', *Review of Economic Studies*, vol. 13, pp. 1–9.

World Bank (1993) *The East Asian Miracle* (Washington DC: World Bank).

Young, A. (1991) 'Learning by Doing and the Dynamic Effects of International Trade', *Quarterly Journal of Economics*, vol. 106, pp. 369–406.

Young, A. (1993) 'Lessons From the East Asian NIC's: A Contrarian View', Working Paper no. 4482 (Cambridge, Mass.: Bureau of Economic Research).

7 Modern Economic (Endogenous) Growth and Development

Moshe Syrquin

The topic of the Siena workshop on which this chapter is based was 'Endogenous Growth and Development'; I shall argue here that the two elements of growth and development have proceeded along parallel lines, leaving the potential for cross-fertilisation largely unrealised.

Modern economic growth (MEG) is the term used by Simon Kuznets (1966) to describe the economic epoch of the last 250 years, distinguished by the pervasive application of science-based technology to production. The principal characteristic of MEG, one that sets it apart from all previous economic epochs, is 'a sustained increase in per capita or per worker product, most often accompanied by an increase in population and usually sweeping structural changes' (Kuznets, 1966, p. 1).

The process of modern economic growth has wide ramifications besides the rise in productivity and the structural changes that will occupy us below. Concomitant changes of MEG include the concentration of economic activity in urban centres, with the consequent displacement of population; a switch to large-scale enterprises, with a corresponding change from self-employment to employee status; and a move towards universal education. These and related trends lead to changes in the structure of families and in their roles as providers of 'safety nets', and to changes in the social positions, expectations and aspirations of various groups in the population. The required adaptations are intrinsically conflictive, hence the necessity for mechanisms for conflict resolution and the emergence of the state as arbiter among group interests, and as mitigator of the adverse effects of economic change.

The spread of MEG has been a gradual process. Originally, it was confined to the group we identify today as developed countries: countries in western, northern and central Europe; the European offshoots overseas (the United States, Canada and Australia); and Japan. Over the past fifty years, several additional countries in various regions have traversed a substantial part of the transition from a low-income agrarian economy to an industrial urban economy with a substantially higher income. There have also been cases of frustrated take-offs, while for many others the process of modern economic growth has remained an elusive one. It would be difficult to suggest the feasibility of one, simple and parsimonious unified theory that could encompass and make intelligible the great variation in country experiences observed over the past fifty years.

In the 1950s economic theorists returned to the analysis of long-term dynamics or growth after decades of being absorbed by issues related to microeconomics and to short-term stabilisation. The following decade saw an explosive growth in growth theories which, however, were only marginally influential or relevant to development economics. Growth models from that older vintage were of little help in explaining the variability of growth rates among countries and over time. But then, as argued by F. H. Hahn and R. C. O. Matthews in their magisterial 1965 survey, 'model-builders [were] not trying to do this, anyway' (p. 112). Instead, they were generally preoccupied with 'an unduly restricted and over-simplified background concept of the phenomenon to be explained ("growth of the US economy since 1865 at a constant rate with constant capital–output ratio and distribution of income")' (ibid.). This narrow focus and the emphasis on the case of steady-state growth 'have drawn the theory into directions which severely limit its direct empirical applications or usefulness. The historical patterns of economic growth as summarized, for example, by Kuznets . . . are too complex to be described in terms of steady growth' (ibid.)

Since the mid-1980s there has been a renewed interest in growth, sparked in part by the claim that some general implications of the older theories apparently failed to agree with observation. The data for this claim and for subsequent empirical studies refer now to a very large number of countries, covering the least and the most developed. Endogenous growth models could therefore appear to be more relevant to development than the older vintage of growth theory on two counts: first, these models incorporate some features that figured prominently in the development literature; and second, the evidence in the empirical applications extends now to LDCs. While these are welcome additions, I will argue below that Hahn and Matthews' evaluation quoted above, applies as much to new growth theory as it did to old growth theory.

I STRUCTURAL CHANGE AND GROWTH

The process of MEG can not be captured in one all-purpose model of development. I shall describe one approach to the study of long-term growth; an approach that emphasises the interrelations between growth and structural change. Its central features are economy-wide phenomena such as industrialisation, urbanisation, and agricultural transformation. Following a brief presentation of its evolution, I shall summarise some of the main findings of this research that seem to be highly relevant for any theory of long-term growth, endogenous or otherwise. I then argue that endogenous growth theory has, by and large, ignored these findings.[1]

In development economics and in economic history, structure commonly refers to the relative importance of sectors in the economy in terms of production and factor use. Industrialisation is, then, the central process of structural change. Following common use, structure also refers to some ratios derived from technological or behavioural relations. Input–output coefficients are an example of the former, and the aggregate saving ratio of the latter. The principal changes in structure emphasised in the development literature are increases in the rates of accumulation (Rostow, Lewis); shifts in the sectoral composition of economic activity (industrialisation) focusing initially on the allocation of employment (Fisher, Clark) and later on production and factor use in general (Kuznets, Chenery); and changes in the location of economic activity (urbanisation) and other concomitant aspects of industrialisation (demographic transition, income distribution). The interrelated processes of structural change that accompany economic development are jointly referred to as the *structural transformation*.

The process of modern economic growth is clearly more encompassing. In addition to the elements of transformation mentioned above, for example, it considers changes in institutions by which structural change is achieved. This wider framework is often acknowledged, though seldom represented in empirical work.

Structural change is at the centre of modern economic growth. It is therefore an essential ingredient for describing the process and for the construction of any comprehensive theory of development. More important is the hypothesis that growth and structural change are strongly interrelated. Most writers recognise their interdependence, and some emphasise the necessity of structural changes for growth. For Kuznets, 'structural changes, not only in economic but also in social institutions and beliefs, are required, without which modern economic growth would be impossible' (Kuznets, 1971, p. 348). The interdependence also appears as a cumulative process: 'Sectoral redistribution of output and employment is both a necessary condition and a concomitant of productivity growth' (Abramovitz, 1983, p. 85); or, more guardedly: 'Neither structural change nor growth in GDP is an exogenous variable; both result from a complex of interacting causes on the supply side and the demand side' (Matthews *et al.*, 1982, p. 250).

Once we abandon the fictional world of homothetic preferences, neutral total factor productivity growth with no systematic sectoral effects, perfect mobility, and markets that adjust instantaneously, structural change emerges as a central feature of the process of development and an essential element in accounting for the rate and pattern of growth. It can retard growth if its pace is too slow or its direction inefficient, but it can contribute to growth if it improves the allocation of resources by, for example, reducing the disparity in factor returns across sectors, or facilitating the exploitation of economies of scale. The potential gains are likely to be more important for developing countries than for developed ones, since the former exhibit more pronounced symptoms of disequilibrium and can achieve faster rates of structural change. In a dynamic context the gains can be far from negligible, accounting for as much as a third of the measured growth in total factor productivity (see Syrquin, 1988). Structural change entails and is fuelled by innovation and adaptation which in a Schumpeterian process of creative destruction lead to the replacement of old by new products founded on novel technologies. This process underlies the explanation of Kuznets (1930) and Burns (1934) of their finding that growth rates of output of particular commodities tended invariably to slow down, while at the same time there was no evidence of retardation of the aggregate level. Arrow's learning by doing can be presented as a generalisation of these early empirical studies.

II THEORIES OF GROWTH AND DEVELOPMENT: OLD AND NEW

Economic historians assign a key role to demand in igniting the process of industrialisation. Landes (1969, p. 77), for example, sums up his discussion of demand and supply factors in the Industrial Revolution in Britain thus: 'it was in large measure the pressure of demand on the mode of production that called forth the new techniques in Britain, and the abundant, responsive supply of the factors that made possible their rapid exploitation and diffusion'. Such an emphasis on demand, reinforced by Keynesian theory, greatly influenced early writings on development economics. The central concepts of the 1950s, including the dynamic version of the Keynesian model (Harrod–Domar), dual-economy models (Lewis), demand complementarity, balanced growth and 'big-push', all feature demand as the centrepiece of analysis, and relegate trade to a minor position. In this vintage of development economics we recognise the two components of the economic core of the transformation: accumulation and sectoral composition. Accelerating and sustaining growth required increasing the rates of accumulation and maintaining sectoral balance to prevent disequilibrium in product markets, or to overcome disequilibrium prevailing in factor markets.

2.1 Accumulation

In the 1950s, accumulation almost invariably referred to physical capital in commodity production and infrastructure. Capital appeared as the critical factor in the Harrod–Domar model. A doubling in the investment rate was seen as being indispensable by Rostow as well as by Arthur Lewis, who wrote that 'The central problem in the theory of economic development is to understand the process by which a community which was previously saving and investing 4 or 5 per cent of its national income or less, converts itself into an economy where voluntary saving is running at about 12 to 15 per cent of national income or more' (Lewis, 1954, p. 155).

Two important early developments can be seen as attempts to specify the role of capital. For the closed economy, Mahalanobis (1953) argued that with non-shiftable capital the key planning problem is the allocation of investment between sectors producing consumption and production goods, or how many machines to use in making machines. A similar model was developed in the mid-1920s by the Soviet economist Fel'dman. (The modern reformulation is attributed to Domar, 1957.) For the open economy, H. B. Chenery and his collaborators introduced foreign-exchange requirements as an additional constraint on growth as well as the limitation imposed by savings (Chenery and Bruno, 1962; Chenery and Strout, 1966). These developments became an integral part of disaggregated dynamic input–output models and of optimising multisector programming models.

The main message of these studies and of the later emphasis on human resources is that a sustained increase in rates of accumulation, while not sufficient, is a necessary requirement for long-run growth and transformation.

At about the same time, neoclassical theory responded to the structuralist challenge posed by the Harrod–Domar model and came out with its own growth theory from the supply side (Solow, 1956). Unlike the Harrod–Domar model and its variants, the impact of neo-classical growth theory on development economics was quite limited. Elaborating on the succinct evaluation of Hahn and Matthews quoted above, I would include among the reasons for this limited impact the explicit focus of growth theory on advanced countries ignoring key features of developing countries, and the fact that some of the main implications of neoclassical growth theory were clearly at odds with the reality of development and underdevelopment. In the aggregate version, there is no surplus labour, and long-run growth is independent of the saving rate; in multisectoral versions of the von-Neumann type, growth, still independent of the saving rate, proceeds in a balanced fashion and no disequilibrium is allowed. Also, growth theory did not really try to devise testable implications and, most important, was totally concerned with asymptotic steady states.

2.2   Sectoral Composition

Accumulation is one of the two main components of the transformation in development economics. The second deals with sectoral composition and its evolution. Modern analyses of sectoral transformation originated with Fisher (1939) and Clark (1940), and dealt with sectoral shifts in the composition of the labour force. They were probably the first to deal with the process of reallocation during the epoch of modern economic growth, and to use the form of sectoral division (primary–secondary–tertiary) which, one way or another, is still with us today. Clark's approach was predominantly empirical, but he did relate the observed shifts to differential productivity growth and Engel effects, the two principal elements in subsequent attempts to account for the transformation in the structure of production. Theories of development of the 1950s also stressed sectoral differences. In Lewis's model, sectoral differences appear as traditional versus modern sectors, and in Nurkse (1959) and Rosenstein-Rodan (1943) as a requirement for balanced growth. These approaches shared a view of the less developed economies as characterised by labour surplus in agriculture, low mobility of factors, price-inelastic demands, export pessimism, and a general distrust of markets. These are the hallmarks of what Little (1982) characterises as the 'structuralist view'. They found a policy echo in the advocacy of inward-orientated strategies and planning, primarily in Latin America and South Asia.

On the empirical side, studies of long-run transformation are best represented by Kuznets' synthesis of modern economic growth in a series of seminal papers ('Quantitative Aspects of the Economic Growth of Nations' (1956–67); more compact statements are the Kuznets (1966) monograph and his Nobel lecture (Kuznets, 1973)). Kuznets established the stylised facts of structural transformation, but was reluctant to offer a theory of development. He saw his analysis as an essential building block towards such a theory. His approach, however, is quite different from the empiricism of earlier writers. Economic theory guided his choice of concepts and the all-encompassing interpretations that accompanied every statistical finding. His essays on modern economic growth are a compendium of ideas on growth, transformation, distribution, ideology, institutions, and their interrelationships. Endogenous growth theorists can find in these essays a rich source of ideas, a guide to specification, and the long-run relationships against which to calibrate their models.

2.3 Sources of Growth

The research programme on structural transformation absorbed and adapted some elements of growth theory. A notable example is the sources of growth analysis where the supply-side elements in the approach of Abramovitz, Solow and others was augmented to include demand-side and other factors that were to reappear as major innovations of new growth theory. Early forerunners of growth regressions, apparently not available to Barro (1991) and his myriad followers, include Chenery *et al.* (1970), Hagen and Havrylyshyn (1969) and Robinson (1971). These studies presented econometric analyses of large samples of countries testing for the significance of structural variables in explaining growth rates. The set of explanatory variables included initial levels of income (to test for convergence), educational attainment, size variables (returns to scale), growth of exports, and the share of agriculture in output. Fifteen years later, Chenery (1986) contrasted the neoclassical approach to growth with a more encompassing structural approach (see Table 7.1). The two views are differentiated by their assumptions regarding disequilibrium and the extent of flexibility in the economy. The structural approach, unlike the neoclassical one, identifies some conditions that make complete and instantaneous adjustments to change unlikely. The slack in the economy resulting from disequilibrium phenomena, such as segmented markets and lags in adjustment, imply that productivity growth can be accelerated by reducing bottlenecks and facilitating the shift of resources to sectors of

Table 7.1 Alternative views of growth

Neoclassical approach	Structural approach
Assumptions	
Factor returns equal marginal productivity in all uses	Income-related changes in internal demand
No economies of scale	Constrained external markets and lags in adjustment
Perfect foresight and continuous equilibrium in all markets	Transformation of productive structure producing disequilibria in factor markets
Empirical implications	
Relatively high elasticities of substitution in demand and trade	Low price elasticities and lags in adjustment
Limited need for sector disaggregation	Segmented factor markets
	Lags in adopting new technology
Sources of growth	
Capital accumulation	Neoclassical sources plus:
Increase in labour quantity and quality	Reallocation of resources to higher productivity sectors
Increase in intermediate inputs	Economies of scale and learning by doing
Total factor productivity growth within sectors	Reduction of internal and external bottlenecks

Source: Chenery (1986).

higher productivity. Table 7.1 was Chenery's 1986 summary of representative research, over the three preceding decades, on the two alternative views of growth. It was published just as new growth was being incubated. Since then the distinction between the two columns has been partially blurred as a result of endogenous growth theory adopting some of the assumptions of the structural approach.

A major implications of comparative studies of structural transformation is that identifying the sources of long-term productivity growth requires a disaggregated, multisectoral approach but in an economy-wide framework. This Kuznetsian approach was adopted in various large-scale comparative studies. An early influential example was the Yale Growth Center comparative study that aimed to cover some twenty-five economies and produced substantial country studies such as the ones for Argentina (Diaz Alejandro, 1970) and Israel (Pack, 1971). Japan, the one developed country not of European origin, has attracted a great deal of attention. K. Ohkawa has been a central figure in various collaborative enterprises to explain long-run growth and transformation in Japan, and the lessons to be derived from this experience for other developing economies (Ohkawa and Rosovsky, 1973; Ohkawa and Ranis, 1985). The Ohkawa and Rosovsky study was part of a large project directed by Abramovitz and Kuznets and sponsored by the SSRC, that focused on long-run growth and transformation in developed countries. In addition to the Japanese study, publications have appeared on the United States (Abramovitz and David, 1973), France (Carre *et al.*, 1975) and, after a long gestation period, the United Kingdom (Matthews *et al.*, 1982).

III LOOKING AT THE STYLIZED FACTS

In this section I shall briefly summarise some of the implications for growth theory from empirical studies of long-term structural transformation which can be regarded as part of the Kuznets research programme on modern development growth (MEG). The presentation is partial and highly subjective. It focuses on aspects that appear relevant for a growth theory that tries to encompass less developed countries even when those aspects may not be the most robust ones identified in the empirical literature.

A basic and robust result which underlies much of the following presentation is that, instead of a sharp dichotomy between less developed and industrial countries, each group having its own distinctive structure, we find that the changes in structure during the process of development are better described by the concept of a transition from a low-income agrarian economy to an industrial urban economy with substantially higher income. The transition may not be smooth and it may follow a variety of alternative paths, but the overall process of structural transformation has enough common elements to justify its representation by a set of stylised facts. This section presents a selection of results on growth and transformation derived from econometric studies, from multisectoral models within countries, and from a combination of both in the form of a simulation model based on cross-country information. The econometric results are based on long historical series for industrialised countries, shorter time series from developing countries, and cross-country comparisons.

At the IEA Corfu conference in 1958, N. Kaldor coined the term 'stylised facts' in his summary of observations about the growth of industrial economies. These 'facts' are empirical regularities observed 'in a sufficient number of cases to call for an explanation that would account for them ... independently of whether they fit into the general framework of received theory or not' (Kaldor, 1985, pp. 8–9). 'Facts or not' (wrote R. M. Solow in 1970), 'they are what most of the theory of economic growth actually explains' (p. 2). Only recently have growth theorists re-examined Kaldor's list of stylised facts by questioning the validity of some of them and adding new entries (Romer, 1989). All along, stylised facts of growth and transformation were being established in the development field, and on occasion summary lists were published (see, for example, Kuznets, 1966, ch. 10; and Taylor, 1989). The following sections give a selection of such stylised facts, first of the pattern of growth of output and TFP, and then of the patterns of structural transformation.

3.1   Growth of Output and Factor Productivity

In the early stages of MEG there was a distinct acceleration in the pace of growth. A more marked acceleration took place after the Second World War in most regions and groups of countries, particularly in middle-income countries, In every decade since 1950 middle-income countries have grown faster than the groups of countries with lower or higher income levels. One implication for convergence studies is that, if at all, convergence takes place among countries beyond a certain income level. (For evidence of growth acceleration among LDCs during the period 1950–83, see Syrquin and Chenery, 1989.)

Turning to the growth of productivity, empirical studies lend support to the following observations which, so far, are not reflected in growth theory but would probably affect significantly theoretical results and policy recommendations:

(a) Most of the acceleration in the growth of output can be traced back to an acceleration in the rate of growth of TFP.
(b) The rate of growth of output is positively associated with the rate of growth of labour productivity and of TFP (Verdoorn effects). While the direction of causality is unclear, the association appears quite robust across countries and over time.
(c) The proportion of output growth attributed to TFP is higher in richer than in poorer countries.
(d) The contribution of capital accumulation to growth is more significant at medium than at higher income levels. This is because of the decrease at higher levels of development of both the rate

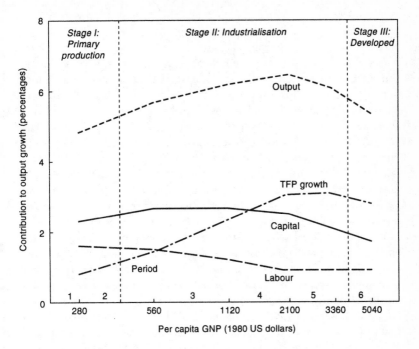

Figure 7.1   Factor contributions to growth

Source: Chenery and Syrquin (1986).

of capital accumulation and the elasticity of output with respect to capital.

The above propositions, and others to come in the next section, can be illustrated through the simulations of the cross-country prototype model of industrialisation presented in Chenery and Syrquin (1986). The results given in Figure 7.1 are more speculative than others in this chapter but, taken with caution, suggest a consistent pattern. The decline in the contribution of labour reflects the slowdown in population growth at high income levels (demographic transition), which outweighs rising labour productivity. The rise in TFP growth in the early periods stems from the existence of underutilised labour and the subsequent shift of resources out of agriculture. The relative constancy of the capital contribution results from the decline in its marginal products, which offsets the rise in the investment rate.

In most countries with available long-term sectoral information, TFP tends to be higher in manufacturing than in agriculture for extended periods. This fact – unbalanced productivity growth – is one of the reasons on the supply side behind the shift in comparative advantage and the transformation of the structure of production during the transition discussed in the following section. The imbalance of TFP notwithstanding, successful industrialisation has always been preceded or accompanied by a significant rise in productivity in agriculture. This point appears to be a most general and very significant result. While there are significant differences among the sectoral rates of TFP, these rates tend to be uniformly higher across sectors in countries with good average performance as well as within countries in periods of rapid growth of aggregate productivity (see also Dollar *et al.* (1988) for similar results and for a discussion of their consistency with the assumption of factor price equalisation). This finding suggests that the overall economic environment, which includes macroeconomic and trade policies, is an important factor in explaining differences in productivity growth.

Disaggregated studies of TFP show that a significant share of the measured rate of aggregate TFP is caused by resource shifts from sectors with low productivity to sectors with higher productivity. At medium income levels the reallocation effect can account for as much as 30 per cent of aggregate TFP. Rapid resource reallocation may not be feasible without high rates of growth and investment; thus the contribution of investment to growth may be underestimated if we do not consider the increase in flexibility due to higher investment rates.

Finally, an observation on the exogeneity of the aggregate rate of productivity growth. For at least two reasons, the aggregate rate of TFP cannot be regarded as exogenous even if the sectoral rates were: first, the output weights needed to aggregate the sectoral rates are clearly not independent of demand; and second, in a disequilibrium situation the aggregate rate of TFP includes the gains from resource shifts.

3.2 Structural Transformation

The central element of structural transformation is the process of industrialisation measured by changes in the sectoral shares in production and factor use. Industrialisation has to be analysed in conjunction with changes in the structures of demand (final and intermediate) and trade. Results from an econometric study of the various elements of structural transformation are summarised concisely in Table 7.2. The patterns of change in the table summarise the relationship that exists

Table 7.2   Shares of economic structure associated with levels of per capita income (percentages)

Component of economic structure	Income per capita (1980 US dollars)				Actual average ≥4000	Total change
	Actual average ≤300	Predicted				
		300	1000	4000		
Final demand						
Private consumption	79	73.3	66.4	60.3	60	−19
Government consumption	12	13.6	13.7	15.4	14	02
Investment	14	18.4	23.3	25.9	26	12
Exports	16	19.3	22.6	26.4	23	07
Imports	21	24.6	26.0	28.0	23	02
Food consumption	39	38.7	29.1	18.9	15	−24
Trade						
Merchandise exports	14	15.2	18.8	21.2	18	04
Primary	13	13.9	15.2	11.8	07	−06
Manufacturing	01	01.3	03.7	09.4	11	10
Production (value-added)						
Agriculture	48	39.4	22.8	09.7	07	−41
Mining	01	05.0	07.7	06.1	01	0
Manufacturing	10	12.1	18.1	23.6	28	18
Construction	04	04.4	05.5	06.7	07	03
Utilities	06	06.7	08.1	09.3	10	04
Services	31	32.4	37.8	44.7	47	16
Labour force						
Agriculture	81	74.9	51.7	24.2	13	−68
Industry	07	09.2	19.2	32.6	40	33
Services	12	15.9	29.1	43.2	47	35

Source: Syrquin and Chenery (1989).

along growth paths where per capita income is the measure of development. In Chenery and Syrquin (1986) we presented a disaggregated model of industrialisation that goes back to some of the underlying relationships determining industrial changes. The main ones are changes in domestic final demand (Engel effects), the growing intermediate use of industrial products, unbalanced productivity growth, and the evolution of comparative advantage as factor proportions change. In this section, I abstract from the interrelated nature of the patterns and present selectively some robust findings that have a bearing on theories of endogenous growth.

Demand   The best-established trends in the composition of final uses of output are the rise in the share of resources allocated to investment and the decline of the share of food in consumption. The latter (Engel's

Law), is among the most robust empirical relationships in economics, but its implication of non-homothetic preference is almost universally ignored in theories of growth and international trade. During the process of development, the use of intermediates relative to total gross output tends to rise. A measure of this change is an increase in the density of the input–output matrix which reflects the evolution to a more complex system with a higher degree of fabrication, and the shift from handicrafts to factory production. Such qualitative changes support the approach of Young (1928), Romer (1986) and Grossman and Helpman (1991). A related robust trend is the significant increase with the level of income of the share of purchased intermediates in the total value of output in agriculture (Deutsch and Syrquin, 1989).

Trade   The rise in the ratio of capital (human and physical) the labour, and the observed higher rate of productivity growth in the more modern sectors of the economy, tend to shift the comparative advantage from primary activities to industrial ones. Accordingly, we find the composition of exports shifting systematically from primary products to manufactures mostly in the upper levels of the transition (Balassa, 1979; Leamer, 1984; McCarthy *et al.*, 1987).

Changes in the structures of production and employment   Changes in demand and trade reinforce each other. They combine with productivity growth to produce a more pronounced shift in the structures of production and labour use. The share of value added in agriculture declines sharply over the transition, whereas manufacturing, construction and utilities double their share and the services sector share raises by about 50 per cent. The decline in the share of agriculture in employment is more pronounced than in production, but since employment starts from a much higher level and its decline takes place at a relatively higher income level, it leads to a decline in the relative productivity of labour in agriculture. Only by the end of the transition does the trend reverse itself and the gap in average productivity begins to narrow. Figure 7.2 presents a graphical summary of the transformation of the structures of production and factor use during the transition.

IV   ENDOGENOUS GROWTH AND DEVELOPMENT

The literature on endogenous growth is vast and still growing rapidly. A large segment of this literature is portrayed as addressing, or being

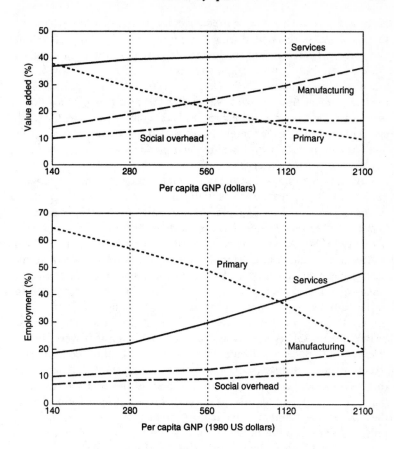

Figure 7.2   Simulations of value-added and employment for cross-country model

Source: Chenery and Syrquin (1986).

of relevance to, growth issues of LDCs. This concern appears sometimes in the analytical formulation and, more often, in growth regressions on samples that span the income range from near subsistence to the highest incomes observed. The following critical comments refer to some dominant trends in this literature, while recognising that it is not monolithic and that (rare) exceptions to those trends exist.

Central issues in new growth theory (external effects, returns to scale, divergence, learning, R&D) were prominent in the mid-1960s in development writings and can also be found in the work of neo-Keynesians such as Kaldor. This earlier preoccupation is ignored by new growth theorists, whose reinvented wheels are now more rigorously developed and have a firmer grounding in microeconomics (often an excessive one). Productivity growth might have been exogenous in Solow (1956), but it was certainly not so in Denison (1967). The long delay in formalising endogenous growth was partly the result of the inability of neoclassical economics to incorporate non-convexities into the analysis. An additional factor might have been the shift in focus of policy and research from growth to equity, and then to short-term stabilisation in the wake of the oil shocks.

Enlarging the sample, probably the main reason behind the attention paid to LDCs, increases substantially the variance of the variables of interest. This can lead to more precise estimates, but at a cost. The cost is that the models now have to be more flexible to incorporate the diversity in the sample. The point is not that a different kind of theory is needed for studying developing countries, but rather that there may be significant differences in the validity of some assumptions and in some behavioural and technological relationships and parameters. Initial conditions are not sufficiently considered in empirical work. In old growth theory, initial conditions wash out at the steady state. In new growth theory this is not always the case, but even if it were, for any relevant horizon and discount rate the effect of initial conditions on structure and growth cannot be ignored. Among the initial conditions that have been shown to influence the path of development are those that effect the extent and nature of participation in international trade: the size of the economy, availability of natural resources, and trade policies. Various other initial conditions are highly correlated with the level of development. Including the level of per capita income at the beginning of a period in a growth regression is therefore a way to capture the effect of some initial conditions, besides those that may represent the potential for catch-up or convergence.

The lack of convergence in the postwar period was an important reason for the renewed interest in growth theory. The renewed interest is welcome even if it was sparked off by a faulty premise. Given the acceleration of growth in the early stages of MEG, convergence should not have been expected for a sample of countries that spans the complete income range. Furthermore, as Kuznets (1966, pp. 390–9) and more recently Pritchett (1995) demonstrate convincingly, the hundred years preceding the postwar period must have witnessed significant divergence rather than convergence.

Empirical studies that are based on aggregate data of uncertain meaning and questionable validity and that, in addition, pool observations from countries in Western Europe and in SubSaharan Africa, can at best yield results that are suggestive, indicative of some associations on average, and give us some rough orders of magnitude. If they appear to be robust under a variety of circumstances they acquire the status of a stylised fact. However, given the heterogeneity of the observations, the assumption that they are random drawings from a single universe appears a bit too strong. The same is true of the notion that a few regressions on such a shaky basis can 'validate' or 'refute' a theory. Levine and Renelt (1992) illustrated the fragility of most of the results derived from growth regressions. Arcand and Dagenais (1995) have recently re-examined the studies of Barro (1991) and Mankiw *et al.* (1992) and concluded that the presence of measurement errors introduce a substantial bias into their results, raising significant doubts about commonly-accepted stylised facts of the determinants of growth.

Cross-country studies of growth have been expanding the list of potential determinants analysed. Variables suggested by political economy analysis include measurements of inequality, corruption and democracy, to list only a few. Almost invariably these augmented studies fail even to acknowledge awareness of a fundamental conceptual problem. Growth rates have low time persistence, while country characteristics such as Gini coefficients are highly persistent. Unless one is prepared to argue that the growth model underlying the regressions is applicable to (say) the post-1960 period but not to earlier periods, the estimates of the inequality variable in a growth regression cease to have the intended meaning.

V CONCLUSION

I conclude as I began, by reiterating the belief that endogenous growth theory and its empirical implementation could become highly relevant and influential for development economics, but that the potential remains largely unrealised. Growth theory could benefit substantially if it were to become more receptive, not just to ideas from the development literature but, even more important, to a large accumulation of empirically established stylised facts of the process of development.

Note

1. Among the many contributions to this research programme I draw primarily from Simon Kuznets, Moses Abramovitz, Angus Maddison and various studies by Hollis Chenery and myself. In particular I draw liberally from Chenery *et al.* (1986) and from Syrquin (1988, 1994).

References

Abramovitz, M. (1983) 'Notes on International Differences in Productivity Growth Rates', in D. C. Mueller (ed.), *The Political Economy of Growth* (New Haven, Conn.: Yale University Press).

Abramovitz, M. and P. A. David (1973) 'Reinterpreting Economic Growth: Parables and Realities', *American Economic Review*, vol. 63, pp. 428–39.

Arcand, J. L. and M. Dagenais (1995) 'The Empirics of Economic Growth in a Cross Section of Countries: Do Errors in Variables Really Not Matter?', University of Montreal.

Balassa, B. (1979) '"A stages approach' to comparative advantage', in I. Adelman (ed.), *Economic Growth and Resources, Vol. 4: National and International Policies* (London: Macmillan).

Barro, R. J. (1991) 'Economic Growth in a Cross Section of Countries', *Quarterly Journal of Economics*, vol. 106, pp. 407–43.

Burns, A. F. (1934) *Production Trends in the United States since 1870* (New York: National Bureau of Economic Research).

Carre, J. J., P. Dubois and E. Malinvaud (1975) *French Economic Growth* (Palo Alto, Calif.: Stanford University Press).

Chenery, H. B. (1986) 'Growth and Transformation', in H. B. Chenery, S. Robinson and M. Syrquin, *Industrialisation and Growth: A Comparative Study* (Oxford University Press), pp. 13–36.

Chenery, H. B. and M. Bruno (1962) 'Development Alternatives in an Open Economy: The Case of Israel', *Economic Journal*, vol. 72, pp. 79–103.

Chenery, H. B. and A. Strout (1996) 'Foreign Assistance and Economic Development', *American Economic Review*, vol. 56, pp. 679–733.

Chenery, H. B. and M. Syrquin (1986) 'Typical Patterns of Transformation', in H. B. Chenery, S. Robinson and M. Syrquin, *Industrialization and Growth: A Comparative Study* (New York: Oxford University Press), pp. 37–83.

Chenery, H. B., H. Elkington and C. Sims (1970) 'A Uniform Analysis of Development Patterns', Harvard University, Center for International Affairs, Economic Development Report 148 (Cambridge, Mass.).

Chenery, H. B., S. Robinson and M. Syrquin (1986) *Industrialization and Growth: A Comparative Study* (New York: Oxford University Press).

Clark, C. (1940) *The Conditions of Economic Progress* (London: Macmillan).

Denison, E. F. (1967) *Why Growth Rates Differ* (Washington DC: Brookings Institution).

Deutsch, J. and M. Syrquin (1989) 'Economic Development and the Structure of Production', *Economic Systems Research*, vol. 1, pp. 447–64.

Diaz Alejandro, C. F. (1970) *Essays on the Economic History of the Argentine Republic* (New Haven, Conn.: Yale University Press).

Dollar, D., E. N. Wolff and W. J. Baumol (1988) 'The Factor Price Equalization Model and Industry Labor Productivity: An Empirical Test Across Countries', in R. Feenstra (ed.), *Empirical Methods for International Trade* (Cambridge, Mass.: MIT Press), pp. 23–47.

Domar, E. (1957) 'A Soviet Model of Growth', in *Essays in the Theory of Economic Growth* (New York: Oxford University Press).

Fisher, A. G. B. (1939) 'Production, Primary, Secondary and Tertiary', *Economic Record*, vol. 15, pp. 24–38.

Grossman, G. M. and E. Helpman (1991) *Innovation and Growth in the Global Economy* (Cambridge, Mass. and London: MIT Press).

Hagen, E. E. and O. Havrylyshyn (1969) 'Analysis of World Income and Growth, 1955–1965)', *Economic Development and Cultural Change*, vol. 18, pp. 1–96.

Hahn, F. H. and R. C. O. Matthews (1965) 'The Theory of Economic Growth: A Survey', in American Economic Association and Royal Economic Society, *Surveys of Economic Theory* (New York: St Martin's Press).

Kaldor, N. (1985) *Economics Without Equilibrium* (New York: M. E. Sharpe).

Kuznets, S. (1930) *Secular Movements in Production and Prices* (Boston, Mass. and New York: Houghton Mifflin).

Kuznets, S. (1956–67) 'Quantitative Aspects of the Economic Growth of Nations', *Economic Development and Cultural Change* (a series of ten articles).

Kuznets, S. (1966) *Modern Economic Growth* (New Haven, Conn.: Yale University Press).

Kuznets, S. (1971) *Economic Growth of Nations: Total Output and Production Structure* (Cambridge, Mass.: Harvard University Press).

Kuznets, S. (1973) 'Modern Economic Growth: Findings and Reflections', *American Economic Review*, vol. 63, pp. 247–58.

Landes, D. (1969) *The Unbound Prometheus: Technological Change and Industrial Development in Western Europe from 1750 to the Present* (Cambridge University Press).

Leamer, E. E. (1984) *Source of International Comparative Advantage* (Cambridge, Mass.: MIT Press).

Levine, R and D. Renelt (1992) 'A Sensitivity Analysis of Cross-Country Growth Regressions', *American Economic Review*, vol. 82, pp. 942–63.

Lewis, W. A. (1954) 'Economic Development with Unlimited Supplies of Labor', *Manchester School of Economic and Social Studies*, vol. 22, pp. 139–91.

Little, I. M. D. (1982) *Economic Development: Theory, Policy and International Relations* (New York: Basic Books).

Mahalanobis, P. C. (1953) 'Some Observations on the Process of Growth of National Income', *Sankhya*, vol. 12, pp. 307–12.

Mankiw, N. G., D. Romer and D. N. Weil (1992) 'A Contribution to the Empirics of Economic Growth', *Quarterly Journal of Economics*, vol. 107, pp. 407–37.

Matthews, R. C. O., C. Feinstein and C. Odling-Smee (1982) *British Economic Growth* (Oxford University Press).

McCarthy, F. D., L. Taylor and C. Talati (1987) 'Trade Patterns in Developing Countries, 1964–82', *Journal of Development Economics*, vol. 27, pp. 5–39.

Nurkse, R. (1959) 'Notes on "Unbalanced Growth"', *Oxford Economic Papers*, vol. 7, pp. 295–7.

Ohkawa, K. and G. Ranis (eds) (1985) *Japan and the Developing Countries: A Comparative Analisis* (Oxford: Basil Blackwell).

Ohkawa, K. and H. Rosovsky (1973) *Japanese Economic Growth: Trend Acceleration in the Twentieth Century* (Palo Alto, Calif.: Stanford University Press).

Pack, H. (1971) *Structural Change and Economic Policy in Israel* (New Haven, Conn.: Yale University Press).

Pritchett, L. (1995) 'Divergence, Big Time', Policy Research Working Paper No. 1522 (Washington, D.C. World Bank).

Robinson, S. (1971) 'Sources of Growth in Less Developed Countries', *Quarterly Journal of Economics*, vol. 85, pp. 391–408.

Romer, P. (1986) 'Increasing Returns and Long-Run Growth', *Journal of Political Economy*, vol. 94, pp. 1002–10.

Romer, P. (1989) 'Capital Accumulation in the Theory of Long Run Growth', in R. Barro (ed.), *Modern Business Cycle Theory* (Cambridge, Mass.: Harvard University Press), pp. 51–127.

Rosenstein-Rodan, P. (1943) 'Problems of Industrialization in Eastern and South-Eastern Europe', *Economic Journal*, vol. 53, pp. 202–11.

Solow, R. M. (1956) 'A Contribution to the Theory of Economic Growth', *Quarterly Journal of Economics*, vol. 70, pp. 65–94.

Solow, R. M. (1970) *Growth Theory: An Exposition* (New York and Oxford: Oxford University Press).

Syrquin, M. (1988) 'Patterns of Structural Change', in H. B. Chenery and T. N. Srinivasan (eds), *Handbook of Development Economics*, vol. I. (Amsterdam: North-Holland), pp. 203–73.

Syrquin, M. (1994) 'Structural Transformation and the New Growth Theory', in L. L. Pasinetti and R. M. Solow (eds), *Economic Growth and the Structure of Long-Term Development* (New York: St Martin's Press).

Syrquin, M. and H. B. Chenery (1989) 'Three Decades of Industrialization', *The World Bank Economic Review*, vol. 3, pp. 145–81.

Taylor, L. (1989) 'Theories of Sectoral Balance', in J. G. Williamson and V. R. Panchamukhi (eds), *The Balance between Industry and Agriculture in Economic Development, vol. 2* (London: Macmillan), pp. 3–31.

Young, A. A. (1928) 'Increasing Returns and Economic Progress', *Economic Journal*, vol. 38, pp. 117–32.

8 Growth and Development Theories*

Lance Taylor

The sun rarely shines on new ideas in economics; the days are even fewer when economists' novel thoughts contribute value-added to those that came before. These truisms reflect the nature of the discipline. The expand upon Robert Heilbroner's (1991) classic description, worldly philosophers are philosophers still, doomed to mull over concepts that do not envolve at any rapid pace.

Contrary to the discipline's current practice, this observation means that economics should be conscious of its history. Real philosophers ponder Plato and Aristotle with benefit, just because they happened to get to most of the good ideas first. Economists proposing 'new' theories of growth, trade or development could gain from their more un-worldly colleagues' example. Good minds have grappled for two centuries with obstacles to development and causes of growth. In the long run, their insights are likely to prove more useful than the models that fit this decade's fashions best.

Such thoughts are especially relevant when one recognises that there are many distinct theories of growth, only a small selection of which are reflected in the new mainstream literature. Somewhat arbitrarily, six theoretical traditions are categorised in summary fashion in Sections A–F of Figure 8.1, with additional effects catalogued in Section G. 'Filiation' (a phrase coined by Schumpeter, 1954) runs roughly horizontally in the different sections, with cross-category linkages pointed out by solid lines. Dashed lines show oppositional reactions of importance.

The diagram provides a background for the three main themes of this chapter. The first is that past thinking about growth and development encompasses diverse lines of thought; many are relevant to the current policy debate. 'New' growth theories draw upon just a few of these ideas, and are correspondingly deficient. Second, 'new' or 'market friendly' development strategies which became popular in the 1980s suffer from the same problem. Their orthodox advocates have an extremely limited perspective. How both mainstream discourses might be widened is the final topic. It can be clarified in part by considering

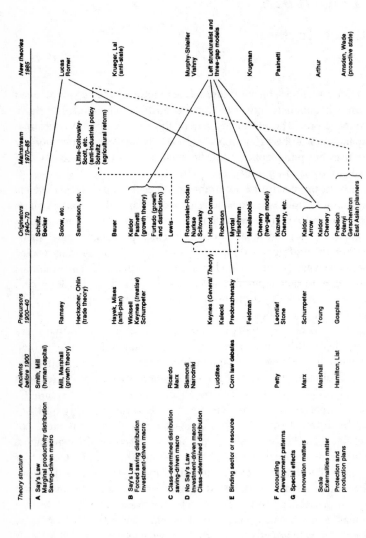

Note: Solid lines denotes filiations, and dashed lines oppositions.

Figure 8.1 Filiations and oppositions in growth and development theory

specific issues with regard to generation and absorption of technical progress. These are mentioned at various points, with semi-formal models banished to three appendixes.

I NEW GROWTH MODELS AND SAY'S LAW

Section A is the Tory Row of Figure 8.1 – mainstream growth theorists dwell almost exclusively there. They postulate Say's Law, that all scarce production inputs are fully utilised, and claim that flexible prices in markets dominated by optimising 'agents' vary to permit the economy to arrive at such a state. In macroeconomic terms, the supply of saving is determined by forces of productivity and thrift, and capital formation adjusts correspondingly (perhaps aided by a variable interest rate in the market for 'loanable funds' with laws codified by John Stuart Mill). As charted by Chakravarty (1980), from Mill through Marshall to Solow and beyond, this vision of the economic system has animated orthodox thought. It supports an engine of considerable analytical power; the trouble is that all its energy is easily dissipated on manipulating models with weak connections to the institution- and ignorance-ridden economies in which we live.

The concerns of new growth theory appear to be twofold. The first is to break away from Solow's (1956) regime in which output and employment (plus exogenous productivity) growth rates are forced to be equal in steady state. Mathematical tricks have been employed to widen the spectrum of possible output growth rates.

The second goal is to 'endogenise' productivity growth by tying it to other variables in the system, ideally through the use of rational actor 'microfoundations'. One approach has been to relate the level of productivity to a stock variable such as physical capital, or the human capital built into the (fully-employed) labour force. Some sort of externality may be postulated to this end. A question that might seem natural to enthusiasts of market processes is why an externality which increases a variable as important as macroeconomic productivity is not internalised by perceptive economic actors. However, it is not posed by new growth theorists.

The other way to endogenise productivity has been to tie its observed increases to realised economies of scale. To carry out this task, tractable formal models of imperfect competition are required. Most are borrowed from the new industrial organisation literature, with their verisimilitude subject to doubt.

We can begin by discussing macro-level relationships, with micro-foundations addressed below. Let X stand for output and K the capital stock; *pace* Cambridge controversies we treat both as being made from the 'same' (malleable) commodity. The output–capital ratio $u = X/K$ becomes a measure of input substitution (not capacity utilisation as in the demand-driven models discussed in Appendixes 1 and 2). If there is full employment of labour L at all times, then the labor–capital ratio $\lambda = L/K$ follows from dynamic equations for L and K respectively. Let ξ be the output–labour ratio, or average labour productivity, and s be the economy-wide saving rate, which can be decomposed as $s = s_\pi \pi + s_w(1 - \pi)$ where π is the share of non-wage income in total product and s_π and s_w are savings rates from wage and non-wage incomes respectively (empirically, the inequality $s_\pi > s_w$ is well-founded). For future reference, let $\theta = 1 - \pi$ be the labour share.

The 'old' growth models that flourished in the 1950s and 1960s based themselves on a string of accounting balances:

$$\frac{\text{Saving}}{\text{Output}}\frac{\text{Output}}{\text{Capital}} = \frac{\text{Investment}}{\text{Capital}} = \frac{\text{Increase in capital}}{\text{Capital}} = \frac{\text{Increase in output}}{\text{Output}}$$

$$= \frac{\text{Increase in Employment}}{\text{Employment}} + \frac{\text{Increase in (Output/Employment)}}{\text{(Output/Employment)}}$$

or

$$su = I/K = \hat{K} = \hat{X} = n + \rho, \qquad (8.1)$$

where a 'hat' denotes a growth rate ($\hat{K} = (dK/dt)/K$) and depreciation is ignored for simplicity. With exogenous growth rates of employment and labour productivity after the last equals sign (with values $n = \hat{L}$ and $\rho = \hat{\xi}$ respectively) and savings-determined investment, then either the saving–output ratio s or output–capital ratio u has to adjust to allow all the equalities to hold in a steady state.

Solow's road to a such an equilibrium is based on the assumptions that the saving rate s is fixed, while the output–capital ratio u is an increasing function $f(q)$ of the 'effective' labour–capital ratio $q = \xi\lambda = \xi L/K$ via which the labour input of employed workers is scaled by their average productivity ξ. A well-behaved neoclassical production function is usually invoked to explain the dependence of u and q.

Using Equation (8.1), the growth rate of q becomes

$$\hat{q} = \rho + n - \hat{K} = \rho + n - su = \rho + n - sf(q). \qquad (8.2)$$

For easy comparison with the models set up in Appendixes 1 and 2. Equation (8.2) describes the growth process in terms of changes in the effective labour–capital ratio q as opposed to the more commonly used capital–labour ratio.

Although, as will be discussed presently, many new growth models presume otherwise, the usual hypothesis is that the function $f(q)$ is increasing; that is, for a given capital stock, output rises when there is a bigger labour input. One implication – a proof is sketched below – is that, subject to proper boundary conditions (the 'Inada conditions'), there will be a stable steady-state growth path with $\hat{q} = 0$ and $n + \rho = su = sf(q) = \hat{K}$. Because u is constant at steady state, we also have $\hat{X} = \hat{K}$.

One of the new theory's advertised advances is to get away from boring steady growth at an exogenous rate $n + \rho$ by relaxing the Inada conditions (a possibility already recognised by Solow). For example, u can simply be made constant, as in Rebelo's (1991) 'AK' model. The implication is that $\hat{X} = \hat{K} = su$ automatically, in a restatement of the 'Harrod–Domar equation' used to crank out growth rates in numerous development planning exercises since the 1950s (the quotation marks signal the fact that the equation does not reflect the stability questions raised by both Harrod and Domar).

To satisfy Equation (8.1), the productivity growth rate ρ becomes an endogenous variable in an AK world, adjusting as a true 'residual' (in the traditional sense of that word) to satisfy the growth-accounting balances. The fact that Solow's introduction of capital-labour substitution was originally billed as an improvement over Harrod's and Domar's formulations is usually not mentioned in descriptions of AK models. Affinities between AK machines with several capital goods and von Neumann's (1938) and Sraffa's (1960) formulations are not pointed out either.

A more dramatic break with Solow is to render his growth equation unstable so that q diverges from a steady growth path toward either infinity or zero – a knife-edge, with policy implications to be developed later. For example, Romer (1986) asserts that externalities generated by investments in R&D can be a source of aggregate increasing returns. In a typical formal representation, this hypothesis is observationally equivalent to Kaldor's (1957) 'technical progress function' $\xi = f(K/L)$, discussed in Appendix 1. In log-linear or growth rate form we have $\hat{\xi} = \phi_0 + \phi_1(\hat{K} - \hat{L})$, so that faster capital stock growth relative to labour speeds the growth of labour productivity.

It is simplest to work out the implications of Romer-style increasing returns or externalities on the assumption that they generate labour-augmenting or Harrod-neutral technical progress, as is done herein with ξ. We thereby preserve the possibility of steady-state growth in convergent Solow models. In log-differential or growth rate notation, the details in the traditional neoclassical production specification are as follows.

The production function is:

$$\hat{X} = \theta(\hat{L} + \hat{\xi}) + (1 - \theta)\hat{K}.$$

This formula can be derived as an accounting identity from the national income and product accounts (Taylor, 1979) or else on the hypothesis that production inputs are paid their real marginal products. Either way, it shows that:

$$\hat{u} = \hat{X} - \hat{K} = \theta(\hat{L} + \hat{\xi} - \hat{K}) = \theta\hat{q},$$

a result used later. It is of interest to trace through another derivation in terms of the neoclassical theory of demands for labour and capital. They are, respectively,

$$\hat{L} - \hat{X} = -\sigma\hat{\omega} + (\sigma - 1)\hat{\xi}$$

and

$$\hat{K} - \hat{X} = -\sigma\hat{r},$$

where ω is the real wage; r the rate of profit; and σ the elasticity of substitution. Plugging the input demand functions into the production function gives the wage–profit curve,

$$\hat{r} = [\theta/(1 - \theta)](\hat{\omega} - \hat{\xi}),$$

that is, there is an inevitable inverse trade off between ω and r, contrary to the structuralist models discussed later.

With saving-driven investment, the capital stock growth rate g will be:

$$g = sX/K = [s_\pi(1 - \theta) + s_w\theta](sX/K) = [s_\pi(1 - \theta) + s_\omega\theta]u.$$

The differential equation for increases in q thus becomes:

$$dq/dt = q[\hat{L} + \hat{\xi} - g]. \tag{8.3}$$

Before bringing in the technical progress function, it makes sense to review how the model performs when both growth rates $\hat{L}$ and $\hat{\xi}$ are exogenous. We want to know the sign of dg/dq. To get it, begin by putting together the input demand functions to derive a wage equation,

$$\hat{\omega} - \hat{\xi} = [(1 - \theta)/\sigma](\hat{K} - \hat{L} - \hat{\xi}) = -[(1 - \theta)/\sigma]\hat{q},$$

which shows that ω/ξ is an inverse function of q, with a stronger response for smaller values of σ.

From the wage–profit curve and the capital input demand function, we have

$$\hat{u} = \sigma\hat{r} = -[\sigma\theta/(1 - \theta)](\hat{\omega} - \hat{\xi}) = \theta\hat{q},$$

the result derived above. It shows that $du/dq > 0$ and thereby $\partial g/\partial q > 0$, at least with regard to the effect through u. The implication is that $d(dq/dt)/dq < 0$, or the growth equation is stable, as noted previously.

Besides u, we also have to trace effects of q on g via changes in the labour share. The wage equation above can be used to show that $d\theta/dq$ is positive when $\sigma > 1$ and negative when $\sigma < 1$, that is, the real wage does not have to fall very much for producers to hire additional labour when it substitutes easily with existing capital. So for high σ there could be instability: a higher q could reduce the profit share and the savings-driven growth rate enough to increase dq/dt. This sort of divergence is akin to the Jones and Manuelli (1990) version of endogenous growth discussed later.

Now bring in the technical progress or increasing returns function,

$$\hat{\xi} = \phi_0 + \phi_1(\hat{K} - \hat{L}). \tag{8.4}$$

The wage and wage–profit equations stay the same, but the growth rate equation, Equation (8.3), takes the form:

$$dq/dt = q[(1 - \phi_1)(\hat{L} - g) + \phi_0],$$

so that stability is going to depend on the sign of $1 - \phi_1$. For $\phi_1 < 1$, the reasoning goes as above. An increase in q means that ω/ξ falls, so that r rises and u goes up as well, increasing g. There is convergence to a steady state with a capital stock growth rate $g = L + \phi_0/(1 - \phi_1)$, as in the Kaldor model of Appendix 1. Note that as ϕ_1 approaches one from below, the growth rate tends toward infinity.

The Romer case is $\phi_1 > 1$. Now a higher q still increases g and reduces dq/dt, but before that happens ξ goes up enough to make $dq/dt > 0$ – an instability of the sort that occurs in traditional Keynesian models when the marginal propensity to consume is greater than one. A similar form of 'endogenous' growth can be extracted from Kaldor's model. Forty years ago, he just didn't think of a catchy label for the divergent case of his growth equation.

Most new growth theorists, of course, go beyond Solow and Kaldor in treating savings rates not just as fixed coefficients. Rather, they believe that they are the outcomes of dynamic optimisation exercises carried out over infinite time by representative immortal 'agents' with perfect foresight and perfect knowledge about the economic system. Begging the question as to how anybody who has read history could possibly think that such a stylisation of economic behaviour underlies recorded human events – Frank Ramsey, the inventor of optimal growth analysis, certainly did not – we can run through the details of an illustrative example because it permits new founts of endogeneity to come into play.

Let $k = K/L = \lambda^{-1}$ and assume that the aggregate production function takes the form $X = F(K, \xi L)$. If the 'level' form of the technical progress function is $\xi = k^\phi$, then with the usual assumption that F is homogeneous of degree one, we have $X/L = f(k, k^\phi)$, where f is the intensive form of the production function.

The world is supposed to be populated by small, identical firms that do not perceive the externality implicit in the k^ϕ argument of f. As far as its own plans are concerned, each firm believes that the marginal product of capital is just f_1, the first partial derivative of $f(k, k^\phi)$. On this hypothesis, the Euler equations emerging from typical modernised versions of Ramsey's (1928) original optimal growth model take a form such as:

$$dk/dt = f(k, k^\phi) - c - nk \qquad (8.5a)$$

and

$$dc/dt = (c/j)[f_1(k, k^\phi) - i], \qquad (8.5b)$$

where c is consumption per capita; $-j$ is the elasticity of the marginal utility of consumption (with respect to c); n is the rate of population growth; and i is an exogenously given rate of time preference or social rate of discount that consumers are supposed to apply to their choices regarding consumption now and later. Equation (8.5a) is another version of the growth equation, Equation (8.3), while the optimisation exercise replaces fixed savings rates with the dynamic consumption equation, Equation (8.5b).

The Jacobian of this system is:

$$\begin{bmatrix} f_1 + f_2\phi k^{\phi-1} & -1 \\ (c/j)[f_{11} + f_{12}\phi k^{\phi-1}] & 0 \end{bmatrix}.$$

Without the externality terms (those with '2' in their subscripts), this matrix would have a positive trace ($f_1 > 0$, capital has a positive marginal product) and a negative determinant ($f_{11} < 0$, capital has decreasing returns). In other words, it would have one positive and one negative eigenvalue and demonstrate what is now called 'saddlepoint stability'. By invoking appropriate transversality conditions (possibly with c jumping acrobatically to the 'saddlepath'), the system (Equations (8.5a) and (8.5b)) can be made to converge to a steady growth solution with $dk/dt = dc/dt = 0$ (or $\hat{C} = \hat{K} - n$, where C is total consumption).

Bringing in the externality takes a step further the mainstream's optimal growth gambit of specifying a locally unstable dynamic system and then driving it to a desirable solution via transversality conditions. Typically f_{12} will be positive (a stronger externality raises the marginal product of capital). With a big enough ϕ, therefore, the southeast entry in the Jacobian can become positive and the determinant becomes positive as well. In other words, the Jacobian has two positive eigenvalues and the dynamic system, Equations (8.5a) and (8.5b), has an unstable node about the steady growth path $dk/dt = dc/dt = 0$.

Barro and Sala-i-Martin (1995), among others, inscribe the incantations about transversality conditions that will bring this locally and completely unstable dynamic system to a steady growth path with $\hat{c} = \hat{k}$, that is, consumption and capital per head grow at the same rate (determined by the larger of the two positive eigenvalues). Output and consumption per unit of capital also stay constant, on the assumption that f_1 tends toward a constant level as k goes to infinity. Restating Equations (8.5a) and (8.5b) in growth rate form and equating $\hat{c}$ and $\hat{k}$ shows that saving per unit of capital becomes $su = u - c/k = n + (1/j)$ $(f_1 - i)$. From Equation (8.5b), for positive growth of c we need $f_1 > i$, or the marginal product of capital as perceived by firms must exceed the social rate of discount. In terms of the traditional accounting of

Equation (8.1), the residual ρ will equal $(1/j)(f_1 - i)$ – perhaps a lucid explanation for a variable which has always provide difficult to understand.

How can these convenient outcomes be arranged? One device is the *AK* model already mentioned. So long as the average (= marginal) product of capital *A* exceeds *i*, endogenous growth is assured. Slightly more generally, Jones and Manuelli (1990) in effect postulate that the production function $f(k)$ has a range strictly bounded from below. A constant elasticity of substitution (CES) production function will do the trick so long as the elasticity exceeds one. Econometric estimates of CES functions usually reject this hypothesis, but endogenous growth adepts suggest that this difficulty can be circumvented if 'capital' is construed to mean not just machines and buildings but also productive assets more generally.

Whether these endogenous growth formulations – with either fixed savings rates or dynamically optimising consumers – are credible empirically is an interesting question. For example, Equation (8.5b) of the optimal growth variant suggests that consumption and saving decisions will be sensitive to differences between the private return (f_1) and cost (i) of capital. Such sensitivity has been hard to demonstrate in practice for both saving and investment decisions. Moreover, marginal products of capital and interest rates do not vary over wide ranges. It is not obvious that basing big national differences is estimated rates of productivity growth (ρ) on such foundations is a fruitful endeavour.

These observations are sharpened by the fact that both optimising and fixed saving coefficient endogenous growth models demonstrate knife-edge dynamics – $\hat{c}$ can equal $\hat{k}$ for both positive and negative rates of growth as both variables diverge from the zero (per capita) growth path. In the optimising models, does it make sense to say that knife-edges result from observed cross-country differences in savings parameters and rates of return? Can they come from small deviations above and below unity on the part of a parameter such as ϕ_1 in Equation (8.4)? Asserting that big differences across national economies in growth performance depends on such factors sidesteps a mass of historical experience, some of it discussed below.

Second, knife-edges have long been postulated in growth theory from the side of investment demand, which cannot figure in neoclassical models based on Say's Law. Investment has been said to be highly sensitive either to the profit rate (see Appendix 1 on Kaldor's growth model) or to the level of capacity use (the source of potential instability in Harrod's pioneering model of 1939). From a Keynesian perspective, knife-edges are more likely to be sharpened by investment rather than saving behaviour, but none have been empirically observed to date.

Finally, unstable growth dynamics can arise from many other sources. In the 1950s, Leibenstein (1954) and Nelson (1956) pointed out that high labour/capital ratios accompanied by Malthusian population dynamics and an absence of externalities can lead to poverty traps. Following many Latin American authors, Taylor and Bacha (1976) argued in an investment-driven model that the growth rate may rest on a knife-edge determined by distributional conflicts and tastes for different sorts of commodities by different social classes – a poverty trap or unequalising growth led by luxurious consumption can result.

Turning to microfoundations, two sorts of behavioural rationales have been proposed for endogenous productivity growth. One is externalities, via which a productivity level such as ξ can be tied to a stock or state variable in a growth model. As already observed, such specifications long pre-date Romer (1986). Besides Kaldor's (1957), an important precursor is Arrow (1962), who tied ξ to 'learning by doing', as proxied by accumulated output over the years. To fit such phenomena into optimal growth models, however, a dilemma that plagued Marshall has to be resolved.

One horn of the dilemma is the desire of neoclassical economists to retain marginal productivity distribution theory under conditions of perfect competition. To carry out that project, they have to assume that economic agents behave as if there are non-increasing (preferably constant) returns to scale for all production inputs. Otherwise, second-order conditions for dynamic optimisation cannot be satisfied and marginal productivity distribution rules make no sense. As Schumpeter (1947) pointed out long ago, such niceties are irrelevant to real capitalist practice, in which firms are disciplined not by anonymous prices but rather by 'creative destruction' caused by the 'unending gale' of technical change. For better or worse, this disequilibrium, dialectical process is alien to the concerns of neoclassical economics.

The dilemma's other horn is that positive externalities give rise to increasing returns. For example, in his well-known new-growth model, Lucas (1988) postulates an aggregate production function of the form

$$X = K^{\beta}[(1 - \tau)H]^{1-\beta}(H^*)^{\gamma}, \qquad (8.6)$$

where H is the total stock of human capital and τ is the share of their time that agents devote to acquiring new H (ambitious beings, they are fully employed in commodity production the rest of the time).

'Normal' production takes place according to constant returns of scale for work effort $(1 - \tau)H$ and physical capital K, but via the externality factor $(H^*)^\tau$, more human capital raises the overall productivity level. The asterisk in the H^* term is a reminder that human capital is subject to personal decisions but also boosts overall productivity.

The agents make their saving and time allocations by maximising the discounted utility of consumption subject to Equation (8.6) and accumulation equations over infinite time. Leaving aside this exercise's ontological absurdity, these agents (like Romer's small, identical firms discussed previously) *cannot* recognise the externality due to H^*, or else their calculations fall apart for the reasons just noted.

Solving infinite horizon optimal growth problems with unrecognised externalities has been billed as a mathematical step forward, a claim that would make a real applied mathematician smile. More disconcerting should be the smiles that externalities even as transcendent as human capital (or the fruits of R&D) provoke from severe neoclassical economists, including members of the 'Austrian' school. If extra learning generates more output, Austrians argue, sooner or later somebody should start making money from that fact (say, by providing education more cheaply than the state can). Were such internalisation of the benefits of a higher H^* to occur, Lucas's rationale for the importance of human capital accumulation ceases to make sense.

At least one ambitious piece of data analysis points to an absence of externalities. In a multidecade project, Jorgenson (1990) has tried to grade components of the United States' labour and capital stocks in detail by their 'quality' in a sources-of-growth accounting framework; the owners of these inputs have full claim to their returns. For the USA at least, his results consistently show a minor contribution of the residual (or 'technical progress') to growth. In other words, the mathematical contortions required to fit the externality in Equation (8.6) into an optimal growth framework may not be worth the effort – on strictly neoclassical empirical grounds.

A final comment on the Lucas model is that it bases its growth dynamics on human capital as a produced means of production. The rate of growth is ultimately determined by how much human capital is reinvested to produce more human capital. This causal scheme is the same as that of two important families of development planning models – Fel'dman–Mahalanobis–Domar (FMD) two-sector specifications focusing on the allocation of scarce capital goods between production of consumer goods and more capital goods ('machines to make machines') and 'gap' models concentrating on internal, external and fiscal balance restrictions on capital formation ('foreign exchange to make foreign exchange'). Whether human capital, physical capital goods or foreign exchange is best treated as 'the' binding restriction on growth in a developing economy is a question taken up later.

An alternative approach to explaining productivity growth is to drop perfect competition to bring in decreasing average production costs. For example, Romer (1987) assumes that production depends on a number of intermediate inputs, with each one supplied subject to constant marginal cost plus a fixed capital cost which can be 'spread' over a greater production volume. Subject to strong behavioural assumptions, Romer shows that this form of decreasing costs translates into an aggregate production function for final goods in which the capital tied up in intermediates shows up as an externality such as H^* in Equation (8.6).

Romer's empirical spirit is willing, but the analytical flesh is weak. Realistic analyses of decreasing costs under imperfect competition point to two strong conclusions. First, authors such as Sraffa (1926), Young (1928) and Kaldor (1972) emphasised that scale economies can under-lie 'cumulative processes' which upset the unbalanced, mutual and self-adjusting equilibria characteristic of Walrasian theory. Firms that initially exploit decreasing costs can gain a commanding position, or else un-stable price and investment cycles can arise (as noted below, Japanese and Korean planners in their push for scale economies in production avoided such problems by hands-on market interventions to preclude what they called 'excessive competition'). Under such circumstances, there is no reason for exit and entry of firms to drive 'pure' profits to zero.

Second, as development economists such as Hirschman (1958) em-phasised, and Chenery (1959) formalised, relative product prices can shift over wide ranges depending on which production processes with increasing returns are present or absent in the economy (think of the decision whether to import, produce for the domestic market, or pro-duce for export some tradable good; or the impact of decreasing costs on the price of a usually non-traded good such as electricity). Cost-based prices arising from one configuration involving presence or ab-sence of members of a set of possible decreasing cost production processes are not an adequate guide for investment project decisions to create another configuration with a markedly different price vector.

Like many recent modellers of imperfect competition, Romer relies on a specification devised by Dixit and Stiglitz (1977), which cleverly sweeps these problems under the rug. In his version, final goods pro-ducers choose 'varieties' of intermediates which substitute for one another subject to a CES function. The more varieties put into operation, the greater is supposed to be the level of final output (just why a farmer using several brands of petrol instead of just one in his tractor will produce more crops is not explained carefully). Firms with identical cost structures enter symmetrically into production of intermediates until pure profits are driven to zero. The tradeoff between a decreasing marginal product of greater input diversity and decreasing supply cost limits the size of each firm – there is no possibility for cumulative processes to get going!

Aghion and Howitt (1992) extend the model to take into account the search for cheaper technologies to produce intermediates, with 'innovations' arriving according to a stochastic process. Their model is tractable just because of the convexifying properties of the Dixit–Stiglitz specification. Without it, potential innovators would face an insoluble computational problem in infinite horizon stochastic dynamic programming because of the potentially wide range of relative price configurations discussed above. The inspiration that true entrepreneurs possess to cut through this computational knot was what Schumpeter (1934, 1947) celebrated. Aghion and Howitt do not get the point.

The Romer and Aghion–Howitt models serve a useful function in emphasising the importance of intermediate inputs in production processes. Although in practice intermediates enter technologically with highly asymmetric input–output coefficients, their share in the gross value of output does rise with income, going from about a third to a half in poor and rich countries respectively. Moreover, a big proportion of the macroeconomic residual is 'explained' by shifts in the sectoral composition of output from low to high productivity sectors in an input–output framework.

The problem is that the new growth models leave out the dynamic, cumulative effects of decreasing costs coupled with backward and forward production linkages that underlie these changes, which were fully recognised by Hirschman, Chenery and a host of other early development economists. *The Strategy of Economic Development* is a far better guide to these connections than are exercises in optimal growth with the lack of behavioural realism that they impose – just to smooth out the imbalances that Hirschman thought were at the heart of the development matter.

II SAY'S LAW WITHOUT MARGINAL CONDITIONS

Other growth theories can be situated in opposition to the mainstream – not because they are less relevant to a serious questions, but because orthodoxy provides a well-known standard of reference. Schumpeter (1934), as detailed in Section B of Figure 8.1, for example, did not adhere to marginal productivity theory when he described an economy 'developing' from one configuration of steady state growth or 'circular flow' to another. Rather, he took over much of Marx's supply-side vision (discussed below) and combined it with a provocative analysis of technical innovation to forge a spirited defence of capitalism. A sketch of his *Theory of Economic Development* goes as follows.

As just hinted, the starting point is rather like Mill–Marshall–Solow steady growth shown in Section A of Figure 8.1 – this is Schumpeter's own interpretation of 'circular flow'. An economy in circular flow may be growing, but in his terminology it is not 'developing'. Development occurs only when an entrepreneur unveils an innovation – a new technique, product, or way of organising things – and shifts production coefficients or the rules of the game. S/he gains a monopoly profit until other people catch on and imitate, and the economy moves to a new path of steady growth.

A key analytical question about this process refers to both the financial and real sides of the economy – how does the entrepreneur obtain resources to innovate? An endogenous money supply and redistribution of real income flows are required to support the new mode of economic operation.

To get the project going, the entrepreneur must invest – an extra demand imposed upon an economy already using its resources fully in circular flow. To finance investment, s/he obtains loans from the banks; new credit, and thereby money, are created in the process. The bank loans are used to purchase goods in momentarily fixed supply. Prices are driven up, so that real incomes of other economic actors decline. The most common examples are workers receiving temporarily fixed nominal wages, or the cash flows of non-innovating firms. There is 'forced saving' as workers' lower real incomes force them to consume less; groups which receive windfall income gains are assumed to have higher saving propensities, so that demand apart from the enterpreneur's declines. Meanwhile, routine investment projects may be cut back.

In summary, the transition between states of circular flow is demand-driven from the investment side (though, of course, the innovation may involve production of new goods or increases in productivity) and short-run macro adjustment takes place through income redistribution via forced saving with an endogenously varying money supply. This story illuminates the Section B typology in several ways.

First, the forced saving adjustment story is not just Schumpeter's; he shared it with Wicksell, the Keynes of the *Treatise on Money*, and a whole host of other 'post-Wicksellian' macroeconomists (Amadeo, 1989). In the guise of the widow's cruse, forced saving survived the Second World War into Kaldor–Pasinetti growth theory. Together with related mechanisms such as the inflation tax (faster inflation erodes wealth in the form of real money balances and induces people to save more), forced saving is virtually the only means that can bring an independent investment function together with supply-constrained output. If investment or some other demand injection goes up, consumption must be crowded out by changing (typically rising) prices; the marginal productivity distribution rules that underpin new growth theory go by the board.

Just what determines output from the supply side is another question. Institutions as in Pasinetti's (1981) accounting-based descriptive model, or else a shortage of a critical input such as capital goods or foreign exchange are two possibilities discussed later.

Kaldor's (1957) theories in Section B complement Schumpeter's through their emphasis on technical progress stemming from economies of scale and new investment. As has been noted, his 'technical progress function' and 'Verdoorn Law' relating the rate of productivity growth respectively to the rate of growth of capital per worker and rate of growth of manufacturing output fit directly into new growth theory models (typically without citation, since mainstream authors seem to find it necessary to refer only to themselves!). Although they may be subject to instability problems in the short run, Kaldor's models form a nice synthesis of forced saving macroeconomic adjustment and endogenous technical change. They tie together his 'stylised facts' of a stable capital–output ratio and profit rate in the long run, together with a falling labour–output ratio and a rising capital–labour ratio over time. For the record, a brief formal presentation is given in Appendix 1.

Finally, the Schumpeter–Kaldor causal scheme can be extended to several sectors, as by Latin-American structuralists such as Furtado (1972). If industrialisation beyond production of simple goods such as food and textiles is to occur, they said, then under present social conditions greater income concentration is necessary to sustain demand for more sophisticated commodities, since their production is likely to be subject to minimum cost-effective size requirements because of economies of scale. The Taylor and Bacha (1976) knife-edge mentioned above comes from increasing income concentration through a variant of forced saving. It provides macroeconomic adjustment in response to (and feeds back into) rising investment in a luxury goods sector catering to rich people's demands.

III DISTRIBUTION AND GROWTH

Section C of Figure 8.1 refers to a line of growth theories that take income distribution as determined by institutional factors prior to the economic system. This idea, of course, traces back to the Classics, and found vibrant form in the hands of Karl Marx.

To summarise Marx's views on growth (or anything else, for that matter) in a way acceptable to all his readers is impossible. All we can do here is set out a number of points that he raised, which can be inserted into simple, formal models that fall well short of capturing the complexity and internal contradictions of his perceptions of growth under capitalism and other modes of production.

  (i) Indeed, the first thing to note is that Marx emphasised that economies change in irreversible historical time in an overall institutional framework such as 'capitalism', 'feudalism', or 'oriental despotism'. Any such mode of production can be characterised by specific social devices for appropriation of surplus product over necessary consumption. This classical insistence on the primacy of processes determining the income distribution is adopted by many non-mainstream authors.

 (ii) Marx concentrated on the capitalist mode, in which growth results from both accumulation and endogenous technical change. Producers adopt new methods to edge out competitors, or because rising labour power can wipe out surplus value, thereby wiping out laggard capitalists as well. Schumpeter gave a specific form to such processes when he wrote about innovation-induced 'creative destruction' of obsolete technologies and firms.

(iii) Competition among capitalists tends to equalise profit rates across sectors. However, sectoral demand and supply levels may not mesh, giving rise to a 'disproportionality crisis'. Similarly, aggregate demand may not equal supply. Money provides a vehicle for hoarding purchasing power, which can lead to a 'realization crisis' or slump.

(iv) Both kinds of crisis interact in a cyclical theory of growth, well described by Sylos-Labini (1984). At the bottom of a cycle, the real wage is held down by a large 'reserve army' of unemployed workers, and capitalists can accumulate freely. However, as output expands, the reserve army is depleted and the real wage may rise. Capitalists search for new labour-saving technologies and also invest to build up the stock of capital and reduce employment via input substitution. Excessive funds tied up in machinery, sectoral imbalances, and lack of purchasing power on the part of capitalists to sustain investment (or of workers to absorb the output that new investment produces) can all underlie a cyclical collapse.

(v) Although he cited Ricardo and ignored Marx, Lewis (1954) translated this story of cyclical upswing into a long-run theory of economic growth, with 'surplus labour' replacing the reserve army. This view, from Section C of the diagram, provoked a strong reaction from the neoclassical line A, as discussed later. More recent, explicitly Marxist authors stress the fall in investment that may occur in response to a profit squeeze as labour gains in bargaining power over a sequence of cycles. This view shows up in the demand-driven growth models discussed in Section D. They provide an interesting alternative to mainstream stories.

(vi) Finally, accumulation and growth may occur as these processes unfold, perhaps accompanied by a falling rate of profit, increased immiserisation of the working class, or both. Marx and more recent authors see cyclical profit squeezes culminating in a steadily declining rate of profit over time.

IV MODELS WITHOUT SAY'S LAW

In their macroeconomics, both Marx and Lewis largely stick with saving-determined capital formation; in this regard, they differ little from neoclassicists. But why, after Kalecki and the Keynes of the *General Theory*, should we believe that growth dynamics are determined by saving from the supply side? In the short run, output can vary to bring saving into line with investment, with prices and income distribution relatively fixed. Over time, distribution can evolve according to conflicting income claims; if the process is dynamically stable (a counterexample will be discussed shortly), the economy will tend toward a 'long-run' steady state with constant relative shares.

'Stagnationist' or 'left structuralist' growth models built upon these ideas show up in Section D. They underlie much discussion of the economic development process, as by Lustig (1980) and Chakravarty (1987). In rich countries, Kalecki (1971) and Robinson (1962) are among the original exponents of this tradition (with forerunners tracing back to Malthus and beyond). Robinson, for example, determines short-run equilibrium at the intersection of saving and investment functions which depend positively on the rate of profit (the first functional relationship can reflect forced saving). A Marx-inspired dynamic evolution of factors influencing the profit share can drive such a model over time, as discussed by Marglin (1984).

Figure 8.2 is a natural extension of the Robinson diagram – discussed by Gordon (1995), Taylor (1991) and others – which puts a distributional variable (the profit rate or real wage) on the vertical axis, and output or capacity utilisation on the horizontal axis. An output response or IS schedule plots points along which investment equals saving (at some endogenous output level) for a given distribution. A supply-related curve then shows how distribution responds (either in the short run or steady state) to changing output. Figure 8.2 has a rising 'Cost' schedule in the capacity utilisation versus real wage plane, as the latter variable responds positively to increases in the former.

Within this structuralist framework, the slope of the IS curve becomes an interesting parameter, as pointed out by Rowthorn (1982) and Dutt (1984). For example, its sign determines whether or not the economy can easily absorb labour productivity growth, which in the first instance wipes out jobs and workers' spending power. Capitalism's classic compensatory mechanism for falling labour–output ratios has been growth of real wages to support aggregate demand. Almost two centuries ago, members of the Luddite movement, reflected by economists such as Malthus and Ricardo, recognised that this process can break down when full employment is not presupposed (as by Kaldor, Schumpeter, and the economists who operate in Figure 8.1's Section A).

Luddite arguments can be valid if an economy with less than full employment is 'wage-led' in the sense that a higher real wage or wage share stimulates aggregate demand. In an economy closed to foreign trade, an increase in the wage share has two immediate effects on effective demand: (i) if the propensity to consume from wage income exceeds the propensity from non-wage income (an econometric truism), then consumer demand will increase, possibly stimulating investment through the accelerator as well; and (ii) the reverse, the corresponding reduction in the non-wage share may cut back on investment via reduced

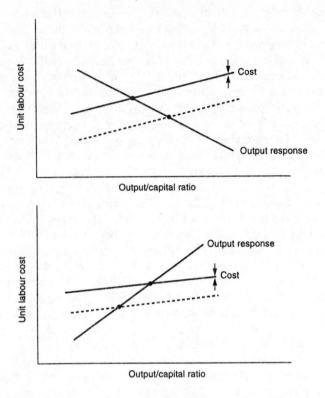

Figure 8.2   Effects of faster labour productivity growth in profit-led (top) and wage-led (bottom) economies

profitability. If the first effect dominates, then demand will increase with the wage share. By an obvious contrast, the economy becomes 'profit-led' if the second effect is more important.

If the economy is open to trade, further complications arise. One follows from the fact that the wage share, or the product of the real wage and the overall labour–output ratio, is a good approximation to labour costs per unit output. An increase in the share, therefore, may provoke higher export costs and a reduction in effective demand via falling sales abroad, that is, an economy in which exports are cost-responsive is more likely to be profit-led.

The econometric evidence (such as it is) suggests that developing economies are typically wage-led. A positive wage/output linkage can complicate adjustment to increase in labour productivity; this is how

Luddite arguments come in. If unemployed labour is present, a productivity gain (or a fall in the labour–output ratio) is not likely to be accompanied immediately by a higher real wage. At the initial level of output, total wage payments will decline as the Cost schedule shifts downward (to the dashed line) in the lower diagram of Figure 8.2. The output–capital ratio decreases along the Output response curve as unit labour costs fall towards their new steady-state level where the schedules cross. There is reduced consumption demand and possibly lower investment and potential output growth via the accelerator, as shown in more detail in Appendix 2.

Wage-led economies are also subject to distributional instability, which occurs when the Cost schedule is steeper than the Output response. A wage increase then raises aggregate demand, which in turn bids up wages further as labour markets tighten. This positive feedback can upset macroeconomic stabilisation efforts, as it did, for example, after 'heterodox shock' anti-inflation programmes in Latin America in the mid-1980s. By freezing prices, these packages offset forced saving and the inflation tax, leading to an initial jump in output caused by consumption demand. The resulting wage pressures contributed to making the freezes melt rapidly.

If exports are sensitive to local production costs, they may jump up enough to raise total output in the profit-led adjustment shown in the upper diagram. The price elasticity of 'our' exports becomes a crucial parameter, key to absorbing productivity growth. In practice, market mechanisms alone are not likely to make export demand responsiveness rise. A government agency or publicly-backed large enterprise such as a South Korean *chaebol* or a transnational corporation may be needed to search out buyers and pressure local producers into making goods and services that sell.

Finally, profit-led economies also may not be easy to guide, especially if the Cost curve in the upper diagram is non-linear, with a steep slope at high levels of capacity utilisation (Gordon, 1995). Attempts to raise output by shifting the Output response curve outwards will then mainly be diverted into real wage increases in a full employment profit squeeze. Investment demand may well decline if it is more sensitive to profitability than output through the accelerator. In a profit-led world, attempted expansionary policy can lead to slower potential output growth, just as faster productivity advance can have a similar effect when effective demand is led by wages.

Another set of models in Section D can be developed on a multisectoral basis, with steady states defined by stable income distributions, and all sectors expanding at the same rate. Such a framework for redistribution lies behind reform proposals that have appeared over the years. The French-Swiss reformer Sismonde de Sismondi (1815) recommended progressive redistribution in the wake of the Napoleonic Wars to stimulate French industrialisation – more prosperous workers would demand clothing and textiles, and propel investment in those sectors. Similar themes appeared in the writings of the nineteenth century's *Narodniki* or Populists in Russia and is debated in India today.

As with Furtado's work mentioned above, the key idea here is that demand and distributional changes can stimulate cumulative processes a là Myrdal (1957) and Kaldor (1972) to alter the nature of supply. Many authors have pointed out that redistribution and/or public investment projects may raise demand enough to make profitable production processes with fixed overheads that have constant marginal but decreasing average costs. Activating economies of scale in this fashion can have profound economy-wide effects of the sort invoked by Young (1928) and his student Rosenstein-Rodan (1961) with his 'Big Push'.

New growth theorists such as Murphy *et al.* (1989) came late in picking up such possibilities, which were commonly accepted by the post-Second World War generation of development economists. Unhindered by Say's Law, they shared a set of ideas that fit well with the growth theories of Sections B to E, and included the following:

1. Schumpeter's views about the disequilibrium nature of the development process are valid, and provide an underlying framework that can be applied widely.
2. One can postulate conditions under which development will be increasingly rapid, capital-intensive and reliant upon a greater role of the state. In nineteenth-century Europe, for example, greater relative 'backwardness' called forth more dramatic transitions (Gerschenkron, 1962).
3. Economies of scale are important. As already noted, co-ordinated investment across many sectors in a Big Push may be required to give balanced output and demand expansion to take advantage of decreasing average costs economy-wide (Rosenstein-Rodan, 1943; Nurkse, 1953). Building on Schumpeter's metaphor, the idea was to get the economy from a 'vicious' to a 'virtuous' circle of growth.
4. The investment must be planned, since pervasive market failures such as decreasing costs and imperfect tradability mean that price-driven, decentralised investment decisions will not be socially optimal (Scitovsky, 1954).

5. Once modern analytical tools such as input–output models and social cost–benefit analysis make public investment planning possible (Chenery, 1959).
6. On the other hand, planning tools are at best approximations, so that one should be on the lookout for inflationary, balance of payments, and other bottlenecks, and figure out how to break them in a process of perpetually unbalanced expansion (Hirschman, 1958).

The distinction between Hirschman's dialectical world view and Rosenstein-Rodan's 'balanced growth' ideas was sharp. But to anticipate later discussion, neither Hirschman nor Rodan disappeared from the mainstream's view because his work was insufficiently formalised, contrary to what Krugman (1993) asserts. Indeed, the mathematics of Chenery's (1959) and contemporaries' planning models with economies of scale was more sophisticated than the apparatus Krugman habitually works with. The difference is that Chenery and friends used integer or dynamic programming methods to solve centralised or firm-level planning problems, while Krugman (with the new growth theorists) used devises such as the Dixit and Stiglitz (1977) formulation outlined above to convexify a putative general equilibrium in which firms have fixed costs. Once again, the interesting questions of multiple equilibrium posed by non-convexities are simply ignored.

Contrary to Krugman's arguments, the old development literature lost impact because it had two ideological drawbacks. One was that while it was rich with diagnoses of development problems, it provided little concrete policy advice. Circular flow, cumulative processes, relative backwardness, balanced and unbalanced growth and so on were intriguing metaphors but did not help much with practical decisions. Planning models and cost–benefit analysis proved to be more of academic interest than managerial worth. Later neoclassical approaches claimed (falsely) to be more practical.

The second problem is that the early development economists placed limitless faith in the capacity of the state to intervene in the economic system. Its inability to carry out its assigned development role(s) became apparent, almost equally fast. This defect had already been emphasised by, first, Mises (1935) and then Hayek (1935) in the 'calculation debate' about socialist planning. Their teachings were reanimated by Bauer (1972) in the developing country context; the neoliberal resurgence of the 1980s brought them to prominence later on.

Realistically or not, neoclassical economics at most requires that the state should be a 'night watchman'. The early development economists needed the state to be proactive and effective, but provided no reasons why it could or should fulfil its tasks. This omission was soon seized upon by neoclassical economists, who forged a new 'market-friendly' consensus about how to further development and growth, a topic to be addressed below.

V   MODELS WITH BINDING RESOURCE OR SECTORAL SUPPLY CONSTRAINTS

In models which do not postulate Say's Law, specific supply limits can still provoke distributional changes such as those underlying forced saving. Examples include shortages of crucial inputs such as capital goods or foreign exchange, or interactions between sectors adjusting to excess demand respectively via changes in output and a flexible price. Growth models along these lines have been elaborated by economists as shown in Section E of Figure 8.1. Those emphasising limiting factors such as foreign exchange or capital goods make an interesting contrast with new growth theory models such as Lucas's (1988) described in Section I.

The ever-present danger of 'external strangulation' in developing economies is an old theme in structuralist thought, dating back at least to the work of the Economic Commission for Latin America in Santiago in the 1950s. The notion was formalised by Chenery and Bruno (1962) in their two-gap model incorporating separate foreign exchange and saving restrictions on growth.

The saving constraint follows naturally from Harrod–Domar or *AK* algebra: investment has to be financed by either national saving or capital inflows from abroad. But the inflows also cover the trade deficit. Industrialisation via import substitution (the only way that has been discovered so far to build up local production capacity) means that the economy becomes dependent on imports of intermediate goods – without them, local factories cannot work. At the same time, import substitution rarely extends to capital goods, so that up to half of investment spending takes the form of purchases from abroad. There is a sharp tradeoff between current production and capital formation, which only additional foreign exchange can relieve. If domestic output is limited by scarcity of convertible dollars or yen, inflationary forced-saving macroeconomic adjustment often occurs. As a consequence, during the 1980s, real wages fell by some 50 per cent in many economies externally strangled by the debt crisis.

The saving and foreign gaps have been extended in recent work (Bacha, 1990; Taylor, 1991) to take into account two important fiscal effects. First, after the debt crisis, many governments nationalised foreign obligations – the state was liable for external payments on debt. Second, econometric work in the 1980s typically showed that there is a strong 'crowding-in' effect of public on private capital formation (contrary to the crowding-out of private by public spending through rising interest rates in financial markets that is frequently presumed). The consequence is a 'fiscal gap' limiting growth because public (and therefore total) capital formation is cut back. Attempts to relieve fiscal burdens by relying on forced saving or the inflation tax became ever more frequent in the 1980s. The multiple interacting problems posed by saving, foreign exchange, fiscal and inflation gaps are a source of much current policy concern. They are not addressed adequately by growth models in the mainstream tradition, which typically assume that sufficient relative price flexibility will make such woes go away.

Besides foreign exchange, a shortage of physical capital can be an impediment to growth. This point was raised forcefully by the economist G. A. Fel'dman during the intense – and for many of its participants, tragic – debate about industrialisation in the Soviet Union in the 1920s. His contribution was brought to Western attention by Domar (1957), at about the same time as Mahalanobis (1953) applied a similar diagnosis to India.

The FMD model assumes that capital is essential to support production of both new capital goods and consumer goods. Diverting machines to make more machines means that present-day consumers will suffer; on the other hand, the long-run growth rate will be faster, the greater the reinvestment rate. Blessed with a long (infinite?) horizon, an optimising planner would therefore concentrate efforts on machine building at the start of his or her tenure, to build up a base for consumption in the future. It is possible that Stalin thought along such lines when he was 'owner' of the Soviet Union (his associates' phrase).

By similar logic, a planner in a foreign exchange constrained economy would concentrate initial efforts on building up export capacity. If human capital is the key to economic success, then everybody should be educated as intensively as possible (subject to the teacher constraint) during the initial phases of growth. Country histories can be analysed in terms of all three models – thanks to external assistance and early export success, South Korea never faced a tight external constraint, but its planners did consciously build up both human and physical capital early on – suggesting that single factor explanations of growth are not likely to bear much fruit.

Like most new-growth theorists, Lucas (1988) focuses on steady states, thus ignoring planning issues of the sort just discussed. Moreover, much new theory falls into the single factor trap. Human capital is frequently asserted to be the fundamental growth factor, and it is certainly true that there is a cross-country correlation between education levels and the level (and maybe even the rate of growth) of per capita income. Country histories, however, belie any tight causal link. The Philippines has a well-educated population, but it is the laggard in East Asian growth; well-educated Sri Lanka grew slowly before external assistance eased the foreign exchange constraint in the late 1970s; and poorly-educated Brazil grew very fast until the debt crisis struck.

Turning to Section E models, with two broad commodities supplied domestically, a frequently used specification is based on one sector where supply is limited by available capacity and the price adjusts to clear the market, plus a second sector in which production meets demand. This two-sector setup blends forced saving. Engel demand effects and output adjustment in an illuminating fashion. It can be applied in various contexts, for example, to analyse the agricultural terms of trade, to discuss 'Dutch disease' problems when a traded goods sector has its price fixed from the world market and a non-traded sector has an adjusting price, and to do global macroeconomics between a 'North' exporting industrial goods and a 'South' selling primary products. The nature of the model can be illustrated with the first interpretation here.

Models focusing on the relative price of food (or agriculture's terms of trade) date at least from the controversy between David Ricardo and Thomas Malthus about whether England's Corn Laws limiting grain imports should or should not be repealed. To address this question, we assume that 'industry' has prices fixed by a mark-up over prime costs and its output is determined by demand, while 'agriculture' has fixed supply and a market-clearing price in the short run.

To see how the model works, we can ask how the two markets interact. Suppose that the terms of trade shift towards agriculture – because of a reduction of food imports, say industrial output can either rise or fall. It will be pushed up by increased demand from higher agricultural income, but also held down by reduced real non-agricultural spending power (real wages drop because of forced saving from dearer food). The latter effect will be stronger in so far as Engel's Law makes food demand income-inelastic, so that the loss in workers' spending power primarily forces down their demand for industrial goods. Under such circumstances, letting more imports into the economy would doubly benefit the industrial sector – food prices fall and output expands. Although he used a different model to argue his case, this outcome is consistent with Ricardo's advocacy of the repeal of the Corn Laws.

The alternative view was espoused by Malthus in his *Principles of Political Economy*, where the argument can be interpreted in terms of distributional effects on aggregate demand. Agriculture is responsible for a large proportion of income and consumer spending. Farmers (or, for Malthus, landlords) hit by adverse of trade will cut their purchases, reducing economic activity overall. Whether a Ricardian or Malthusian distributional configuration applies in developing countries today is highly relevant for policy – the answer according to applied computable general equilibrium models seems to go either way.

Besides import policy, other state interventions can affect the terms of trade. Fiscal expansion or increased investment, for example, will bid up the flexible price to generate forced saving to help meet the increased injection of demand. Ellman (1975) argues that food-price-induced forced saving supported the Soviet industrialisation push of the 1930s, in contrast to Preobrazhenski's (1965) suggestion that the terms of trade be shifted *against* agriculture by a monopsonistic state to extract an investable surplus.

Fix-price/flex-price models (a terminology coming from Hicks, 1965, one of the many co-inventers of such specifications) can also be used to describe growth. Determination of the growth rate depends crucially on how causality in the macroeconomic system runs. If saving–investment balance in the North, for example, regulates expansion of the world economy, then the primary export terms of trade and capital formation in the South will tag along as adjusting variables. Similarly, slow growth in a dominant fixed-supply sector can determine behaviour of the whole system. How the agrarian question may (or may not) be resolved is an obvious application not taken up by recent mainstream theories.

A final observation about Section E is that ideas such as Myrdal's cumulative processes and Hirschman's succession of bottlenecks fit well into a category of models based on binding sectoral performances and constraints. Whether they can be formalised tractably is another question. The fact that the answer is often in the negative does not detract from the usefulness of disequilibrium or dialectical approaches to thinking about the world.

VI ACCOUNTING FOR GROWTH

Section F in Figure 8.1 appears to emphasise that accounting schemes and contemplation of how the entries within them change over time can provide insight into the development process. The discovery that it makes sense to peruse the numbers was made centuries before running endless regressions of GDP growth rates on a host of right-hand-side variables (re)appeared as a recent fad. It dates back 300 years to the 'political arithmetick' of William Petty and his contemporaries who, for example, recognised that the GDP share of agriculture declines as per capita income goes up – a consequence of now predictable technological trends and Engel's Law. Kuznets and Chenery were able uncoverers of similar regularities, and their findings are well summarised by Syrquin (1988).

The other theme that should be mentioned in connection with Section F is that manipulation of accounting schemes themselves can provide useful insights. In a recent example, Pasinetti (1981) closes the input–output accounts by assuming that operating surpluses of firms at the sectoral level just finance their investment demands. This hypothesis (a disaggregated version of the widow's cruse) is not a bad approximation to the nature of investment finance under industrial capitalism, and points to several interesting conclusions (details of the model appear in Appendix 3):

1. A labour theory of value broadly applies, with mark-up rates on labour costs varying across sectors according to their capital intensity and capacity growth rates.
2. If one aggregates gross outputs over sectors using direct and indirect labour inputs, and taking into account investment requirements as weights, a material balance of the form $\Sigma h_i c_i = 1$ emerges, where the h_i are 'hyperintegrated' labour inputs (in Pasinetti's usage) and the c_i stand for public and private sectoral consumption levels per worker (ignoring net exports).
3. In this accounting scheme, Pasinetti first observes that the h_i coefficients decrease when there is labour productivity growth, which historically runs between zero and a few per cent per year under modern capitalism. Second, although per capita demand for a given commodity or service may rise for a time, ultimately it tends to slow, or even decline. For example, in the United States in the 1920s and Europe after the Second World War, surging consumption of cars and associated products supported employment growth,

even though productivity was going up. But by now, cars are no longer income-elastic items and their c_i coefficient is stable or going down, while their h_i also continues to fall.

Both trends can stifle employment expansion – in Marx's hoary language, the material balance condition can fail to be satisfied because of either a realisation or a disproportionality problem. Even if enough work is available in principle, disproportional demand and productivity trends across sectors may require substantial labour force reallocations is full employment is to be maintained. Such movements are never socially simple; most countries rely on public action to make them as painless as possible.

Similarly, if the employment realisation – or stagnation – problem is severe, it can be offset in several ways, but all entail their own complications. One similar mechanism is capitalism's continual introduction of new goods that people feel impelled to buy – for example, few households had video-cassette recorders (VCRs) and compact disc (CD) players even a few years ago. Whether or not entrepreneurs can continue to deluge us with novel temptations with rapidly growing c_i coefficients is always an open question. Second, real wages can rise to offset lower h_i coefficients. We have seen how, when the economy is wage-led, Luddite barriers can impede this process. Finally, policy-makers can attempt to demand stimulation; in a profit-led economy such an effort can easily break down. Contrary to the facile optimism underlying the models of Figure 8.1's Section A, there is no automatic mechanism which makes the $h_i c_i$ terms for currently functioning sectors add up to one.

4. Finally, Pasinetti uses his labour theory of value to rediscover and generalise the theory of the terms of trade proposed by Lewis (1969). The gist is that there is a common set of traded goods for which poor countries have relatively low productivity (levels or growth) in comparison with rich countries. Poor countries have somewhat higher productivity in their exclusive traded goods (tropical food crops, raw materials, for example) than in the common ones, while the reverse is true for rich countries. The result is to swing the terms of trade and real income relative to the common traded goods against poor countries. The moral is that real income growth in developing economies depends crucially on their attaining rapid rates of productivity increase for the common set of traded goods.

A variant trade story concentrates not so much on primary exports as on manufactures. Following Japanese and South Korean practice, how successful have developing economies been in shifting demand composition toward export commodities with high income elasticities in trading partners and rapid productivity growth (perhaps a result of decreasing per-unit costs)? A material balance with the c_i terms decomposed into domestic demands and exports (and imports treated as leakages) would be a natural means to address this question.

VII OTHER PERSPECTIVES

Concern about the forces supporting East Asia's economic success carries over to Section G, along with restatements of the scale economy and technical innovation mechanisms already discussed. These feed indirectly into endogenous growth theory, and with more force appear in Arthur's (1989) observations about the likely irreversibility of sensibly modelled processes of technological advance (especially when there are production non-convexities). Harking back to the balanced/unbalanced growth debate, his results suggest that the unbalanced team was closer to getting the story right.

A related and distinctly non-mainstream view about the importance of 'productive forces' traces back to exponents of protectionism as a basis for industrial development, such as Hamilton and List. Along parallel lines, Polanyi (1944) argued that the state played an essential role in building up the institutions that supported nineteenth-century growth.

From the orthodox point of view, such notions sound heretical, but they certainly encouraged people such as Prebisch (1959) in their advocacy of import-substituting industrialisation (ISI). Friedrich List on *The National System of Political Economy* was more widely read than Anglo-Saxon economists in Japan in the 1930s, and his ideas strongly undergird the East Asian 'model' which emerged at that time. Studies of South Korea and Taiwan by Amsden (1989) and Wade (1990) respectively describe the model's features. Because East Asia raises issues which any realistic growth or development theory should address, it is worthwhile summarising the basic points.

1. A theme continually developed in South Korea's official documents was that 'the market mechanism cannot be entirely trusted to increase competitive advantage by industries', so that branches likely to enjoy high productivity growth and/or income-elastic demand were to be promoted as 'promising strategic industries' (Chang, 1993). They were given custom-designed financial, technical and adminis-

trative support. Picking winners turned out to be an operational concept in an economy such as South Korea's (and, earlier, Japan's), which was not operating on world technological frontiers. As Dore (1986) emphasises in the Japanese case, in 'catching up' situations, it is fairly easy to pick out which sectors to favour and what kinds of support they need for success.

Corrective feedback to the selection process was provided by ongoing, broad reporting of activities of 'priority' firms to the government. The economic bureaucracy thus had access to detailed business information, which proved essential for effective industrial policy. 'Creative destruction' was assured by the government's use of its business information to weed out inefficient production operations in successive waves of rationalisations, mergers and liquidations. Individual *chaebols* were clearly subject to discipline, even though as a group they had privileged access to state resources. Noise and static in dealings between the state and producers were reduced by the fact that apex organisations were engaged on both sides of the dialogue.

2. In line with this strategy, intense effort was devoted to acquiring technology (the huge public investment in education was mobilised economically exactly in this fashion). For this reason, direct foreign investment was strictly regulated, while foreign technologies were banned in sectors in which domestic counterparts were available. Firms were encouraged to practice reverse engineering, along with licensing and purchase of technologies not available at home – all under bureaucratic guidance.

3. There was a consistent emphasis on attaining economies of scale. This goal was reflected in many mergers of small firms initiated or subsidised by the government, for example, in the chemical, automobile, fertiliser and other sectors. There was an ongoing campaign to restrict entry and control capacity expansion in various sectors to curtail 'excessive competition' in the form of big swings and destabilising cumulative processes in investment and price wars in industries with decreasing costs.

4. Within the generally expansionary macroeconomic environment, credit allocation was aggressively practised. The banking system was nationalised early in the Korean industrial drive, giving the state effective control over all important financial flows (aided by tight foreign exchange restrictions). 'Policy loans' with subsidised interest rates and/or priority rationing accounted for over half of bank credits in the 1960s and 1970s.

These features of East Asian industrial planning suggest several conclusions relevant to other developing economies. One is that there can be a bargaining solution among peak organisations to restrain 'rent-seeking' à la Krueger (1974), with rapid output growth and the state's power to punish recalcitrants in the background. Rents (or, better, Marshallian quasi-rents or Marxian/Schumpeterian profits) were certainly created for the *chaebols* by their privileged position, yet they became production powerhouses and not leeches thriving on public largesse. Moreover, they were guided effectively by the bureaucracy, since channels were created for it to get access to business information.

The economic bureaucracy itself was an essential player. In the terminology of economic sociology of the sort pioneered by Polanyi (Evans, 1992), it was 'embedded' in the society in the sense that it could act autonomously for the public good as it saw fit, without completely being taken over by patronage and rent-seeking.

Dialogue among the bureaucracy and enterprises permitted the East Asian nations to practice economic planning effectively in a capitalist environment. Short-term allocative efficiency ('getting prices right') was often sacrificed to long-term productive efficiency or rapid productivity growth. Conscious rent creation on the part of the state was the key to constant industrial upgrading and realisation of economies of scale. In the long run, huge steel mills and shipyards made sense.

Finally, following Japan, the institutional basis for other East Asian miracles was put into place over a relatively short time. *Chaebols*, trading companies, planning bureaucracies and the macroeconomic policy mix all emerged in a creative burst in the early 1960s. Obviously, such institutions cannot be transferred without modification to other national contexts, but partial functional equivalents may well prove relevant elsewhere in the world. Exploring such possibilities would be a proper domain for realistic theories of economic growth.

VIII   THE MAINSTREAM POLICY RESPONSE

The theories of Sections B–F of Figure 8.1 might conceivably be up to such an exploration, but the same cannot be said for the orthodox views summarised in Section A. In fact, they emerged as part of a strong reaction against public guidance of the economy, which got under way in its most recent form in the 1960s. Of course, Mises, Hayek and predecessor liberals had raised the same ideas long before, while the Polanyis of their times fired back.

The first wave of recent critics concentrated on the 'inefficiency' of state intervention as it had evolved, particularly in the emphasis that development economists of the Rosenstein–Rodan vintage placed on ISI. Trade theorists, who are imbued with the evils of protectionism at an early age, took the lead. Using then novel analytical tools such as effective rates of protection and domestic resource costs, authors such as Little *et al.* (1970), Krueger (1984), and many others showed that the incentive structures created by import substitution were highly unequal for different economic actors. They further sought to correlate 'distorted' policy regimes with poor economic performance. Their modest success in this endeavour is a continual embarrassment for the school (Fanelli *et al.* (1993) criticise the latest attempts in the World Bank's 1991 *World Development Report*).

One of the empirical problems is worth flagging now. The 'welfare losses' caused by distortions emerging from solutions of computable general equilibrium models – the 'highest tech' analytical tools – are usually meagre: 100 per cent price wedges might reduce GDP by half a per cent. Implicitly, then, the initial neoclassical critique reduced to an assertion that eliminating distortions will lead the economy to jump to a noticeably more rapidly growing configuration of circular flow. But just how is such a transition supposed to occur? The dynamics of miracles by the invisible hand are not easy to describe, perhaps because they seldom happen.

Regardless of this difficulty, when the critics showed that many industries in developing countries had 'negative value-added' at world prices, they took the profession by storm. But they also transmitted a more powerful message. Reading between the lines, these economists advocated *laissez-faire* as the only viable alternative to an incentive mare's nest. The rapid growth rates of Taiwan and South Korea – at the time unrealistically postulated as having non-interventionist governments – were cited in support of the free market. Although they are not easy to substantiate, the notions that observed distortions inhibit growth and that rapid growers are non-interventionist now permeate the rhetoric and advice of mainstream development scholars and lending institutions; they are built solidly into the policy recommendations offered by the World Bank and International Monetary Fund.

Similar developments took place on the agricultural front, where Lewis and Preobrazhensky-style concerns about the dual economy were swept aside by authors emerging from an anti-interventionist American Middle Western agricultural economics tradition, such as Schultz (1964). Their diagnosis was that farm-gate prices had been held down in developing countries, in comparison to world market prices (however distorted by rich country interventions), as a point of reference. Accumulation processes as well as income distribution within the sector and politico-economic difficulties in altering the way it works were alien to the new price mechanists' ways of thought. Although food production in some countries was aided by subsidies to big farmers to utilise the new technologies offered by the Green Revolution, price reform alone has not been capable of stimulating agriculture over much of the developing world. Africa is the saddest case.

In the 1980s, the debate on economic policy took another turn. Echoing Bauer (1972), who had questioned the efficacy of early state intervention, recent authors postulate that 'bureaucratic failure' is worse than 'market failure'.

For example, Olson (1982) argues that because of bargaining costs and the presence of free riders, coalitions within the society form to protect their own interests. They seek to redistribute income towards themselves, instead of increasing efficiency in the national interest. A weak state cannot intervene, so the system tends towards a highly distorted market structure with the coalitions distributing the spoils. Developing countries that have helped coalitions form themselves around ISI or other strategic interventions may drift toward infernal situations as the subsidised groups take over decision-making: Argentina comes to mind for this pathology (along with numerous others).

The public-choice school led by Buchanan (1980) follows Krueger (1974) in elevating 'rent-seeking' induced by government interventions – lobbying for state favours, paying a bribe to get an import quota or a Pentagon contract, fixing a ticket for a traffic violation – to a deadly social ill. If real resources are devoted to pursuing rents or 'directly unproductive profit-seeking' (DUP) activities in the jargon, the outcome can be a form of suboptimality resembling Olson's for the society as a whole.

Inventing DUP was a technical advance, since deep wells of postulated corruption allowed numerical models to give satisfyingly large estimates of welfare losses from distorion. Moreover, the saving social grace becomes a thoroughly night-watchmanly state supervising a competitive market – the latter condition to be guaranteed by international free trade. Under these conditions, DUP activity supposedly becomes unrewarding, and the invisible hand will guide society toward optimal resource allocation.

In reality, unfortunately, elites have taken advantage of the liberalisation process to further enrich themselves. As Boratav *et al.* (1996)

observe, 'in most Third World countries the bourgeoisie itself is a creation of the state and this historical phenomenon has created cultural, sociological, and economic traits which do not disappear with changes in the policy model'. From this observation they deduce that market liberalisation is not likely to do away with rents in the form of advantageous positions for specific business groups, because 'the very process of rent-seeking emanates from the bourgeoisie, [and] not the state per se'.

A second form of bliss takes a more authoritarian cast. For Buchanan, the ideal state mimics the Cheshire Cat by vanishing to avoid being taken over by the interests. Alternatively, the state can force the interests to vanish, or, in Lal's (1983) words, 'A courageous, ruthless, and perhaps undemocratic government is required to ride roughshod over these newly-created special interest groups' – before Chiapas, the current Mexican leadership may have shared such dreams. It is not clear why Lal's ruthless, etc. generals and bureaucrats will abstain from taking over the market too. The record of Third-World authoritarian states in avoiding corruption and distortions is not encouraging in this regard.

Indeed, a market distorted by the state for its own ends is a final extreme possibility, which can be associated with North's (1981) theories of economic history – not to mention Kennedy's (1987) good read about how their military–industrial complexes force great powers into economic decline. In a typical North example, a state may choose to raise revenue by creating monopolies and then marshall political arguments in their support. The fate of Leninist centrally-planned systems suggests that economic damnation may well lie at the end of such a path.

The conclusion is that the state and market in principle can arrive at extreme configurations that are easy to characterise. However, the Buchanan combination of a purely night-watchman state and a completely undistorted market has never been observed in practice (certainly not in eighteenth-century Britain and contemporary Hong Kong – the two most widely cited putative examples). If it were ever created, a Lal equilibrium would probably not be stable and recent events suggest that the same is true of statist extremism along North's lines.

Indeed, existing societies combine mixtures of state activism with market distortions. If it were possible to assign numerical scores to nations on the two accounts, statistical analysis would almost certainly detect scant association between their degrees or movements of state presence and market imperfections with indicators of economic performance, such as GDP growth rates, except for the likelihood of poor growth in countries with extremely distorted markets.

Beyond this hypothetical regression, a much more fundamental point is that the new neoclassical theory of the state is anhistorical and timeless – although it may shed light on tendencies, it elides the messy dynamics of transitions. As with the new growth theory, a typical model would please Dr Pangloss: all its 'agents' optimise successfully over all possible choices so that the system inevitably arrives at the best (and only, presuming uniqueness) possible world. Not much hope for 'development' in Schumpeter's sense the jumping from one pattern of circular flow to another, in such specifications.

IX WHERE THEORY MIGHT SENSIBLY GO

We are left to ponder how formal growth theory might incorporate some of the foregoing ideas, to become practically useful for policy formation. No instant answers are at hand, but a few thoughts are worth noting.

1. Mechanisms supporting growth and factors restraining it clearly vary from place to place and time to time. The different ways in which the broadly similar accounting schemes which underlie all growth models can be 'closed' by behavioural assumptions along the lines laid out in Figure 8.1 do matter, as pointed out by Sen (1963) and elaborated by Marglin (1984), Taylor (1991) and many others.

   Formalisations of the ideas in all the sections of Figure 8.1 can be fitted to any single economy's data and will give different answers about its likely evolution and sensitivity to policy moves. Statistical techniques such as Granger causality (or lead-lag) tests are of little use in sorting the closure question out, because the absent data and multiple causal patterns. When they are applied, however, they rarely support the macroeconomic vision underlying Figure 8.1's Section A (Gordon, 1995). Serious political economy or institutional discussion provides a better means to consider the causal patterns at hand.

2. Even so, the ideas of Mises and Hayek as propagandised by Margaret Thatcher and Ronald Reagan continue to dominate the current policy scene. In growth and development theory, the corollaries are an emphasis on price-induced supply responses and the wonders of the invisible hand. The big role played by human capital accumulation in new growth models is a case in point.

The idea that more education can have productive payoffs was raised by Smith and Mill and popularised by Schultz (1963) and Becker (1964). Dissidents such as Amsden (1989) similarly stress the role that a skilled labour force played in East Asia's economic success. The question is whether education is more a necessary or concomitant condition for economic development, than sufficient for it to occur. Examples already mentioned suggest possible answers.

South Korea's numerous engineers may well have been unemployed or unemployable, had the Economic Planning Board not practised its Hamiltonian (as in Alexander, not William Rowan) strategies for growth. Brazil, with its poor education performance, grew rapidly until it hit a foreign resource bottleneck in the 1980s; and well-educated Sri Lanka only began to grow fast when external donors turned on the hard currency tap at about the same time. These stories suggest that economic growth is a multifactoral process, and that all available inputs will not automatically be used à la Say. However impressive their manipulations of nineteenth-century mathematics, models ignoring these mundane observations fail the credibility test.

3. As many authors listed in Figure 8.1 pointed out, growth can be strongly influenced by distributional processes unfolding within the social, political and economic structures that exist. Old Ricardo and Marx were not wrong in setting up models based on socioeconomic classes; the not-so-old *General Theory* was built upon an institutional vision of capitalism that is still valid to a great extent. Structuralist modellers are inspired by these examples, which strike them as far richer than the world of Walras.

   Indeed, structure as reflected in low-order dissipative differential equation systems may be more tractable to deal with than the not-necessarily well-behaved Hamiltonian (à la William Rowan, this time) dynamics utilised by neoclassicists. In phase spaces of $2n$ dimensions where n exceeds one, chaos can easily arise to confute the saddlepaths beloved of optimal growth adepts (Lorenz, 1989). On a less formal level, it makes sense to heed the *justes limites* to Walras's programme raised by Poincaré himself: 'you regard men as infinitely selfish and infinitely farsighted. The first hypothesis may perhaps be admitted in a first approximation, the second may call for some reservations' (letter of 1 October 1901, cited by Ingrao and Israel, 1990).

4. In the 'really existing' world, even the first approximation is not very good – the planet is evidently populated by impurely 'economic'

men and women, who certainly have neither unlimited computational capabilities nor perfect foresight. In such a place, development is a transformation with which deep minds besides Mises' and Hayek's have tried to understand, without clearcut success. None the less, one can learn from the theories of capitalism proposed by Marx, Weber, Polanyi and others. As already observed, Marx stressed the importance of the institutions supporting accumulation and technical advance. Despite Bretton Woods tutelage since 1992, they show no signs of emerging in much of the developing world under allegedly 'market friendly' reform programs.

The mature Weber (1968) pointed to a complex causal pattern underlying capitalism's origins: 'All in all, the specific roots of Occidental culture must be sought in the tension and peculiar balance, on the one hand, between office charisma and monasticism, and on the other between the contractual character of the feudal state and the autonomous bureaucratic heirarchy'. All were essential in setting up capitalism as a system of institutionalised strife among shifting but well-defined social groups (Collins, 1980). At a more practical level, all successful or semi-successful reform programmes in semi-industrialised countries in recent decades – Spain, Chile, Korea, Taiwan – have involved complex causal patterns and contingent historical events.

Polanyi's great insight has also been noted, that the institutions supporting the market system arose historically with state guidance from within society, which also defended itself against their worst excesses – child labour laws were passed early in the nineteenth century and the collapse of real wages in Eastern Europe was arrested at 30–40 per cent late in the twentieth century. 'Double movements' of this sort will continue to occur as other countries develop – peacefully only if the tensions of change do not become unbearable.

As society's superordinate actor, the state will also have to play a central role in forcing both sides of the double movement – markets will be neither created nor regulated without public action. The experience of developing countries surely shows that states can fail in several dimensions (Evans, 1992). They operate under fundamental uncertainty, and may or may not respond to the uneven advances of different sectors, disproportionalities, and balance of payments and inflationary pressures that will inevitably arise (Hirschman, 1958). They can try to do too much, thereby achieving little. They can become purely predatory, as in countless petty dictatorships around the world. None the less, as theoreticians of backwardness, from Gerschenkron to Amsden, have pointed out, when backward economies do catch up the process is mediated by the state, in particular by an autonomous bureaucracy accepted by (and embedded in) the society overall.

Somehow, new growth theory manages to ignore all these considerations, while authors operating in Sections B to F of Figure 8.1 have kept them at the front of their minds.

Appendix 1 Kaldor's Growth Model

Let π be the share of profits in output and b the labour–output ratio. Then, using the notation developed in the discussion of new growth models, the breakdown of the value of output (ignoring intermediate inputs, indirect taxes, etc.) takes the form $PX = wbX + \pi PX$, or

$$P = wb/(1 - \pi), \qquad (A8.1)$$

where w is the money wage. The factor $1/(1 - \pi)$ can be interpreted as a mark-up on labour costs, a point developed further in Appendix 2. The real wage ω is $\omega = w/P$, and we can define the profit rate $r = \pi PX/PK = \pi u$, where the output–capital ratio u now measures the level of economic activity as opposed to the results of factor substitution as in neoclassical growth models. Since $\omega b = 1 - \pi$, any one of the three distributional variables r, π, and ω determines the other two.

Assume that the aggregate saving function, reflecting class distinctions, is

$$g^s = \text{Savings}/PK = [s_\pi^\pi + s_w(1 - \pi)]u, \qquad (A8.2)$$

in which s_π is the saving rate from profit income; s_w is the rate from wage income, and $s_\pi > s_w$.

Investment can be assumed to respond to capacity utilisation, as in Kaldor (1940) and Steindl (1952) as well as to the profit rate r:

$$g^i = I/K = g_0 + \alpha r + \beta u = (\alpha\pi + \beta)u, \qquad (A8.3)$$

where we ignore depreciation.

Macroeconomic equilibrium is determined by the condition $g^i - g^s = 0$. With u predetermined, we can solve for π as:

$$\pi = \frac{g_0 + (\beta - s_w) u}{[s_\pi - (s_w + \alpha)]u} . \tag{A8.4}$$

The macroeconomic stability condition with π as the adjusting variable in the short run in $\partial(g^i - g^s)/\partial\pi < 0$. Mindless differentiation shows that this inequality is equivalent to:

$$\delta = s_\pi - (s_w + \alpha) > 0. \tag{A8.5}$$

For the private non-residential US economy with variables scaled by potential output, rough values for long-run investment and saving parameters are in the order of $\alpha = 0.25$, $\beta = 0.1$, $s_\pi = 0.5$, $s_w = 0.3$ (Gordon, 1995). Subject to the vagaries of econometrics and the difficulties of blowing up these parameters to take into account tax and import leakages, other forms of investment and so on, stability of the Kaldorian adjustment process (were the economy really at full employment with forced saving as the main adjustment mechanism) would be precarious in the USA. As will be seen in Appendix 2, where u is the adjusting variable with π fixed in the short run, Kaldorian instability translates into the statement that the economy is profit-led. In the present context, the message of instability is that an increase in π releases demand pressures which make it increase further still.

Be that as it may, Equation (A8.4) when the stability condition in Equation (A8.5) is satisfied shows that the profit share rises with all three parameters of the investment function for given u; this is forced saving. The standard widow's cruse result shows up as $\partial\pi/\partial s_\pi < 0$.

When output is the macro adjusting variable in the short run, the usual Keynesian stability condition or $\alpha(g^i - g^s)/\partial u < 0$ says that saving should respond more strongly than investment to a change in u, or

$$\Delta = s_\pi^\pi + s_w(1 - \pi) - (\alpha\pi + \beta) > 0, \tag{A8.6}$$

which is satisfied for the parameters above with a 'reasonable' value of π (say between 0.1 and 0.2).

If this inequality is valid, then the sign of $\partial\pi/\partial u = -\delta/\Delta u$ will be negative when Equation (A8.5) is satisfied. In a moment, we shall want to assume that the derivative of the capital stock growth rate $g = (dK/dt)/K$ with respect to u is positive. From the investment function in Equation (A8.3), this requirement will be fulfilled for a small positive δ.

As observed in Section I, Kaldor's technical progress function can be written as $\xi = f(K/L)$, or in log-linearised differential form as:

$$\hat{\xi} = \phi_0 + \phi_1(g - \hat{L}), \qquad (A8.7)$$

where a 'hat' denotes a growth rate: $\hat{\xi} = (d\xi/dt)/\xi$. Assume that $\hat{L}$ is exogenous. Since $u = \xi\lambda = \xi(L/K)$, we can write:

$$\hat{u} = (1 - \phi_1)(\hat{L} - g) + \phi_0. \qquad (A8.8)$$

Away from the 'trivial' solution where $u = 0$, we find that the differential equation for du/dt is stable around an equilibrium where $g = \hat{L} + \phi_0/(1 - \phi_1)$ as long as $dg/du > 0$ and $\phi_1 < 1$. Along such a steady state growth path, π and u are constant and the rest of Kaldor's stylised facts mentioned in the text hold true. Because $\pi = 1 - \omega b = 1 - \omega/\xi$ and is constant, we have $\hat{\omega} = \hat{\xi}$, or the real wage increases at the rate of productivity growth. In the spirit of his times, Kaldor concentrated on these steady-state outcomes, rather than on the possibilities of 'endogenous' growth or contraction occuring in the unstable case when $\phi > 0$.

Appendix 2   A Left Structuralist Growth Model

If we drop the hypothesis of full employment, then it is natural to treat u as the adjusting variable in the short run, with the income distribution evolving over time according to the dynamics of labour-management bargaining, conflicting claims to output, or class conflict (depending on which perspective one prefers). With π constant in the short run, Equation (A8.1) above becomes a mark-up price theory along Kaleckian lines.

An immediate question that arises is how output responds to changes in distribution. For the model set out in Appendix 1 but closed by constant π and variable u, the answer is that the economy is 'wage-led' with $\partial u/\partial \omega > 0$ when the inequality in Equation (A8.5) is satisfied and the stability condition in Equation (A8.6) is valid. In words, wage-led adjustment happens when there is a big difference in saving parameters from profit and wage incomes, and the response of investment to the profit rate is weak. (As noted in the text, one should also take into account export demand as well as the fact that imported intermediate inputs into the production process represent a saving leakage not tied to wage income. Both factors push developing economies in the direction of being wage-led – their exports are not price-responsive and they become highly dependent on intermediate imports via ISI. In simple models, an output increase in response to a higher wage occurs when there is an output decrease in response to real devaluation. Devaluation is often, but not always, contractionary in the Third World.)

To explore how productivity growth influences long-run macro developments, we have to bring in distributional dynamics explicitly. Let $\theta = \omega b = 1 - \pi$ stand for the labour share (or, equivalently, labour cost per unit output in a simple model). Conventional wisdom after the famous Dunlop and Tarshis papers of the late 1930s suggests that the real wage ω increases with the level of economic activity; more recent 'full employment profit squeeze' Marxists would argue the same for the labour share. If the social processes underlying wage determination are self-stabilising (the world is stable), then wage dynamics might take the form:

$$\hat{\omega} = h(\theta, u), \qquad (A8.9)$$

with negative and positive first partial derivatives for θ and u respectively. Higher capacity utilisation puts upward pressure on the wage, and a bigger labour share damps it down.

If there is ongoing labour productivity growth, a technical progress function could take the form

$$\hat{b} = -\phi(\theta, u) < 0, \qquad (A8.10)$$

replacing Equation (A8.7). Typically, one would suppose that $\partial\phi/\partial\theta > 0$, as more expensive labour spurs the search for productivity gains. Higher capacity utilisation leading to greater investment from Equation (A8.3) should aid productivity growth, as in Kaldor's formulation.

With productivity rising, unit labour costs become the natural object of distributional conflict. The relevant dynamic equation is:

$$\hat{\theta} = \hat{\omega} + \hat{b} = h(\theta, u) - \gamma\phi(\theta, u) = h(\theta, u) + \gamma\hat{b}. \quad (A8.11)$$

In these expressions, γ is the share of productivity growth that is passed through to lower unit cost in the short run (another tricky social question). We assume that $h_\theta - \gamma\phi_\theta < 0$ and $h_u - \gamma\phi_u > 0$, that is, induced changes in productivity do not outweigh the distributional effects on real wage changes mentioned above. Alternatively, Equation (A8.11) can be written as:

$$\hat{\omega} = h(\theta, u) + (1 - \gamma)\phi(\theta, u),$$

so that a share $1 - \gamma$ of higher productivity feeds into real wages. In Korean experience, for example, γ takes a value around a half.

A steady state for Equation (A8.11) is defined by $\hat{\theta} = 0$, so that $\hat{\omega} = -\hat{b}$ and there is a constant profit share. Changing levels of u and θ allow the steady state to be obtained via the adjustment process illustrated in Figure 8.2 in the text. A wage-led scenario appears in the lower diagram, in which $du/d\theta > 0$ along the 'Output response' curve. The diagram shows a stable equilibrium in which the 'Cost' schedule along which $\hat{\theta} = 0$ is less steep than the output response curve.

A burst of technical advance can be represented by an upward shift of the ϕ function, making real unit labour cost decline faster in Equation (A8.11). To bring $\hat{\theta}$ back up to zero, θ itself would have to fall. The Cost schedule shifts downwards, and at the new steady state both unit costs and capacity use are lower. If investment demand is relatively more sensitive to capacity utilisation than the profit rate (the exact condition is $\beta(s_\pi - s_w) > \alpha s_w$), then the steady state capital stock growth rate would also decline.

The upper diagram in Figure 8.2 is based on the hypothesis that the economy is profit-led – for example, because exports are highly responsive to falling unit labour costs. As a consequence, aggregate demand is an inverse function of θ. Faster productivity growth leads to a new steady state where u is higher and the capital stock growth rate speeds up. Such a virtuous shift in circular flow can occur in a nation at any income level, and has been typical in East Asia. How to find the export strategy that converts local rent-seekers into aggressive entrepreneurs is the corresponding industrial policy task.

Appendix 3   Pasinetti's Accounting

Following Taylor (1995), Pasinetti's (1981) model is restated here in input – output notation, illustrated with a social accounting matrix (SAM) for two sectors in Table A8.1. The first two columns give breakdowns of sectoral costs $P_i X_i$ into intermediate input costs $P_i a_{ij} X_j$ (where the a_{ij} are the usual input–output coefficients), labour costs $w d_i X_i$ (where the d_i coefficients stand for 'direct' labour inputs per unit of gross outputs X_i), and profits or operating surpluses $\pi_i P_i X_i$. The first two rows show that values of sectoral outputs are exhausted by intermediate, consumption and investment demands. The c_i coefficients give

Table A8.1   Input–output accounts for two sectors with investment demands

							Totals
$P_1a_{11}X_1$	$P_1a_{12}X_2$	P_1c_1L			$P_1b_{11}I_1$	$P_1b_{12}I_2$	P_1X_1
$P_2a_{21}X_1$	$P_2a_{22}X_2$	P_2c_2L			$P_2b_{21}I_1$	$P_2b_{22}I_2$	P_2X_2
wd_1X_1	wd_2X_2						Y_w
$\pi_1P_1X_1$	Y_π^1						Y_π^1
	$\pi_2P_2X_2$						Y_π^2
			S_π^1				$P_I^1I_1$
				S_π^2			$P_I^2I_2$
Totals P_1X_1	P_2X_2	Y_w	Y_π^1	Y_π^2	$P_I^1I_1$	$P_I^2I_2$	

Note: $P_I^i = P_1b_{1i} + P_2b_{2i}$.

consumption of sector i's product(s) per employed worker (total employment is L). The b_{ij} coefficients transform investment levels 'by destination' I_i into commodity demands by sectors 'of origin'. They obey the columnwise restrictions $b_{1j} + b_{2j} = 1$, and represent a version of Leontief's 'B' matrix. They also underlie price indexes for investment goods of the form $P_I^j = P_1b_{1j} + P_2b_{2j}$ ($j = 1, 2$).

The third row defines labour income Y_w, and the third column shows that it is exhausted by consumption demand, so that workers are assumed not to save.

The remaining rows and columns summarise Pasinetti's key assumptions that (i) sector i's investment is exactly financed by its operating surplus; and (ii) each sector operates at full capacity use. Ignoring depreciation, in each sector we then have $I_i = k_ig_iX_i$, where g_i is the growth rate of capacity and k_i is an investment/incremental capacity ratio.

The savings assumption can be stated as $\pi_iP_iX_i = P_I^iI_i = P_I^ik_ig_iX_i$. The implication is that the operating surplus share π_i is given by the formula $\pi_iP_i = P_I^ik_ig_i$. The usual expression for the profit rate r_i would be $r_i = \pi_iP_i/P_I^ik_i = g_i$, so that fast-growing sectors are assumed to be more profitable. Such an observation is often made in practice; Pasinetti's saving–investment hypothesis is also consistent with the fact that sectors with high mark-up rates tend to be capital-intensive. Finally, an increase in a sector's capacity growth rate has to be met by a higher profit share, in a disaggregated version of forced saving.

Pasinetti undertakes two main tasks with this set-up – mapping labour costs into prices (or solving a 'transformation problem'), and finding an expression relating labour – output and consumption–labour coefficients. Implications of both are discussed in the text.

It is simplest to do the transformation problem in matrix notation. Let A be the square matrix of the a_{ij}, B the matrix of the b_{ij}, and $\gamma_i = k_i g_i$ a 'growth factor' for sector i. The square matrix γ^* has the growth factors along its main diagonal with zeros elsewhere and the row vector of operating suprlus shares can be written as $(\pi P)' = (\pi_1 P_1, \pi_2 P_2, \ldots)$. The price–cost breakdown in the first two columns of the SAM can be written as $P' = P'A + wD' + (\pi P)'$, where D' is the row vector of direct labour input coefficients.

The saving–investment assumptions imply that $(\pi P)' = P_I' \gamma^* = P'B\gamma^*$, where $P_I' = (P_I^1, P_I^2, \ldots)$ is the vector of investment goods price indexes. The price vector P' solves out as:

$$P' = wD' (I - A - B\gamma^*)^{-1} = wH', \qquad (A8.12)$$

where H' is a vector of 'vertically hyper-integrated labour' coefficients in Pasinetti's nomenclature. As long as the growth factors in γ^* are not 'too big', the matrix $(I - A - B\gamma^*)^{-1}$ will be non-negative and the price vector P' in (A8.12) will make sense. We get a multi-sectoral mark-up formulation not far in spirit from Equation (A8.1) in Appendix 1.

A vector of 'vertically integrated' labour coefficients or Marxian values can be defined as $V' = D'(I - A)^{-1}$. To express prices in terms of vertically integrated as opposed to hyperintegrated labour, we can write $(I - A - B\gamma^*)^{-1} = (I - A)^{-1}(I + \Theta)$, where $\Theta = B\gamma^*(I - A - B\gamma^*)^{-1}$. These manipulations give $H' = V'(I + \Theta)$. The matrix Θ (with non-zero rows for all sectors producing capital goods) marks up the vertically-integrated labour vector V' into its hyperavatar H'. A sector's price depends on accumulation in all sectors,

$$P' = wV'(I + \Theta) = w(V' + \Lambda'),$$

where $\Lambda' = V'\Theta$ is a vector with a typical element λ_i representing the labour tied up in capital goods going into new investment projects in sector i.

Pasinetti's relationship between labour and consumption parameters is:

$$\Sigma(v_i + \lambda_i)c_i = 1. \qquad (A8.13)$$

It is easy to derive from the first rows of the SAM after prices are divided out to give the material balance equation $(I - A - B\gamma^*)X - cL$, where X and c are column vectors of output levels and consumption coefficients respectively. Premultiplying both sides of the output solution $X = (I - A - B\gamma^*)^{-1} cL$ by D' gives $D'X = H'cL$. Recognising that employment $L = D'X$, we can divide out the (scalar) L terms to get $H'c = 1$, which is equivalent to Equation (A8.13).

Note

* This chapter is a revised version of a paper presented at a workshop on 'Endogenous Growth and Development', sponsored by the International School of Economic Research, University of Siena, Italy, 3–9 July 1994. Discussions with the workshop's participants are gratefully acknowledged.

References

Aghion, Philippe and Peter Howitt (1992) 'A Model of Growth through Creative Destruction', *Econometrica*, vol. 60, pp. 323–51.

Amadeo, Edward J. (1989) *Keynes's Principle of Effective Demand* (Aldershot: Edward Elgar).

Amsden, Alice (1989) *Asia's Next Giant: South Korea and Late Industrialization* (New York: Oxford University Press).

Arrow, Kenneth J. (1962) 'The Economic Implications of Learning by Doing', *Review of Economic Studies*, vol. 29, pp. 155–73.

Arthur, W. Brian (1989) 'Competing Technologies, Increasing Returns, and Lock-in by Historical Events', *Economic Journal*, vol. 99, pp. 116–31.

Bacha, Edmar L. (1990) 'A Three-Gap Model of Foreign Transfers and the GDP Growth Rate in Developing Countries', *Journal of Development Economics*, vol. 32, pp. 279–96.

Barro, Robert J. and Xavier Sala-i-Martin (1995) *Economic Growth* (New York: McGraw-Hill).

Bauer, P. T. (1972) *Dissent on Development* (London: Weidenfeld & Nicolson).

Becker, Gary S. (1964) *Human Capital* (New York: Columbia University Press).

Boratav, K., O. Turel and E. Yeldan (1996) 'Dilemmas of Structural Adjustment and Environmental Policies under Instability: Post-1980 Turkey', *World Development*.

Buchanan, James (1980) 'Rent-Seeking and Profit-Seeking', in J. M. Buchanan, R. D. Tollison and G. Tullock (eds), *Toward a Theory of Rent-Seeking Society* (College Station TX: Texas A&M University Press).

Chakravarty, Sukhamoy (1980) *Alternative Approaches to a Theory of Economic Growth* (Delhi: Orient-Longman).

Chakravarty, Sukhamoy (1987) *Development Planning: The Indian Experience*, (Oxford: Clarendon Press).

Chang, Ha-Joon (1993) 'The Political Economy of Industrial Policy in Korea', *Cambridge Journal of Economics*, vol. 17, pp. 131–57.

Chenery, Hollis B. (1959) 'The Interdependence of Investment Decisions', in

Moses Abranovitz, *et al.*, *The Allocation of Economic Resources* (Palo Alto, Calif.: Stanford University Press).

Chenery, Hollis B. and Michael Bruno (1962) 'Development Alternatives in an Open Economy: The Case of Israel', *Economic Journal*, vol. 72, pp. 79–103.

Collins, Randall (1980) 'Weber's Last Theory of Capitalism: A Systematization,' *American Sociological Review*, vol. 45, pp. 925–42.

Dixit, Avinash and Joseph Stiglitz (1977) 'Monopolistic Competition and Optimum Product Diversity', *American Economic Review*, vol. 67, pp. 297–308.

Domar, Evsey D. (1957) 'A Soviet Model of Growth', in E. Domar, *Essays in the Theory of Economic Growth* (New York: Oxford University Press).

Dore, Ronald (1986) *Flexible Rigidities: Industrial Policy and Structural Adjustment in the Japanese Economy 1970–1980* (Palo Alto, Calif.: Stanford University Press).

Dutt, Amitava K. (1984) 'Stagnation, Income Distribution, and Monopoly Power', *Cambridge Journal of Economics*, vol. 8, pp. 25–40.

Easterly, William (1994) 'Economic Policies, Economic Shocks, and Economic Growth', Paper presented at a workshop on 'Endogenous Growth and Development', International School of Economic Research, Siena, Italy.

Ellman, Michael (1975) 'Did the Agricultural Surplus Provide the Resources for the Increase in Investment during the First Five Year Plan?', *Economic Journal*, vol. 85, pp. 844–64.

Evans, Peter B. (1992) 'The State as Problem and Solution: Predation, Embedded Autonomy, and Structural Change', in Stephen Haggard and Robert Kaufman (eds), *The Politics of Economic Adjustment* (Princeton, NJ: Princeton University Press).

Fanelli, Jose Maria, Roberto Frenkel and Lance Taylor (1993) 'The World Development Report 1991: A Critical Assessment', in *International Monetary and Financial Issues for the 1990s* (New York: United Nations).

Furtado, Celso (1972) *Analise do 'Modelo' Brasileiro*, (Rio de Janeiro: Civilização Brasileira).

Gerschenkron, Alexander (1962) *Economic Backwardness in Historical Perspective* (Cambridge, Mass.: Harvard University Press).

Gordon, David M. (1995) 'Putting the Horse (Back) Before the Cart: Disentangling the Macro Relationship Between Investment and Saving', in Gerald A. Epstein and Herbert M. Gintis (eds), *Macroeconomic Policy After the Conservative Era* (Cambridge University Press).

Harrod, Roy (1939) 'An Essay in Dynamic Theory', *Economic Journal*, vol. 49, pp. 14–33.

Hayek, Freiderich von (ed.) (1935) *Collectivist Economic Planning* (London: Routledge & Kegan Paul).

Heilbroner, Robert (1991) *The Worldly Philosophers* (6th revised edn) (New York: Simon & Schuster).

Hicks, John R. (1965) *Capital and Growth* (Oxford: Clarendon Press).

Hirschman, Albert O. (1958) *The Strategy of Economic Development*, (New Haven, Conn.: Yale University Press).

Ingrao, Bruna and Giorgio Israel (1990) *The Invisible Hand: Economic Equilibrium in the History of Science* (Cambridge, Mass.: MIT Press)

Jones, Larry E. and Rodolfo Manuelli (1990) 'A Convex Model of Equilibrium

Growth: Theory and Policy Implications', *Journal of Political Economy*, vol. 98, pp. 1008–38.

Jorgenson, Dale (1990) 'Productivity and Economic Growth', in Ernst R. Berndt and Jack E. Triplett (eds), *Fifty Years of Economic Measurement: The Jubilee of the Conference on Income and Wealth* (University of Chicago Press).

Kaldor, Nicholar (1940) 'A Model of the Trade Cycle', *Economic Journal*, vol. 50, pp. 78–92.

Kaldor, Nicholas (1957) 'A Model of Economic Growth', *Economic Journal*, vol. 67, pp. 591–624.

Kaldor, Nicholas (1972) 'The Irrelevance of Equilibrium Economics', *Economic Journal*, vol. 82, pp. 1237–55.

Kalecki, Michal (1971) *Selected Essays on the Dynamics of the Capitalist Economy* (Cambridge University Press).

Keynes, John Maynard (1930) *A Treatise on Money* (London: Macmillan).

Keynes, John Maynard (1936) *The General Theory of Employment, Interest, and Money* (London: Macmillan).

Kennedy, Paul (1987) *The Rise and Fall of Great Powers* (New York: Random House).

Krueger, Anne O. (1974) 'The Political Economy of the Rent-Seeking Society', *American Economic Review*, vol. 64, pp. 291–303.

Krueger, Anne O. (1984) 'Comparative Advantage and Development Policy 20 Years Later', in M. Syrquin, L. Taylor and L. Westphal (eds) *Economic Structure and Performance: Essays in Honor of Hollis B. Chenery* (New York: Academic Press).

Krugman, Paul (1993) 'Towards a Counter-Counter-Revolution in Development Theory', *World Bank Economic Review*, x (supplement), pp. 15–38.

Kuznets, Simon S. (1971) *Economic Growth of Nations: Total Output and Production Structure* (Cambridge, Mass.: Harvard University Press).

Lal, Deepak (1983) *The Poverty of 'Development Economics'* (London: Institute of Economic Affairs).

Leibenstein, Harvey (1954) *A Theory of Economic–Demographic Development*, (Princeton, NJ: Princeton University Press).

Lewis, W. Arthur (1954) 'Economic Development with Unlimited Supplies of Labor', *Manchester School of Economics and Social Studies*, vol. 22, pp. 139–91.

Lewis, W. Arthur (1969) *Aspects of Tropical Trade, 1883–1965* (Stockholm: Almqvist and Wicksell).

Little, Ian M. D., Tibor Scitovsky and Maurice Scott (1970) *Industry and Trade in Some Developing Countries: A Comparative Study* (London: Oxford University Press).

Lorenz, Hans Walter (1989) *Nonlinear Dynamical Economics and Chaotic Motion*, Lecture Notes in Economics and Mathematical Systems No. 334, (New York: Springer-Verlag).

Lucas, Robert E. (1988) 'On the Mechanisms of Economic Development', *Journal of Monetary Economics*, vol. 22, pp. 3–42.

Lustig, Nora (1980) 'Underconsumption in Latin American Economic Thought: Some Considerations', *Review of Radical Political Economics*, vol. 12, pp. 35–43.

Mahalanobis, P. C. (1953) 'Some Observations on the Process of Growth of National Income', *Sankhya*, vol. 12, pp. 307–12.

Marglin, Stephen A. (1984) *Growth Distribution and Prices* (Cambridge, Mass.: Harvard University Press).

Mises, Ludwig von (1935) 'Economic Calculation in the Socialist Commonwealth', in F. von Hayek (ed.), *Collectivist Economic Planning* (London: Routledge & Kegan Paul).

Murphy, Kevin M., Andrei Shleifer and Robert Vishny (1989) 'Industrialization and the Big Push', *Journal of Political Economy*, vol. 97, pp. 1003–26.

Myrdal, Gunnar (1957) *Economic Theory and Underdeveloped Regions* (London: Duckworth).

Nelson, Richard R. (1956) 'A Theory of the Low-Level Equilibrium Trap in Underdeveloped Economies', *American Economic Review*, vol. 46, pp. 894–908.

Neumann, John von (1938) 'A Model of General Economic Equilibrium', *Review of Economic Studies*, vol. 13, pp. 1–9.

Olson, Mancur (1982) *The Rise and Decline of Nations* (New Haven, Conn.: Yale University Press).

North, Douglass C. (1981) *Structure and Change in Economic History* (New York: W. W. Norton).

Nurkse, Ragnar (1953) *Problems of Capital Formation in Underdeveloped Countries* (Oxford: Basil Blackwell).

Pasinetti, Luigi L. (1981) *Structural Change and Economic Growth* (Cambridge University Press).

Polanyi, Karl (1944) *The Great Transformation: The Political and Economic Origins of Our Times* (New York: Rinehart).

Prebisch, Raul (1959) 'Commercial Policy in the Underdeveloped Countries', *American Economic Review*, vol. 49, pp. 257–69.

Ramsey, Frank (1928) 'A Mathematical Theory of Saving', *Economic Journal*, vol. 38, pp. 543–59.

Rebelo, Sergio (1991) 'Long Run Policy Analysis and Long Run Growth', *Journal of Political Economy*, vol. 99, 500–21.

Robinson, Joan (1962) *Essays in the Theory of Economic Growth* (London: Macmillan).

Romer, Paul M. (1986) 'Increasing Returns and Long-Run Growth', *Journal of Political Economy*, vol. 94, pp. 1002–37.

Romer, Paul M. (1987) 'Growth Based on Increasing Returns Due to Specialization', *American Economic Review (Papers and Proceedings)*, vol. 77, pp. 56–62.

Rosenstein-Rodan, Paul N. (1943) 'Problems of Industrialization of Eastern and South-Eastern Europe', *Economic Journal*, vol. 53, pp. 202–11.

Rosenstein-Rodan, Paul N. (1961) 'Notes on the Theory of the Big Push', in H. S. Ellis and H. C. Wallich (eds), *Economic Development for Latin America* (New York: St Martin's Press).

Rowthorn, Bob (1982) 'Demand, Real Wages, and Economic Growth', *Studi Economici*, vol. 18, pp. 2–53.

Schumpeter, Josef A. (1934) *The Theory of Economic Development* (Cambridge, Mass.: Harvard University Press).

Schumpeter, Josef A. (1947) *Capitalism, Socialism, and Democracy* (New York: Harper and Brothers).

Schumpeter, Josef A. (1954) *History of Economic Analysis* (New York: Oxford University Press).

Schultz, T. W. (1963) *The Economic Value of Education* (New York: Columbia University Press).

Schultz, T. W. (1964) *Transforming Traditional Agriculture* (New Haven, Conn.: Yale University Press).

Scitovsky, Tibor (1954) 'Two Concepts of External Economies', *Journal of Political Economy*, vol. 62, pp. 143–51.

Sen, Amartya K. (1963) 'Neo-Classical and Neo-Keynesian Theories of Distribution', *Economic Record*, vol. 39, pp. 54–64.

Sismonde de Sismondi, J. C. L. (1815) 'Political Economy', in *Sir J. D. Brewster's Edinburgh Encyclopedia* (Edinburgh)

Solow, Robert M. (1956) 'A Contribution to the Theory of Economic Growth', *Quarterly Journal of Economics*, vol. 70, pp. 65–94.

Sraffa, Piero (1926) 'The Laws of Returns under Competitive Conditions', *Economic Journal*, vol. 36, pp. 535–50.

Sraffa, Piero (1960) *Production of Commodities by Means of Commodities* (Cambridge University Press).

Steindl, Josef (1952) *Maturity and Stagnation in American Capitalism* (Oxford: Basil Blackwell).

Sylos-Labini, Paolo (1984) *The Forces of Economic Growth and Decline* (Cambridge, Mass.: MIT Press).

Syrquin, Moshe (1988) 'Patterns of Structural Change', in H. B. Chenery and T. N. Srinivasan (eds), *Handbook of Development Economics*, vol. I (Amsterdam: North-Holland).

Taylor, Lance (1979) *Macro Models for Developing Countries* (New York: McGraw-Hill).

Taylor, Lance (1991) *Income Distribution, Inflation, and Growth* (Cambridge, Mass.: MIT Press).

Taylor, Lance (1995) 'Pasinetti's Processes', *Cambridge Journal of Economics*, vol. 19, pp. 697–713.

Taylor, Lance and Edmar L. Bacha (1976) 'The Unequalizing Spiral: A First Growth Model for Belindia', *Quarterly Journal of Economics*, vol. 90, pp. 197–218.

Wade, Robert (1990) *Governing the Market: Economic Theory and the Role of the Government in East Asian Industrialization* (Princeton, NJ: Princeton University Press).

Weber, Max (1968) *Economy and Society*, G. Roth and C. Wittich (eds) (New York: Bedminster Press).

Young, Allyn (1928) 'Increasing Returns and Economic Progress', *Economic Journal*, vol. 38, pp. 527–42.

Part III

Economic Policies, the Role of the State, and Growth

9 Economic Policies, Economic Shocks and Economic Growth*

William Easterly

Why do we care so much about economic growth? Figure 9.1 shows the path of output in the most famous recent case of successful development, South Korea. The graph shows how Korea compares at different points in time to the per capita incomes of nations today. In a generation Korea has gone from being at the income level of Somalia to being at the income level of Portugal. With that kind of revolution in living standards possible, one can sympathise with Lucas, that 'once you start to think about growth, it's hard to think about anything else'.

How much do actions by governments explain growth outcomes like these? How much does growth depend on purely random events? In new conceptual views of economic growth that have become popular among economists, initial conditions, random shocks and changes in expectations can change economic growth rates drastically. At a casual level of observation, the highly volatile growth rates in the real world seem to bear this out. This sensitivity of growth to shocks may seem to limit the ability of national policies to affect long-run growth. Yet the conceptual views that acknowledge growth to be sensitive to surprises also show how growth can be transformed by policy changes. Statistical evidence confirms that national policies do have very strong effects on a country's long run growth.

Section I discusses the role of shocks and policies in new and old views of economic growth; Section II looks at growth experiences across countries for evidence of the role of shocks; and Section III surveys statistical evidence on national policies and economic growth.

I NEW AND OLD VIEWS OF GROWTH

This section sets out in a highly simplified way some of the differences in implications between new and old views of economic growth.

227

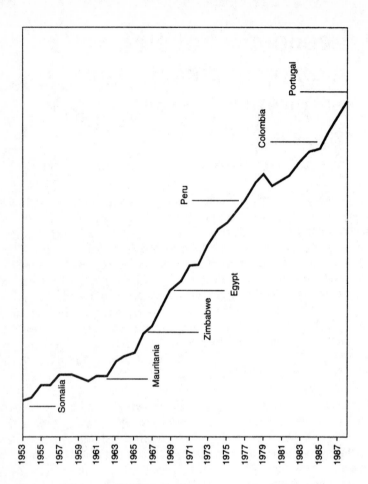

Figure 9.1   GDP per person in Korea compared with level in other countries, 1988

The economists' view of economic growth has undergone a lot of change in recent years. A group of iconoclasts has suggested a new view of growth whose implications are very different from the old.[1] To put it succinctly, the old view assumed that capital scarcity implied high returns to capital; the new view assumes that capital scarcity implies low returns.

The old view of growth assumed that where capital is scarce, it has a high return. There was a natural plausibility about this: when you give a machine to a worker who previously did not have one, it has a big productivity effect. Together with the assumptions of constant returns to scale and the existence of unalterable factors such as labour supply, the assumption of diminishing returns has a sharp prediction. During the transition to a new steady state, growth in capital-scarce countries will be high because of the high returns to capital. So poor countries should catch up fairly rapidly to richer countries.

Just to write down the algebra, the neoclassical production function is

$$y = A \, k^{\alpha}, \tag{9.1}$$

where y and k are output per worker and capital per worker, respectively.

Let us follow the convention of the literature in assuming identical consumers and producers maximising utility (assumed a logarithmic function of consumption for simplicity) over an infinite horizon, with a discount rate of ρ. We also assume zero labour growth for simplicity.[2] We also do not allow any exogenous technological change, so A is fixed. The optimal rate of growth is then:

$$dy/y = (Ak^{\alpha-1} - \rho). \tag{9.2}$$

Growth is high when capital per worker k is low, then declines as k rises. Growth stops when the rate of return to capital is just equal to the discount rate ρ. The constant-k steady state is unique and stable. Figure 9.2, Panel 1 shows the equilibrium where the rate of return line crosses the horizontal discount rate line.[3] There is no growth in the long run if there is no change in A, but neoclassical theory usually supposes a constant rate of change in A that will generate long-run growth. In this figure, that corresponds to a continuous shifting out of the marginal product line.

The new growth theorists have suggested that capital has a higher return where it is already abundant, because of various externalities to capital accumulation, and resulting strategic complementarities. I shall list some of the possible mechanisms below, but let us start with the algebra. If there is an externality to output k^{β} from the average level of per capita stock in the economy, then optimal growth becomes:

$$dy/y = (Ak^{\alpha+\beta-1} - \rho). \tag{9.3}$$

If the externality is sufficiently strong such that $\alpha + \beta > 1$, then the rate of return to capital rises with the level of capital per worker.

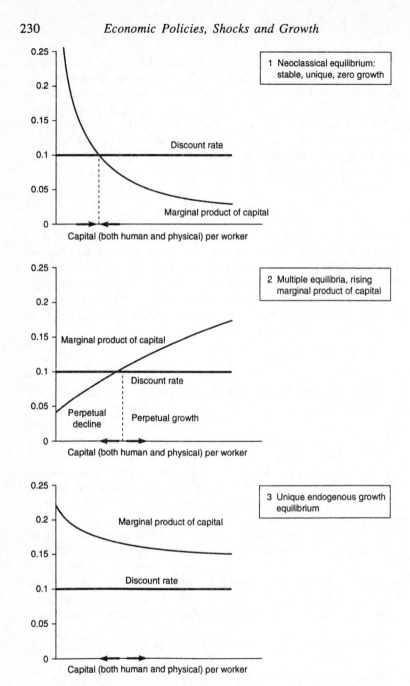

Figure 9.2   Exogenous and endogenous growth, alternative scenarios

Figure 9.2, Panel 2 shows the corresponding rate-of-return line. The point where the rate-of-return line crosses the discount-rate line is no longer a stable equilibrium; there are now multiple equilibria. If consumers start to the right of this point, they will want to accumulate capital for ever, thus generating endogenous growth. Growth will be a virtuous circle of capital accumulation attracting yet more capital accumulation. For this to happen, a critical mass of human and physical capital has to be in place. If consumers start to the left of this crossover, they will want to decumulate capital continuously – generating endogenous decline. The economy has to pass a minimum threshold level of human and physical capital in order to be able to grow.[4]

The need to pass a threshold makes growth sensitive to shocks. Suppose a country is in the growing regime, then suffers a civil war that wipes out a large fraction of the capital stock, moving the economy into the declining regime. A temporary shock such as a civil war could permanently alter the fortunes of the economy, moving it from growth to decline.

Other shocks common to developing countries could work in similar ways. Without working out all the details, let us think about a severe permanent drop in the world price of the commodity in which a country is heavily specialised, rendering unprofitable and useless part of the capital stock devoted to the production of that commodity. To make this hand-waving example work, we suppose that capital investment is irreversible, that capital in commodity production is associated with a range of exogenous production costs such as extraction difficulty, and hence that some of the capital simply has to be junked at the new world price. The drop in world price will have an effect like the civil war, effectively wiping out from the economic point of view part of the capital stock. In the neoclassical model, this would just be a temporary setback – after losing some of your capital, you just start accumulating again. In the new growth models, the terms of trade shock can permanently reverse the direction of the economy from growth to decline. Losing some of your capital may take you below the threshold where it is no longer worthwhile to accumulate capital.

On the good side, an infusion of capital, foreign aid, or a favourable terms of trade shock could bring you above the threshold and enable you to take off. Even a temporary receipt of aid or a temporary commodity windfall that passes into saving could be enough to do the trick if one is close to the threshold.

What are the mechanisms for such a fateful externality in the new growth literature? The list is a long one. Moreover, not all of the growth models simplify exactly to Equation (9.3). But at the risk of oversimplification, it is true that many of the new growth models will have similar predictions to Equation (9.3). The original suggestion of Romer (1986) was that there was a strong learning-by-doing externality to capital. Romer himself (1993) has subsequently stressed the non-rival nature of knowledge about producing new goods once this knowledge is created. Other views (for example, Lucas (1988), Azariadis and Drazen (1990), Becker *et al.* (1990), and Kremer (1993)) have stressed human capital (we could redefine *K* to include both physical and human capital). The average level of human capital in a society may have a strong externality to the production of new human capital. Returns to human capital may be rising at low levels of human capital because there is some minimum threshold for economically useful human capital. With strong complementarities in production, an educated person may have a higher return where there are other educated people for him or her to work with than where there is no one else with his or her skills.

Other models stress geographic interactions (Krugman 1991, 1994). Where there is a lot of capital is where the market is, where the suppliers are, and where the specialised business services are. With fixed costs to starting a new factory and non-zero transportation costs, there are strategic complementarities in capital accumulation in a given location. A similar idea is that technology choice by firms (between 'traditional' and 'advanced' technologies) depends on the size of the market if the advanced technology has fixed costs (Murphy *et al.*, 1989). The size of the market in turn depends on how many firms choose the advanced technology (since the latter is more productive and raises income). Thus there are strategic complementarities between firms, with multiple equilibria of all firms choosing advanced technology and all firms choosing advance technology. A 'big push' could move the economy from one equilibrium to another; so could a big shock.

The new growth models create a large role for luck and history. But policies also matter. Policies that lower the rate of return to private capital – such as high taxes on income, exchange or import controls, financial repression that penalises financial intermediation – make the threshold for take-off higher, and take-off less likely. With an income tax *t* on income from production, for example, Equation (9.3) becomes

$$dy/y = ((1 - t)Ak^{\alpha + \beta - 1} - \rho. \tag{9.4}$$

Higher *t* shifts the rate of return line down, which makes the threshold for growth at higher *k*. In other words, a higher tax expands the region in which there will be decline and shrinks the region in which there will be growth. Moreover, we can see from Equation (9.4) that higher taxes make growth lower even if a country is in the growing region, and make decline steeper if it is in the declining region.

If countries are close to the threshold, growth is likely to be volatile. Good luck on terms of trade, good policies that make investment attractive, and favourable expectations could all interact to get a country above the threshold and create rapid growth. Then a shift in policies, a bad shock on terms of trade or a political crisis that reverses the favourable expectations could abort the rapid growth and send the economy down again.

1.1 Models in the Middle

The new growth models are appealing because they offer a rationalisation of the failure of development of very low income economies such as the African ones, and they could explain reverse flows of capital and human skills from poor to rich countries. However, the new growth models also have at least one unappealing prediction, which is that growth accelerates as economies get richer. We can see from Equation (9.3) that growth should keep accelerating as per capital stock rises if $\alpha + \beta > 1$. Now in the very big picture, it is true that world growth has accelerated since the 1700s, with each successive fastest grower (United Kingdom, United States, Germany, Japan) experiencing higher growth rates. A model such as Equation (9.3) may thus be roughly consistent with the stylised facts of very-long-run world economic growth. Kremer (1993) discusses how population growth has certainly accelerated over time (since 1 million BC, for example), and relates this to predictions of accelerating growth with increased scale. However, the stylised fact of rising world growth seems a little shakier from the less long-run point of view because of the slowdown in world growth since 1973. And the prediction of accelerating growth certainly seems counter-factual from the viewpoint of cross-section comparisons, where the rich economies grow no faster on average than the middle-income economies. The convergence literature has argued, in fact, that rich countries grow more slowly once we control for initial stocks of human capital and other factors (Barro and Sala-i-Martin, 1992).[5]

Some authors have sought to modify the unappealing prediction of accelerating growth in new growth models. Some suggest that the externalities are only important at low income levels, making the production function concave–convex (Becker *et al.*, 1990; Azariadis and Drazen,

1990). There will still be multiple equilibria, but countries in the good equilibrium will experience declining growth, just as in the Solow model.

There is also the popular and tractable model proposed by Rebelo (1991), in which $\alpha + \beta$ is exactly equal to unity. This might at first seem like a rather implausible constraint on a purely technological parameter (as argued by Stiglitz (1992) and others). But what Rebelo in fact argued was something a little different: he suggests that the neoclassical assumptions of constant returns and diminishing returns to physical capital were fine – it was the assumption of an exogenous fixed factor (raw labour) that we should get rid of. If all factors can be accumulated – labour can be accumulated by increasing human capital without limit – and there are constant returns to scale, then output will be proportional to the aggregate of human and physical capital. That is, if K is reinterpreted as including both human and physical capital, then $Y = AK$. In this model, equilibrium is unique and stable, and there is neither convergence nor divergence of economies. Policies will have growth effects, since growth in Equation (9.4) now becomes $(1 - t)A - \rho$.

Another attempt at a middle ground was by Jones and Manuelli (1990), who suggested an even smaller modification to the neoclassical model. They noted that endogenous growth was feasible in the neoclassical model if the marginal product of capital diminishes not to zero, but to some positive constant. This positive constant will asymptotically play the role of A in Rebelo's model. One model that can have this feature is output as a CES production function of K and L:

$$Y = A(\gamma K^{\varepsilon} + (1 - \gamma)L^{\varepsilon})^{1/\varepsilon}. \tag{9.5}$$

If we suppose that $\varepsilon > 0$, so that the elasticity of substitution between labour and capital is greater than one in absolute value, then the marginal product of capital goes asymptotically to the following as the capital–labour ratio goes to infinity:[6]

$$\partial Y/\partial K \Rightarrow A\gamma^{1/\varepsilon} \text{ as } K/L \Rightarrow \infty. \tag{9.6}$$

The assumption $\varepsilon > 0$ could be seen as a weaker version of Rebelo's assumption that all factors are reproducible: only at the limit can we substitute away from the non-reproducible factors.

Figure 9.2, Panel 3 shows that when the marginal product of the capital curve lies above the discount rate, there will be a unique, positive growth equilibrium. If the marginal product of the capital line cuts the discount rate line, then the economy will stagnate at a steady state with constant capital per capita.

What are the implications of these models in the middle for the effects of shocks and policies on growth? All these models predict strong policy effects on growth, just like the increasing returns to capital models. The concave–convex production functions also imply a big role for shocks if countries are close to the threshold that determines which of the multiple equilibria one goes to. The Rebelo and Jones–Manuelli models have unique equilibria, and shocks should not be very important. A one-time shock could pass permanently into income if the proceeds of the shock are saved (or dissaved for a bad shock), but even then the effect of growth will be modest and transitory.

II GROWTH IS OFTEN A SURPRISE

Let's now look at some characteristics of growth experiences in the real world. Ideally, one would like to use empirical evidence to distinguish between new and old models of economic growth, and between different new models. Unfortunately, this has not been accomplished very successfully in the literature, and indeed has hardly even been tried. In this and the next section, the goal is much more modest. Evidence of the effects of shocks and policies on growth rates will be discussed, leaving the reader to interpret the findings in the light of the various alternative models discussed in the first section. We shall look first at shocks.

The evidence for the importance of shocks is fairly strong. We see, first of all, that growth rates are remarkably unstable.[7] Figure 9.3 shows the per capita growth rates of countries in both 1960–73 and 1974–88.[8] We see a mess of data with no clear pattern – countries that were in the top half in 1960–73 fell into the bottom half in 1974–88, and vice versa. It is *not* true that the same countries are consistent good performers, or consistent bad performers. Rather, countries are success stories in one period and disappointments in the next, often without warning.

The correlation coefficient across the subsequent time periods shown in Figure 9.3 is only 0.2. This coefficient summarises a surprising fact: only 20 per cent of the variation of growth rates over the fourteen-year periods shown here relate to permanent differences between countries; the remaining 80 per cent are the result of factors that change over time. Nations do not have permanent superiority in growth performance

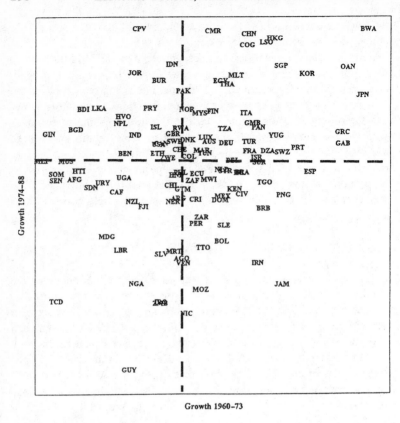

Figure 9.3   Per capita growth rates, 1960–73 and 1974–88

Notes: Dotted lines show median growth rate in each period.

Source: Easterly *et al.* (1993)

because of some unchanging national characteristics, such as cultures, institutions or tradition; growth is eminently changeable.

This low persistence is not an artefact of the breakpoint or period lengths chosen for Figure 9.3. In fact, the fact of low persistence is remarkably unchanging across different periods lengths and break points. Even across subsequent thirty-year periods since 1870, the correlation across periods is only 0.1 – that is, only 10 per cent of the variation in such data results from fixed country characteristics.

The lines drawn in Figure 9.3 show the median world growth rate in each period. We see that a number of the Latin-American countries were above average in 1960–73, only to fall well below world median growth in 1974–88. Examples include Bolivia, Brazil, Costa Rica, the Dominican Republic, Ecuador, Mexico and Peru.

Brazil is one of the more dramatic examples. Brazil was described as a miracle beginning in the late 1960s and through most of the 1970s. Today, people only use the word miracle about Brazil to pray for one to occur.

Chile is an even more dramatic example, where the word miracle has been used more than once over the past two decades. Chile grew per capita by 2.5 per cent between 1960 and 1972, then contracted 6.3 per cent per annum from 1972 to 1976, rose again at 5.5 per cent per annum between 1976 and 1981, dropped 10 per cent per annum from 1981 to 1983, then grew again by 3.2 per cent between 1983 and 1990. The last two expansionary phases have been widely celebrated as the 'Chilean economic miracle'.

Volatile growth is not limited to Latin America. Mauritius, for example, had zero growth in the 1960s, but then became an economic miracle in the 1970s with 7.3 per cent per capita growth. Indonesia was below average in 1960–73 before becoming one of the vaunted East Asian success stories in 1974–88. Nigeria went in the opposite direction: from 2.6 per cent growth in the 1970s to contraction of 4.8 per cent per year in the 1980s. The *typical* country saw its per capita growth change up or down by 3.5 percentage points from the 1970s to the 1980s, after a change of 2.5 percentage points from the 1960s to the 1970s.

The only significant exception to the volatile growth rule is the spectacularly consistent success of Japan and the 'Four Tigers' (Korea, Singapore, Taiwan and Hong Kong).[9] These nations are almost the only ones to remain the the top-right-hand corner of Figure 9.3, indicating persistent success across periods. Yet, in the longer run, even some of these nations fit the rule: Korea's and Taiwan's growth was poor prior to 1960. Japan's growth has been impressive over a longer period, although the recent slowdown could indicate that, even in Japan, success is not for ever.

2.1 Predictions and Surprises

In view of the instability of growth rates, it is not so surprising that we have often been surprised by both success and failure. The first World Bank mission to Korea described the country's first development programme as being absurdly optimistic, in light of the dismal growth in the 1950s: 'there can be no doubt that this development program [the GDP growth of 7.1 per cent forecast for 1962–6] *far exceeds* the potential of the Korean economy . . . it is *inconceivable* that exports will rise as much as projected' (italics added). Korean growth during 1962–6 was in fact 7.3 per cent, after which it accelerated.

In the early 1960s, a group of distinguished economists picked out Sri Lanka as the country most likely to succeed in Asia, certainly more so, than say, Taiwan. Taiwan's growth over the subsequent fifteen years was 7.3 per cent; Sri Lanka's was 0.3 per cent.[10]

The World Bank's early economic reports also picked out as likely stars the Philippines ('second only' to Japan in potential) and Burma (in light of its 'remarkable economic progress', its 'long-run potential compares favorably with that of other countries in South East Asia'). Of course, Burma and the Philippines are among the few South-east Asian countries to which the word 'miracle' has *not* been applied.

Asia as a whole was thought to have the worst prospects among developing countries. A development textbook in 1963 ranked them last in development potential – behind Latin America, subSaharan Africa, and the Middle East.[11]

Africa was considered as a more likely candidate for stardom than Asia. After rapid African growth in the 1950s and 1960s, the World Bank's chief economist predicted in 1967 that Africa's economic future was 'bright'. He even picked out seven particularly promising African economies that had 'the potential to reach or surpass' a 7 per cent growth rate. All the economies he picked out had negative per capita growth from that day to this.[12]

Latin America was considered the region most likely to succeed in the 1960s. A group of economists predicted in the early 1960s that Argentina and Colombia would far outpace Hong Kong and Singapore. Instead, Hong Kong grew twice as fast as Argentina, and Singapore more than twice as fast as Colombia.[13]

2.2 Terms of Trade Surprises

One reason that growth is volatile is because many countries' growth rates are highly sensitive to favourable or unfavourable terms of trade movements. Figure 9.4 makes this point. The countries in the 1980s with the most favourable terms of trade shocks (a gain of about 1 per cent of GDP during each and every year of the 1980s) had positive per capita growth of 1 per cent per annum in the 1980s. The countries with the most adverse terms of trade movements (a loss of about 1.7

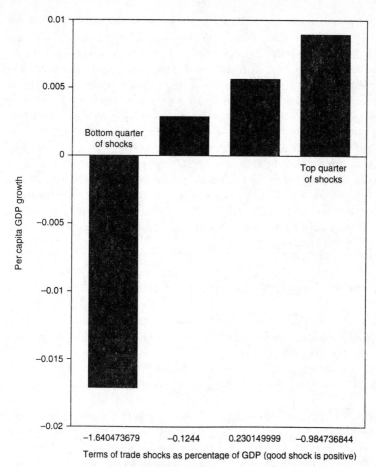

Figure 9.4 External shocks and economic growth in the 1980s

Source: Easterly *et al.* (1993)

percentage points of GDP) had negative per capita growth of 1.6 per cent per annum. This sensitivity to shocks seems consistent with the new view of growth, that one can go very quickly from a virtuous to a vicious circle.

Moreover, to add insult to injury, even some of the variation in our measures of policies is explained by external shocks. For example, the black market premium on foreign exchange – often used as a generalised measure of price distortion – is itself affected by changes in the terms of trade.

Many successes and failures are a function not only of economic policies but also of the shocks that they have experienced. Venezuela's disastrous growth since the mid-1980s has generally been attributed to major policy mistakes, and this is no doubt accurate. But Venezuela's growth has been even worse than it would have been, because bad policies interacted with a very bad shock to the terms of trade – as Venezuela was dependent on oil exports, the collapse of the oil price in the 1980s gave Venezuela one of the world's worst terms-of-trade shocks measured as a percentage of GDP. Conversely, Mauritius is often celebrated as an example of policy-induced success in Africa. Indeed, policies likely have helped Mauritius achieve its rapid growth in the 1980s. But growth was greatly helped by the fact that Mauritius had one of the world's largest terms of trade gains in the 1980s – benefiting from the fall in oil import prices and gains in its sugar export prices.

III   POLICY EFFECTS ON GROWTH

Luck matters, but policy also matters. A large amount of study of national economic policies and economic growth has identified some strong associations.

3.1   Quantifying Policy Effects on Growth

Table 9.1 lists the magnitudes of policy effects on growth that have been identified in several recent studies.[14] An increase in the average years of schooling of the labour force by 1.2 years through increased public provision of primary and secondary education will raise growth by 1 percentage point.[15] A reduction in the role of the central bank in credit allocation – reducing the central bank's share in total credit by 28 percentage points – will raise growth by 1 percentage point.[16] An increase in public investment in transport and communication by 1.7 percentage points of GDP will raise growth by 1 percentage point.[17] Macroeconomic stabilisation that brings inflation down by 28 percentage points will raise growth by 1 percentage point.[18] A reduction in the government budget deficit of 4.3 percentage points will raise growth by 1 percentage point.[19] A unification of the foreign exchange market that eliminates a black market premium of 36 percentage points will raise growth by 1 percentage point.[20]

With such potent policies at the government's disposal, the potential

Table 9.1   Statistical associations between policies and growth

---

An increase in per capita growth of one percentage point is associated with:
An increase in average years of schooling of
   the labor force of: 1.2 years
A reduction in the share of central bank
   credit in total credit of: 28 percentage points
An increase in the ratio to GDP of public
   investment in transport and communication of: 1.7 percentage points
A fall in inflation of: 26 percentage points
A reduction in the ratio of the government
   budget deficit to GDP of: 4.3 percantage points
A fall in the percentage premium of the black
   market over the official exchange rate of: 36 percentage points

---

Sources (respectively): Barro and Lee (1993), King and Levine (1993), Easterly and Rebelo (1993), Fischer (1993), Fischer (1993), and Fischer (1993).

Notes: table shows association with growth of each policy indicator in isolation, other things being equal.

for policies to overcome bad luck on terms of trade is clear (not to mention the potential for ruining good luck with bad policies). Let us set out a hypothetical experiment. Suppose a country has a 50 per cent fall of export prices in a decade. What policy package could offset this? Picking from the menu of policies listed in Table 9.1, the following combination would do the trick: (i) 10 percentage points lower share of the central bank in total credit; (ii) 1 per cent of GDP more public investment in transport and communication investment; (iii) 2 percentage points of GDP lower government deficit; and (iv) elimination of a black market premium of 10 percentage points.

Moreover, it could be that how a country reacts to external shocks can be as important as the shocks themselves. Nigeria and Indonesia provide an effective point–counterpoint. Both are relatively poor economies that relied heavily on oil revenues in the 1980s. But when oil prices collapsed in 1986, Indonesia responded swiftly by cutting budget expenditure; Nigeria delayed its reaction so that macroeconomic imbalances reached crisis stage. Restrictive import policies to redress the exploding Nigerian current account deficit made a bad situation worse. The sensitivity of growth to terms of trade shocks may reflect that most countries behaved more like Nigeria than like Indonesia.

Case study evidence also makes us suspect that specific macroeconomic policy mistakes may be responsible for some of the instability of growth rates; such mistakes may turn successes into failure very quickly.[21]

The 'Chilean economic miracle' of the late 1970s, already mentioned, was undone by an appreciating real exchange rate as the nominal exchange rate was held fixed in the face of continuing inflation. Mexico's high growth of the 1960s and early 1970s was undone by fiscal excess in the late 1970s and early 1980s. Côte d'Ivoire's exemplary growth prior to 1975 was derailed by mismanagement of the coffee and cocoa boom of the mid-1970s.

3.2 Successes and Setbacks

Will policies help us to distinguish between countries or regions that are successes and those that are failures? Can we use policies to explain some of the differences between East Asia and other regions?

3.2.1 East Asia and Latin America

Figure 9.5 decomposes the income gap that opened up between East Asia and Latin America over the period 1965–89. The decomposition is based on a regression taken from Easterly and Levine (1994), used in that paper to explain Africa's disappointing performance also.[22] The regression, which uses pooled decade-average growth rates and policy indicators, is reproduced in the Appendix to this chapter. The growth difference between East Asia and Latin America is decomposed into elements that represent a given policy difference between the two regions multiplied by the estimated effect of that policy on growth. For example, the part of the growth difference associated with budget deficits is calculated as (Latin America's average budget deficit − East Asia's average budget deficit)* (coefficient on budget deficits in growth regression). The regression covers 1960–89, but we show just the time period since 1965, which is when East Asia caught up with Latin America.

The regression includes the policy indicator variables that have proven most robust in statistical analysis (also limiting the policy variables to those for which a reasonably large sample is available).[23] These are the financial depth of the economy, the black market premium (a measure of price distortions), and the government's budget deficit (measured as the central government deficit only to maximise the sample size). The regression also includes several other now-standard variables: the mean years of schooling of the labour force (from Barro and Lee, 1993), a measure of political instability (number of political assassinations), and initial income. Initial income is entered as a quadratic to allow for the possibility that middle-income countries may benefit more than low-

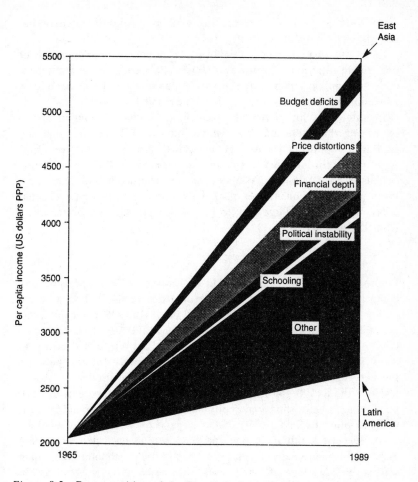

Figure 9.5 Decomposition of the East Asia–Latin America growth gap

Notes: Latin America and East Asia were at the same per capita income in 1965. By 1989, they had diverged greatly – some of this divergence we can explain with policy variables.

income countries from the potential to catch up to advanced countries.

Figure 9.5 makes clear that not everything can be explained with cross-country statistical analysis of policies and growth. Although the regression statistics are very satisfactory, there remains a large unexplained differential between East Asian and Latin American growth (shown as 'other'). This term reflects the statistically significant and negative Latin-American effect that remains in the regression even after controlling for policy variables (as well as a slightly positive but insignificant East-Asian effect).

Latin America's higher political instability does help explain part of the growth differential.[24] However, East Asia's educational attainment does not explain much of the growth differential, as Latin America's educational attainment does not lag far behind East Asia's.

In spite of the limitations of cross-country statistical comparisons, it is striking that there are three simple indicators of policies that can explain a significant fraction of the growth differential between East Asia and Latin America. As shown in Figure 9.5, the lower budget deficits in East Asia, East Asia's higher financial depth, and East Asia's lower price distortions (lower black market premia on foreign exchange) combined to give a large kick to East Asian growth as it pulled away from Latin America.

3.2.2   East Asia and Africa

Figure 9.6 provides the same kind of illustrative decomposition and comparison of the growth performance of Africa versus East Asia, where policy differences are greater. In 1960, Africa's GDP per capita was about $800, while East Asia's was about $1500. By 1989, Africa's GDP per capita was only about $900, while East Asia's had grown to about $5000. Political instability was not significantly different between the two regions, at least according to the measure used here. About $850 of the $4100 gap is due to the original percentage gap in GDP per capita. Policies (financial depth, black market premium and government surplus) explain $1750 of the large gap that emerged over the 1960–89 period. Initial income and schooling in each decade explain $450 of the gap (the disadvantage of lower African schooling more than offsets the advantage of lower initial income in Africa). About $1050 of the $4100 gap between East Asia and Africa remains unexplained.

These two exercises show that much, but not all, can be explained. Growth regressions do explain successfully why East Asia did well, Latin America did worse than expected, and Africa did very badly indeed. At the same time, there remain large and statistically significant growth differences between regions that are unexplained. This may reflect deep-seated country characteristics that are unfavourable for growth, such as Africa's ethnic strife or Latin America's high inequality.[25] The unexplained differential may also reflect how imperfect are the measures of policies by which we try to explain growth differences. Finally, the unexplained residual is consistent with the new views

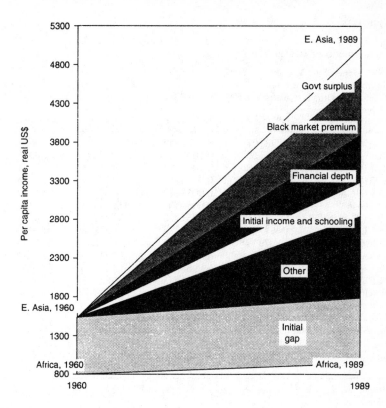

Figure 9.6 Decomposition of the East Asia and Africa growth gap

of growth that allow some role for random events to change growth outcomes even when policies are unchanged.

IV CONCLUSIONS

Theory and evidence tell us that growth is subject to surprises. Commodity windfalls, terms of trade losses or gains, and other forms of luck beyond a country's control do matter quite a bit for growth even in the medium run. But national policies such as financial sector reform, public infrastructure investment, low budget deficits, and maintenance of low and stable inflation also have strong effects on medium-run growth.

Appendix

Table A9.1   Growth regression for decomposition of East Asian versus Latin-American/African Growth

LS // Dependent Variable is GYP
Number of observations: 193
Heteroskedasticity-Consistent Covariance Matrix

Variable	Coefficient	Std. error	T-stat	2-Tail sig.
DUM60	−0.2993107	0.1007544	−2.9706959	0.0034
DUM70	−0.2958322	0.1007023	−2.9376914	0.0037
DUM80	−0.3120710	0.1001451	−3.1161883	0.0021
AFRICA	−0.0135641	0.0053777	−2.5222975	0.0125
LATINCA	−0.0148372	0.0033212	−4.4674337	0.0000
EASIAP	0.0031427	0.0050335	0.6243556	0.5332
LRGDP	0.0914238	0.0261713	3.4932812	0.0006
LRGDPSQ	−0.0064378	0.0017283	−3.7250300	0.0003
LSCHOOL	0.0107039	0.0051292	2.0868446	0.0383
ASSASS	−15.749136	6.5977817	−2.3870350	0.0180
LLY	0.0204562	0.0065385	3.1285762	0.0020
BLCK	−0.0183441	0.0051185	−3.5838986	0.0004
SURP	0.1182126	0.0428476	2.7589100	0.0064

R-squared	0.543118	Mean of dependent var.	0.020842
Adjusted R-squared	0.512659	S.D. of dependent var.	0.025791
S. E. regression	0.018004	Sum of squared resid.	0.058349
Log likelihood	508.1809	F-statistic	17.83123
		Prob (F-statistic)	0.000000

Notes:
Variables:
GYP: Per capita growth, decade averages for 1960s, 1970s and 1980s.
DUM60:   Dummy variable for 1960s.
DUM70:   Dummy variable for 1970s.
DUM80:   Dummy variable for 1980s.
AFRICA: Dummy variable for Africa.
LATINCA: Dummy variable for Latin America.
EASIAP: Dummy variable for East Asia and Pacific.
LRGDP: Log of real GDP (1985 PPP US dollars, Summers and Heston (1991), initial value each decade.
LRGDPSQ: Square of log of real GDP.
LSCHOOL: Log of average schooling attainment in years of labour force (Barro and Lee (1993), initial value each decade.
ASSASS: Numbers of assassinations (Barro (1991)), average each decade.
LLY: Ratio of liquid financial liabilities to GDP (King and Levine (1993)), initial value each decade.
BLCK: Log of black market premium on foreign exchange (Easterly, *et al.*, (1993)), average each decade.
SURP: Central government deficit to GDP ratio (International Financial Statistics, IMF), average each decade.

Source: (for regression) Easterly and Levine (1994).

Notes

* This chapter is based on notes prepared for a summer workshop at the International School of Economic Research, Siena, Italy, 3–9 July 1994.
1. The new literature on economic growth was led by Romer (1986) and Lucas (1988, 1993). As many have pointed out, the 'new' literature contains many echoes of ideas popular in the development and growth literature of the 1950s and 1960s, and even more echoes from Solow's original 1956 article (see Srinivasan (1993)). The idea of constant returns to capital, for example, has always been a staple of growth models in the development literature (see the work of Taylor (1979, 1983, 1991). The methodology of growth regressions was also common in the development literature (for example, Balassa 1978).
2. If labour growth is not zero, then one has to consider deep philosophical issues such as whether consumers maximise the per capita welfare of their descendants, or the sum of absolute welfare of their descendants, or something in between. If it is the first, population growth will have a negative one-for-one effect on optimal per capita growth; if it is the second, population growth will have zero effect on optimal per capita growth.
3. This discussion is in terms of economies closed to capital flows. There are also obvious implications for an open economy model: if capital has high returns where it is scarce, then capital should flow from rich to poor countries.
4. Again, we are only discussing economies closed to capital flows. In an open economy model, if capital has a high return where it is abundant, then capital flows to where it is already abundant. This model predicts both a human capital flow (a brain drain) and a physical capital from poor to rich countries, the opposite of the old growth model prediction.
5. There is also some evidence that the conditional relationship between initial income and growth is hump-shaped, with growth of middle-income countries higher than both low-income and high-income countries (Baumol, *et al.* (1989), Easterly (1994)).
6. The result that growth can be sustained indefinitely in a CES with elasticity of substitution above 1 has been known for over thirty years, but was dismissed as a curiosity.
7. This volatility of growth rates could also be consistent with a neoclassical growth model with a unique steady state, if all countries were close to their own steady states. In that case, random shocks would dominate growth rates. Arguably, however, this condition could not then explain why growth is so sensitive to the levels of policy variables.
8. The evidence cited here and in the succeeding paragraphs is from Easterly *et al.*, 1993.
9. For a recent interpretations of East Asia's success, see the World Bank's (1993a) *East Asia Miracle*; Thomas and Wang, 1993; Young, 1992; World Bank, 1993b; and Pack and Page, 1993.
10. Hicks, 1990.
11. The reference is to Enke, 1963.
12. The quote is from Kamarack, 1967. See the World Bank's (1994) study of Africa, and Easterly and Levine (1994) for a summary of the disastrous growth outcomes.

13. Hicks, 1990.
14. This is not intended to be a survey of the vast empirical literature on policies and growth. I am listing some empirical results from a recent Journal of Monetary Economics special issue on growth (December 1993) as examples.
15. Barro and Lee (1993).
16. King and Levine (1993).
17. Easterly and Rebelo (1993).
18. Fischer (1993). See also De Gregorio (1993, 1994) and Corbo and Rojas (1993).
19. Fischer (1993), Easterly and Rebelo (1993).
20. Fischer (1993). See also Harrison (1993) and Edwards (1992) on openness and growth.
21. Bruno (1993, 1994) and Bruno and Easterly (1994) present evidence on how discrete inflation crises can explain some of the instability of growth rates.
22. This decomposition technique is inspired by a similar exercise by Barro and Lee, 1994.
23. The importance of robustness checks was dramatised by the results of Levine and Renelt, 1992.
24. See the recent survey by Alesina (1994) on the literature on political instability and growth.
25. On equality and growth, see Birdsall and Sabot (1994), Alesina and Rodrik (1994), Persson and Tabellini (1994), and Clarke (1994). On ethnic strife, Mauro (1993), Fay (1994), and Easterly and Levine (1994) find some evidence for ethnic divisions being associated with increased corruption, unfavourable policies, and lower growth.

References

Alesina, Alberto (1994) 'The Political Economy of Growth: What Do We know?', Paper for the Latin-American Seminar on Economic Growth, Bogotá, Colombia, 27–28 June.
Alesina, Alberto and Dani Rodrik (1994) 'Distributive Politics and Economic Growth', *Quarterly Journal of Economics*.
Azariadis, Costas and Alan Drazen (1990) 'Threshold Externalities in Economic Development', *Quarterly Journal of Economics*, vol. 105, pp. 501–26.
Balassa, Bela (1978) 'Exports and Economic Growth: Further Evidence', *Journal of Development Economics*, vol. 5 (June), pp. 181–9.
Barro, Robert J. (1991) 'Economic Growth in a Cross Section of Countries', *Quarterly Journal of Economics* (May).
Barro, Robert J. and Xavier Sala-i-Martin (1992) 'Convergence', *Journal of Political Economy*.
Barro, Robert J. and Jong-wha Lee (1993) 'International Comparisons of Educational Attainment', *Journal of Monetary Economics*, vol. 32, no. 2 (December), pp. 363–93.
Barro, Robert J. and Jong-wha Lee (1994) 'Winners and Losers in Economic Growth', *World Bank Review*.

Baumol, William J., Sue Anne Batey Blackman and Edward N. Wolff (1989) *Productivity and American Leadership: The Long View* (Cambridge, Mass.: MIT Press).

Becker, Gary, Kevin Murphy and Robert Tamura (1990) 'Human Capital, Fertility, and Economic Growth', *Journal of Political Economy*, vol. 98, no. 5, pt 2, pp. S12–37.

Birdsall, Nancy and Richard Sabot (1993) 'Virtuous Circles: Human Capital, Growth and Equity in East Asia', Prepared for the World Bank's project, 'Strategies for Rapid Growth: Public Policy and the Asian Miracle'.

Bruno, Michael (1994) 'Short-run Macroeconomic Management and Long-run Economic Growth', Paper for the Latin-American Seminar on Economic Growth, Bogotá, Colombia, 27–28 June.

Bruno, Michael (1993) 'Inflation and Growth in an Integrated Approach', NBER Working Paper No. 4422.

Bruno, Michael and William Easterly (1994) 'Inflation Crises and Economic Growth', work in progress, World Bank.

Clarke, George (1994) 'More Evidence on Inequality and Economic Growth', *Journal of Development Economics*, forthcoming.

Corbo, Vittorio and Patricio Rojas (1993) 'Investment, Macroeconomic Stability, and Growth: The Latin American Experience', *Revista de Analisis Economico*, vol. 8, no. 1.

De Gregorio, José (1994) 'Inflation, Growth, and Central Banks: Theory and Evidence', Paper for the Latin-American Seminar on Economic Growth, Bogotá, Colombia, 27–28 June.

De Gregorio, José (1993) 'Inflation, Taxation, and Long-run Growth', *Journal of Monetary Economics*, vol. 31, pp. 271–98.

De Long, J. B. and L. H. Summers (1991) 'Equipment, Investment, Relative Prices, and Economic Growth', *Quarterly Journal of Economics* (May) 1991, vol. CVI, no. 2, pp. 445–502.

Easterly, William (1994) 'Economic Stagnation, Fixed Factors, and Policy Thresholds', *Journal of Monetary Economics* (June).

Easterly, William and Ross Levine (1994) 'Africa's Growth Tragedy', Paper presented at the African Economic Research Consortium, Nairobi, May.

Easterly, William, Michael Kremer, Lant Pritchett and Lawrence Summers (1993) 'Good Policy or Good Luck? Country Growth Performance and Temporary Shocks', *Journal of Monetary Economics*, vol. 32, no. 2, (December), pp. 395–415.

Easterly, William and S. Rebelo (1993) 'Fiscal Policy and Economic Growth: An Empirical Investigation', *Journal of Monetary Economics*, vol. 32, no. 2 (December), pp. 417–57.

Edwards, Sebastian (1992) 'Trade Orientation, Distortions, and Growth in Developing Economies', *Journal of Development Economics*, vol. 39, no. 1, pp. 31–57.

Enke, Stephen (1963) *Economics for Development* (London: Dennis Dobson).

Fischer, Stanley (1993) 'Macroeconomic Factors in Growth', *Journal of Monetary Economics*, vol. 32, no. 2 (December).

Harrison, Anne (1993) 'Openness and Growth: A Survey', Mimeo, World Bank.

Hicks, George (1990) 'Explaining the Success of the Four Little Dragons: A Survey', in Seiji Naya and Akira Takayama (eds), *Essays in Honor of Professor*

Sinichi Ichimura (Singapore: Institute of South Asian Studies).

Jones, Larry E. and Rodolfo E. Manuelli (1990) A Convex Model of Equilibrium Growth: Theory and Policy Implications, *Journal of Political Economy*, 98, 5 (October) pp. 1008–1038.

Kamarck, Andrew M. (1967) *The Economics of African Development* (New York: Praeger).

King, Robert and Ross Levine (1993) 'Finance, Entrepreneurship, and Growth: Theory and Evidence', *Journal of Monetary Economics*, vol. 32, no. 2 (December).

Kremer, Michael (1993) 'The O-ring Theory of Economic Development', *Quarterly Journal of Economics*, vol. CVIII, no. 3 (August), pp. 551–76.

Krugman, Paul (1991) *Geography and Trade* (Cambridge, Mass.: MIT Press).

Levine, Ross and David Renelt (1992) 'A Sensitivity Analysis of Cross-Country Growth Regressions', *American Economic Review* (September).

Lucas, Robert E. (1988) 'The Mechanics of Economic Development', *Journal of Monetary Economics*.

Lucas, Robert E. (1993) 'Making a Miracle', *Econometrica*, vol. 61, no. 2, pp. 251–72.

Murphy, Kevin, Andrei Shleifer and Robert Vishny (1989) 'Industrialization and the Big Push', *Journal of Political Economy*, vol. 97, pp. 1003–26.

Pack, Howard and John M. Page (1993) 'Accumulation, Exports and Growth in the High Performing Asian Economies'. Mimeo, World Bank.

Persson, Torsten and Guido Tabellini (1994) 'Is Inequality Harmful for Growth? Theory and Evidence', *American Economic Review*.

Romer, Paul (1986) 'Increasing Returns and Long-Run Growth', *Journal of Political Economy*, vol. 94, pp. 1002–37.

Romer, Paul (1993) 'Ideas and Objects in Economic Development', *Journal of Monetary Economics*, vol. 32, no. 2 (December).

Solow, Robert (1956) 'A Contribution to the Theory of Economic Growth', *Quarterly Journal of Economics*, vol. 70, pp. 65–94.

Srinivasan, T. N. (1993) 'Long-run Growth and Empirics: Anything New?', NBER East Asia Conference.

Summers, Robert and Alan Heston (1991) 'The Penn World Table (Mark 5): An Expanded Set of International Comparisons, 1950–1988', *Quarterly Journal of Economics*, vol. 106, pp. 327–68.

Taylor, Lance (1979) *Macro Models for Developing Countries* (New York: McGraw-Hill).

Taylor, Lance (1983) *Structuralist Macroeconomics: Applicable Models for the Third World* (New York: Basic Books).

Thomas, Vinod and Yan Wang (1993) 'Government Policies and Productivity Growth: Is East Asia an Exemption?' Mimeo, World Bank.

World Bank (1993a) *The East Asian Miracle* (New York: Oxford University Press).

World Bank (1993b) *Sustaining Rapid Development in East Asia and the Pacific* (World Bank, Office of the Vice President, East Asia and Pacific Region).

World Bank (1994) *Adjustment in Africa: Reforms, Results, and the Road Ahead* (New York: Oxford University Press).

Young, Alwyn (1992) 'A Tale of Two Cities: Productivity Growth in Hong Kong and Singapore', *NBER Macroeconomics Annual* (Cambridge Mass.).

10 Growth, Debt and Economic Transformation: The Capital Flight Problem*

Guillermo A. Calvo

An outstanding characteristic of the 1990s is the large number of countries (particularly in the 'East' and the 'South') that are engaged in profound economic transformation processes. These processes entail a considerable amount of *construction* but, also, a considerable amount of *destruction* – or 'creative' destruction, as Schumpeter used to say (see, for example, Calvo and Coricelli, 1993; Kornai, 1993). Although these countries are prepared to 'burn their old idols', they do so in the expectation that they will be rewarded with much better economic performance – that is, more growth and social welfare. The question then arises: are these hopes realistic? Can we identify some key 'traps' lying on the road to successful growth?

This chapter will attempt to shed some light on a type of 'trap' that may be associated directly with the transformation process itself. More specifically, we shall focus on the possible detrimental effects that may result either from initial international indebtedness (the case of highly-indebted countries in the 'South') or from the need to incur in international debt to finance the 'transition' (the case of previously-centrally-planned economies in the 'East'). Furthermore, we shall focus on the case in which servicing the debt requires the imposition of distortionary taxes.

The argument will be couched in terms of a simple model where the country produces homogeneous, perfectly tradable, output by means of capital under constant returns to scale. Capital is perfectly tradable before investment takes place, and cannot be moved afterwards (that is, capital is *putty-clay*). Furthermore, to prevent unbounded growth, we assume that there is a maximum rate at which capital can be accumulated per unit of time. A central insight of the chapter, however, is that growth indeterminacy cannot be dismissed easily. This is so because, in addition to the familiar result that output taxes (the only ones considered in the chapter) are detrimental to growth, we have the opposite line of causation going from growth to taxes. The tax burden (per unit of output) itself is a decreasing function of growth: the higher the growth rate, the smaller will be the tax rate that the government needs to charge in order to service initial debt – thus setting the stage for equilibrium indeterminacy.[1,2]

The model exhibits three distinct debt regions. The first, where debt is low, is unambiguously associated with high growth. Opposite to that, there is the high-debt region, in which only low growth prevails. Finally, there is an intermediate region (that numerical exercises show could be quite large) in which the economy could settle into the low *or* the high growth path – that is, growth indeterminacy obtains.

We define *capital flight* as capital outflows that are detrimental to the country's social welfare.[3] The low-growth equilibrium displayed by our model is a clear example of capital flight, since we shall be able to show that welfare is higher along the high-growth than along the low-growth path.

The paper analyses the implications of imposing controls on capital mobility in order to eliminate capital flight. We show an array of cases in which both growth and welfare would be increased by such controls. However, we also show situations in which, although growth is enhanced, welfare in fact *falls*.

The chapter is organised as follows. Section I presents the basic model under perfect capital mobility. Section II examines the model under no capital mobility, and an hybrid where capital outflows are prohibited but there is no interference with capital inflows. Section III examines the effectiveness of time-varying and vintage-varying tax rates. Finally, Section IV concludes by putting earlier results into a wider perspective.

I THE BASIC MODEL

The central insights of this section can be shown in terms of a simple model. Suppose the economy produces output by means of physical capital, K, and the production function is linear homogeneous: one unit of output is produced by utilizing $1/\alpha$ units of capital. Capital is perfectly internationally mobile *ex ante* (that is, before installation) but not *ex post* (that is, capital is of the putty-clay variety).

The net cash-flow, S, for a firm that accumulates capital at the rate $\dot{K}$ is given by (assuming away capital depreciation):

$$S_t = \alpha(1 - \tau)K_t - \dot{K}_t, \tag{10.1}$$

where τ, $0 \leq \tau \leq 1$, denotes the constant output tax rate (to be more fully discussed below),[4] and subscript t denotes time. Thus, denoting the international real interest rate (that is, the own-rate of return on output) by r, the value of the firm at time zero, V, is given by:

$$V = \int_0^\infty S_t e^{-rt} dt, \tag{10.2}$$

which, setting $z \equiv \dot{K}/K$, yields:

$$V = \int_0^\infty [\alpha(1 - \tau) - z_t] e^{-\int_0^t (r_s - z_s) ds} dt, \tag{10.3}$$

where, without loss of generality, we assume $K_0 = 1$. Notice that z equals the rate of output growth.

The firm is assumed to maximise its value, V, by choosing a non-negative growth path $z(\bullet)$. Inspection of Equation (10.3) quickly reveals that if the maximisation problem has a solution, then it has at least one solution in which z is constant over time. In what follows we shall focus on constant $- z$ solutions.

Assuming a constant z-path, $z < r$, Equation (10.3) takes up the following, much simpler, form:

$$V = \frac{\alpha(1 - \tau) - z}{r - z}. \tag{10.4}$$

Hence, differentiating Equation (10.4) with respect to z, we get:

$$sgn \frac{\partial V}{\partial z} = sgn[\alpha(1 - \tau) - r]. \tag{10.5}$$

Equation (10.5) implies, not surprisingly, that if the marginal (= average) *net* productivity of capital exceeds (falls short of) the real interest rate, then the optimal solution is to grow as fast (as slow) as possible. Therefore, in order to generate well-defined solutions, we need to assume an upper bound for the growth rate z, which will be indicated by $\bar{z}$ (the lower bound for z is zero since we constrained z to be non-negative by the putty-clay assumption).[5]

The next step is to endogenise the tax rate τ. Suppose the economy inherits an initial debt equal to D, and that the government sets the tax rate τ to pay it back (output taxes are the only ones to be examined in this chapter). Assuming the government has full access to international credit markets, and normalising the number of firms to unity, the solvency condition reduces to:

$$D = \alpha\tau \int_0^\infty K_t e^{-rt} dt = \frac{\alpha\tau}{r - z}. \tag{10.6}$$

Thus, using Equation (10.6) in Equation (10.5), we get the following fundamental relationship:

$$sgn \frac{\partial V}{\partial z} = sgn[\alpha - D(r - z) - r]. \tag{10.7}$$

By previous remarks, except in the borderline case in which the expression in Equation (10.7) equals zero, the economy will settle down to either a low-growth equilibrium (LGE), where the growth rate $z = 0$, or a high-growth equilibrium (HGE), where the growth rate $z = \bar{z}$. Furthermore, by Equation (10.7), the condition for HGE is:

$$\alpha - D(r - \bar{z}) - r > 0, \tag{10.8}$$

while the condition for LGE is:

$$\alpha - Dr - r < 0. \tag{10.9}$$

The above conditions are depicted in Figure 10.1 for different levels of initial debt, D. The straight lines correspond to the linear functions in the conditions in Equations (10.8) and (10.9) above. Both start at the same level for $D = 0$, and are downward-sloping with respect to D. The function involved in the HGE condition is flatter than the other because $\bar{z} > 0$. Thus, Figure 10.1 and Equations (10.8) and (10.9) immediately reveal that:

$$\text{HGE exists if } D < D^2, \tag{10.10a}$$

and

$$\text{LGE exists if } D > D^1. \tag{10.10b}$$

The above simple observation implies that the economy will settle down to HGE if initial debt, D, is lower than D^1, and to LGE if initial debt

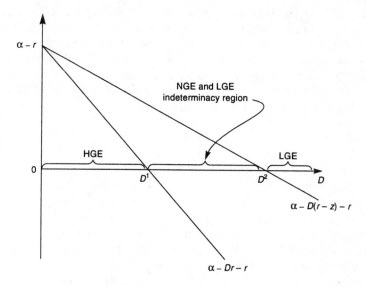

Figure 10.1   Equilibrium: perfect capital mobility

is larger than D^2; furthermore, if initial debt falls between D^1 and D^2 (that is, $D^1 < D < D^2$), then the growth rate is indeterminate, the economy could either settle down to HGE or to LGE.

The intuition behind the above results is straightforward. The higher the initial debt, the higher will be the associated tax burden for servicing the debt, and therefore the lower the rate of return on capital accumulation. So, in principle, one should expect a negative association between initial debt, D, and growth. Furthermore, recalling the solvency condition in Equation (10.6), growth reduces the tax rate necessary for servicing the debt. This inverse causation (from growth to tax burden) lies at the heart of the indeterminacy result. Because, if the economy grows at a low (high) rate, the tax burden will be high (low), the rate of return on capital accumulation low (high), thus giving rise to low (high) growth.

Furthermore, the example shows that a small change in initial debt, D, could have a sizeable effect on growth. This would be the case if, in Figure 10.1, initial debt is larger than, but close to, D^2. Thus the economy would be destined to low growth. However, under these circumstances, a slight debt reduction will place the economy in the indeterminacy region (between D^1 and D^2) where high growth is possible. Interestingly, there is no assurance that the high-growth path will be chosen. Thus the example also suggests that further measures to assure high growth could be necessary. In addition, these measures may also not be very costly, because all it takes is for the private sector to become optimistic about the future of the economy and believe that the economy will lock into a high-growth path.

One can show that the HGE is Pareto superior to the LGE. This is so, because, by Equations (10.4) and (10.6),

$$V = \frac{\alpha - z}{r - z} - D. \qquad (10.11)$$

By Equation (10.8), if HGE exists for some positive initial debt D – implying that $\alpha > r$, a condition that we have implicitly been assuming – then the right-hand side of Equation (10.11) increases with z; thus the firm's present discounted value V is always higher at $z = \bar{z}$ than at $z = 0$. Therefore, since interest rates are the same in the two equilibria, it follows that welfare is higher along HGE than along LGE, as asserted.

Consequently, in all its simplicity, the example illustrates the possible effectiveness of a successful Brady-type debt-reduction plan in which a relatively modest debt cut gives rise to HGE. Moreover, and for similar reasons, the example suggests an explanation for why aid programmes such as the Marshall Plan and the recent G7 plans to help the former Soviet Union – although modest relative to their objectives – may have a sizeable impact on growth.[6]

Let the initial debt GDP ratio be denoted by δ. Hence, $\delta = D/\alpha$. Moreover, let:

$$\delta^i = \frac{D^i}{\alpha}, \ i = 1, 2. \qquad (10.12)$$

Thus, recalling Figure 10.1, δ^i is the initial debt/GDP ratio at the critical value D^i, $i = 1, 2$.

By Equations (10.8), (10.12) and Figure 10.1, we have:

$$\delta^1 = \frac{1}{r} - \frac{1}{\alpha}, \qquad (10.13a)$$

and

$$\delta^2 = \frac{1}{r - z} - \frac{r}{r - z}\frac{1}{\alpha}. \qquad (10.13b)$$

Consequently, a permanent fall in international interest rates increases the size of the region where only the HGE exists, and increases the lower bound on the debt/GDP ratio above which only the LGE exists. Thus, loosely speaking, a permanent drop in the international interest rate makes high growth more likely. In turn, the indeterminacy region (that is, $\delta^1 < \delta < \delta^2$) shifts to the right.

II STOPPING CAPITAL FLIGHT

This section will examine more closely the consequences of stopping capital flight. Consider the case in which the utility of the representative individual takes the following form:

$$\int_0^\infty \ln(c_t)e^{-\rho t}dt, \tag{10.14}$$

where c and $\rho > 0$ denote consumption and the subjective discount rate, respectively, and ln denotes natural logarithm.

In the case of perfect capital mobility, individuals are assumed to face a given (constant) international rate of interest, r, and thus the Euler equation associated with the individual's utility-maximisation problem becomes (from now on, time subscripts will be omitted unless strictly necessary):

$$\frac{\dot{c}}{c} = r - \rho. \tag{10.15}$$

Thus the present discounted value of consumption equals c_0/ρ, independently of the rate of interest.

For the sake of concreteness, we shall examine the situation in which the individual's wealth at time $t = 0$ is given by the firm's value V.[7] Therefore, by Equations (10.11) and (10.15), and the individual's budget constraint, we have

$$c_0 = \rho V = \rho\left(\frac{\alpha - z}{r - z} - D\right). \tag{10.16}$$

By definition, the *current account* (of the balance of payments) of the private sector is the difference between private saving (= disposable income *minus* private consumption) and domestic private investment.

Therefore, the current account at time zero, CA, (recalling that by normalisation $K_0 = 1$) satisfies:[8]

$$CA = \alpha - z - D(r - z) - c_0. \tag{10.17}$$

We are interested in the current account that corresponds to LGE and HGE; that is, $z = 0$ and $z = \bar{z}$. By Equation (10.17), at LGE we have:

$$CA = (\alpha - rD)\left(1 - \frac{\rho}{r}\right). \tag{10.18}$$

We assume that $r > \rho$ which, by Euler Equation (10.15), is a necessary condition for consumption to grow over time. Thus, in the relevant case in which the firm's value $V > 0$ – and, hence, recalling Equation (10.11), $\alpha > rD$ – the initial current account in LGE is positive, and the country initially exports capital to the rest of the world. The intuition is clear. At LGE there is no output growth and, hence, the individual gets a flat disposable income flow equal to $\alpha - rD$. Since the rate of interest exceeds the subjective rate of discount, Euler Equation (10.15) implies that consumption will grow over time. Thus, to satisfy the budget constraint, the individual should start by consuming less than his or her current income, which implies an initially positive current account, that is $CA > 0$.

To analyse the current account at HGE, let us start by looking at the benchmark case in which $\bar{z} = r - \rho$. This is an interesting benchmark because it would correspond to a situation in which the rest of the world has the same utility function of the representative individual (Equation (10.14)) and grows at the maximum rate $\bar{z}$ (we are thus entitled to call this the *homogeneous-world* (HW) case). By, Equations (10.16) and (10.17) the current account in the *HW* case is zero. Again, this has a clear interpretation. In the *HW* case consumption grows at the rate $\bar{z}$ (recall Euler Equation (10.15)) which, at HGE, equals the rate of disposable income growth. Therefore, the budget constraint requires the individual neither to save nor to dissave, implying a zero current account, as asserted. Notice that in the *HW* case, domestic residents would be able to implement the first-best solution without recourse to foreign capital. The same economy, though, would generate capital outflow and no growth at LGE. Therefore, it is appropriate to think of LGE as a case of *capital flight*, that is, a case in which capital outflows are detrimental to the economy's welfare.

In general, current account at HGE could either be positive or negative. The above intuitive discussion suggests – and Equations (10.16) and (10.17) help to prove – the following proposition:

Proposition   At HGE, the initial current account, CA, is negative (positive) if the maximum growth rate, $\bar{z}$, exceeds (falls short of) the growth rate of domestic consumption (that is, if $\bar{z} > (<) r - \rho$).

According to conventional wisdom, the recovery of highly-indebted, and of previously-centrally-planned economies will rely on the ability to attract foreign capital. Therefore, the case in which $\bar{z} > r - \rho$ is an interesting one, because the economy depends on foreign capital inflows in order to implement the first-best solution. We shall thus, refer to $\bar{z} > r - \rho$ as the case of *foreign-capital dependence*. Similarly, we shall refer to $\bar{z} > r - \rho$ (implying $CA > 0$) as the case of *capital surplus*.

We shall now address the issue of stopping capital flight by studying the implications of disallowing capital outflows altogether. To begin, we shall focus on the case in which capital inflows are also disallowed – that is, saving is forced to be equal to physical investment. Under these circumstances, capital accumulation satisfies:

$$\frac{\dot{K}}{K} = z = \alpha(1 - \tau) - \frac{c}{K}. \tag{10.19}$$

Thus, recalling solvency condition in Equation (10.6) and that $K_0 = 1$, we have:

$$c_0 = \alpha(1 - \delta r) - z(1 - \alpha\delta). \tag{10.20}$$

If the debt/GDP ratio is zero, that is, $\delta = 0$, then Equation (10.20) shows that there exists a negative association between the growth rate, z, and initial consumption. Interestingly, if δ is large enough, this association may be reversed (but simulations will be restricted to cases in which the association is negative).

We shall now examine optimal (profit-maximising) firm behaviour. Under present conditions, the domestic interest rate, θ, may differ from the international one, r. Therefore, recalling the definition in Equation (10.4), the domestic value of the firm – which we keep denoting by V – satisfies:

$$V = \frac{\alpha(1 - \tau) - z}{\theta - z}. \tag{10.21}$$

Thus, recalling the solvency condition in Equation (10.6), profit maximisation (that is, maximisation of V in Equation (10.21) with respect to z) implies:

$$\theta = \alpha[1 - \delta(r - z)] \equiv f(z), \text{ if } 0 < z < \bar{z}; \qquad (10.22)$$

moreover,

$$\text{if } \theta \geq \alpha(1 - \delta r) \equiv f(0), \text{ then } z = 0, \qquad (10.23)$$

and,

$$\text{if } \theta \leq \alpha[1 - \delta(r - \bar{z})] \equiv f(\bar{z}), \text{ then } z = \bar{z}. \qquad (10.24)$$

In the no-capital-mobility economy, the Euler equation becomes:

$$\frac{\dot{c}}{c} = \theta - \rho, \qquad (10.25)$$

and, furthermore,

$$\frac{\dot{c}}{c} = z. \qquad (10.26)$$

Therefore, by Equations (10.25) and (10.26), in the no-capital-mobility economy we have:

$$\theta = z + \rho. \qquad (10.27)$$

We are now prepared to characterise equilibria for this economy. An interior equilibrium (that is, $0 < z < \bar{z}$) must satisfy Equations (10.22) and (10.27). Since the latter are straight lines, interior solutions are unique (except in the special case in which the two lines overlap). However, this economy could also exhibit corner solutions satisfying inequalities in Equations (10.23) and/or (10.24). Figure 10.2 depicts the case in which the economy exhibits three equilibrium solutions. In contrast, Figure 10.3 shows a case where there is only one solution, and it is interior. Thus, it should be clear from the analysis that – leaving aside the case where the two straight lines overlap – multiple solutions can only be obtained if we have a configuration like that depicted in Figure 10.2. More formally, equilibrium indeterminacy in the no-capital-mobility economy obtains if:

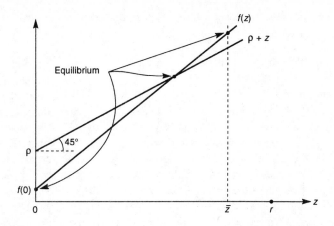

Figure 10.2 Equilibrium indeterminacy: no capital mobility

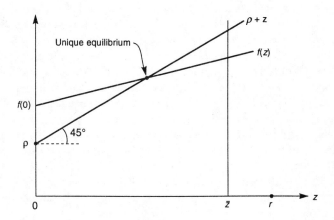

Figure 10.3 Uniqueness of equilibrium: no capital mobility

$$\rho > \alpha(1 - \delta r) \equiv f(0), \qquad (10.28)$$

and, recalling Figure 10.2, the slope of function $f(z)$ must be larger than unity, that is:

$$\alpha\delta \equiv f'(z) > 1. \qquad (10.29)$$

The necessary equilibrium-indeterminacy conditions in Equations (10.28) and (10.29) imply:

$$1 - \delta(r + \rho) < 0, \tag{10.30}$$

which is unlikely to hold in practice. For example, if the unit of time is a year, $r + \rho$ is likely to be less than 15 per cent; thus, for the inequality in Equation (10.30) to hold, the debt/GDP ratio must exceed 6.6! Therefore, we can safely conclude that, for realistic situations, the no-capital-mobility economy exhibits a unique equilibrium.[9]

Let us now consider the *HW* benchmark case (that is, $r - \rho = \bar{z}$). We know from previous considerations that in this case the economy would be able to generate HGE with its own saving, and that the latter is exactly equal to the associated domestic investment required by HGE. Therefore, HGE must also be an equilibrium in the no-capital-mobility situation (since no capital flows are necessary to implement it). The rigorous proof follows from noticing that in the HW benchmark case, HGE condition in Equation (10.8) and Equation (10.27) imply the inequality in Equation (10.24). This is, therefore, an outstanding example of the possible effectiveness of preventing capital flight by imposing capital controls, since it results in the economy being able to attain its first-best. Notice that, by Equation (10.27), once the economy locks into HGE the domestic and international interest rates will be equalised and, hence, there may be no need ever to exercise capital controls actively. Thus, the controls themselves may carry minimal cost.

In general, however, the first-best may not be attained in autarky, and the solution with no capital mobility may actually be *inferior* to LGE. Because, in general, preventing capital flight will result in a growth rate larger than zero (that is, growth at LGE), welfare may decrease if the equilibrium domestic interest rate is substantially below the international one.

Table 10.1 presents some simulations in which the welfare effect of imposing capital-mobility controls varies widely across the cases considered. In our examples we choose parameters that would not have been unrealistic during the 1980s for highly-indebted countries. We assume the international interest rate $r = 10$ per cent and the subjective discount rate $\rho = 1$ per cent (the unit of time is 1 year). Finally, we assume that the initial debt/GDP ratio, δ, is equal to 0.8, and that $\delta = \delta^2$ – that is, the critical debt/GDP ratio beyond which only the LGE holds under perfect capital mobility. In this manner, we capture a situation in which the economy is at the borderline from falling into

Table 10.1   Simulations

CA (%) (1)	Maximum gain (%) (2)	Actual gain (%) (3) = percentage of (2)	δ^1 (4)	Maximun growth z– (5)
7	7.21	–137	0.14	0.08
6	7.30	–83	0.13	0.08
5	7.39	–34	0.12	0.09
4	7.47	10	0.11	0.09
3	7.56	46	0.10	0.09
2	7.65	75	0.10	0.09
1	7.74	93	0.09	0.09
0	7.83	100	0.08	0.09
–1	7.91	88	0.072	0.09
–2	8.00	76	0.064	0.09
–3	8.09	65	0.056	0.09
–4	8.18	54	0.048	0.09
–5	8.26	44	0.040	0.09
–6	8.35	34	0.032	0.10
–7	8.44	24	0.024	0.10

the only-LGE or into the growth-indeterminacy regions. A Brady-type plan would thus put the debt/GDP ratio for this economy squarely into the indeterminacy region. By Equations (10.13a and 10.13b), (10.16) and (10.17), these choices fully determine all the other variables of the model for each level of *CA* (that is, the initial current account under perfect capital mobility if the economy follows the HGE path).

Column 2 of Table 10.1 shows the percentage increase of the firm's value when, under perfect capital mobility, the economy moves from LGE to HGE. This is the maximum welfare gain that can be possibly be attained with, or without, capital mobility.[10] The actual gain from imposing capital controls, as a share of Column 2, is displayed in Column 3. Column 4 shows the critical debt/GDP ratio below which only the HGE prevails under perfect capital mobility, δ^1, while Column 5 shows the associated maximum growth rate.[11,12]

Table 10.1 displays several interesting features. In the first place, under perfect capital mobility, the potential gain from shifting to HGE – if the starting point is LGE – is large: it hovers around 8 per cent. However, the indeterminacy region ($\delta^1 \leq \delta \leq \delta^2$) may also be large, particularly in the foreign-capital dependence region (that is, $CA < 0$). As noted before, if the *HW* conditions hold (that is, $CA = 0$) then controls on capital mobility help securing 100 per cent of the potential gain. However, as the economy becomes increasingly dependent on foreign capital for implementing HGE under perfect capital mobility (that is, as *CA* becomes increasingly negative), actual gains from capital-mobility controls fall relative to the maximum, reaching 24 per cent when *CA* = −7 per cent. However, welfare gains associated with controls on capital mobility are positive in all foreign-capital dependence cases studied, and exceed 2 per cent of LGE consumption. The picture is somewhat different in the capital-surplus region (that is, *CA* > 0). Again, welfare falls off as the economy moves away from the *HW* benchmark (that is, *CA* = 0), but in this region the welfare costs of adopting capital controls may be relatively large (the maximum loss recorded represents about 10 per cent of consumption in LGE, corresponding to the case where *CA* = 7 per cent).

With regard to actual growth, *z*, the latter is always close to, or at, the maximum, $\bar{z}$ (shown in Column 5 of Table 10.1). It coincides with the maximum in the capital surplus region (that is, *CA* > 0), while actual growth stays below the maximum for the foreign-capital dependence region (that is, *CA* < 0). However, the largest difference between $\bar{z}$ and *z* is less than 1 per cent. Thus, capital controls are extremely effective in promoting growth but, as Table 10.1 illustrates, there is no assurance that more growth means more *development* (that is, greater social welfare).[13]

Up to this point, we have studied the two polar cases of perfect international capital mobility and immobility. An interesting intermediate case arises when capital is allowed to flow in, but is prevented from flowing out (in order to stop capital flight). Clearly, this pro-capital-inflows scheme will yield the same equilibria of the no-capital-mobility case if the interest rate associated with the latter, θ, is less than, or equal to, the international interest rate, *r*. To prove it, simply notice that if we start with no capital mobility and then lift controls on capital inflows, there will be no incentives for foreign capital to flow in. Thus results of Table 10.1 apply in the present context because all of them are associated with θ ≤ *r*. The situation would be entirely different, though, if the domestic rate under no capital mobility were to be *larger* than the international interest rate. Under these circumstances, the lifting of capital-inflow controls, alluded to above, will attract foreign capital, leading the economy to HGE under (a regime that would be equivalent to) perfect capital mobility. Thus, the pro-capital inflows scheme would result in the best possible outcome. This suggests that asymmetric capital-mobility controls – discouraging capital flight but not interfering with capital inflows – may be preferable to an all-out prohibition on capital mobility.[14]

III VARIABLE TAX RATES: A SOLUTION?[15]

Up to this point, we have characterised the equilibrium configuration of the economy under the assumption that the tax rate, τ, was held constant over time and over capital vintages. These assumptions will now be relaxed. We shall start by considering the case of time-varying tax rates.

Let τ_t vary over time. Then, by Equation (10.3), the problem of maximising V with respect to the path of z is no longer stationary and, hence, is no longer equivalent to the maximising expression in Equation (10.4). The cost–benefit problem associated with a new piece of investment is nevertheless equally straightforward. On the one hand, investing 'one unit' of capital at time t carries an output cost at t equal to 1. On the other hand, the associated benefits equal the present discounted value of after-tax revenue, $\alpha(1 - \tau_s)$, $s \geq t$. Therefore, the investment decision will be guided by the following expression:

$$\text{sgn}\left[\int_t^\infty \alpha(1 - \tau_s)e^{-r(s - t)} dt - 1\right]. \tag{10.31}$$

If the sign in Equation (10.31) is positive, the investment project will be undertaken (and $z = \bar{z}$) while, if it is negative, no investment will take place (and, hence, $z = 0$). Notice, incidentally, that if τ is constant over time, the sign condition boils down to Equation (10.5), as expected.

An interesting question in this context is whether setting the tax rate lower than at the LGE described above may help eliminating low growth, at least in the medium run. The answer is, unfortunately, negative. Consider the case in which during a 'T-transition', that is, from $t = 0$ to $t = T$, for some $0 < T < \infty$, the tax rate τ is set below its LGE level and, from T on, the tax rate is set constant at whatever rate is necessary to pay back debt remaining at T. We note that if, as in previous sections, the tax rate is constant over time, then at LGE the tax rate τ is such that $\dot{D} = 0$. Thus, a lower τ implies debt accumulation during the T-transition.

Let D_t denote the stock of debt at time t. Thus, the solvency condition (see Equation (10.6)) at time t is given by:

$$D_t = \alpha\int_t^\infty \tau_s K_s e^{-r(s - t)} ds. \tag{10.32}$$

We are now able to test whether low growth at each point in time – that is, $K_t \equiv 1$, is still an equilibrium. By Equations (10.31) and (10.32),

$K_t \equiv 1$ is an equilibrium under time-varying rates if:

$$\alpha - D_t r - 1 < 0, \text{ for all } t \geq 0. \tag{10.33}$$

Thus, if the LGE condition in Equation (10.9) is satisfied, the above inequality holds for $t = 0$ and, consequently, it also holds for all $t > 0$ if, as under the above-mentioned scheme, D grows during a T-transition. Thus, in other words, we have shown that *lower transitional tax rates are not effective for eradicating low growth*.

In contrast, *higher* transitional tax rates could be very effective. Under higher taxes we would have $\dot{D} < 0$ and, thus, the debt/GDP ratio would eventually drop below δ^l, implying that, from that point on, the economy would be able to settle down to HGE with a constant tax rate. However, unless the economy latches on to HGE from the very beginning, there will necessarily be a transition period in which no investment will be taking place and installed capital will pay a heavy tax.

The chances of HGE could be enhanced by, for example, declaring a 'tax holiday' on 'new' capital, and correspondingly raising the tax rate on 'old' capital to ensure that the debt/GDP ratio will eventually fall below δ^l. If the policy is credible, new investment will flow in from the beginning and high growth will be attained at all times. However, the main drawback about a vintage-varying tax policy, or even the transitory-higher-tax-rates policy outlined above, is that the private sector may infer that the government is predisposed to 'time inconsistency'. This is so because these schemes' effectiveness rely heavily on being able to raise taxes on *installed* capital. Thus, to the extent that initial capital would not have been invested if owners anticipated such high taxes, these schemes are effective only because earlier investors are taken by surprise. However, the latter could seriously impair policy credibility – possibly even increasing the chances that the economy will converge to LGE.[16]

In sum, time- and/or vintage-varying tax rates could improve the chances of eventually achieving high growth, but any such policy necessarily relies on taxing more heavily the outstanding stock of capital at the beginning of the programme, risking policy credibility.

IV CONCLUSIONS

The chapter has developed an example in which, under perfect capital mobility, the economy could lock itself into a high- or a low-growth equilibrium depending on the level of the initial government debt. As noted in the Introduction, such a debt could be a result of past policies, or may be the level that the market anticipates will be accumulated by government to wade through an economic transformation process (as in previously centrally-planned economies).

The key factor accounting for growth indeterminacy is the existence of distortionary taxes. This is an aspect of the economy that was not discussed thoroughly in the text, but one that a broader look at the issues should be able to address. In fact, a lesson of the model is that the 'quality' of fiscal policy may play a central role in countries recovering from high debt or undertaking deep economic transformation policies.[17]

This chapter has also illustrated the possibility that schemes designed to stop capital flight may be highly effective in promoting growth. However, the chapter also shows that growth is not equivalent to welfare, by exhibiting examples in which more growth means less, not more, welfare.

There are, however, interesting instances in which eliminating capital flight could have highly positive welfare consequences. The key practical problem in this respect, however, is to find schemes that cannot easily be circumvented by the private sector. This is an issue about which the present chapter has nothing to say. The answer is likely to be highly country-specific. Controls on capital flight, for example, may be very difficult in a world of savvy financiers (as in Latin America) than under somewhat primitive financial conditions (as in Russia).

Finally, there is the issue of credibility, which has been almost completely left out of the analysis. First, as noted above, controls on capital outflows may be hard to enforce. Second, unless these controls are conducive to highly satisfactory solutions (that is, solutions close to first-best), the private sector may expect them to be reversed in the future which – as can be shown formally in the above model – will lead to slower growth and, possibly, smaller welfare gains. One often hears the argument these days that *allowing* capital to flow out freely is a necessary condition to propel the economy into first-best, high-growth, equilibrium. The argument is that ensuring investors can take their money out at the first sign of distress enhances the perceived rate of return on domestic investment. This is another issue, on which this chapter has little to say, because we have provided no theory of why the economy would settle on the high or the low growth equilibrium under perfect capital mobility (which is what is implied by the argument quoted above).[18]

Notes

* I am grateful to Carlos Asilis, Fabrizio Coricelli and Andrés Velasco for useful comments.

1. A close relative of this paper is Eaton (1987) where a similar issue is examined. However, the model is static and cannot handle 'growth' questions. Besides, in the context of Eaton (1987), the elimination of capital flight is always welfare-improving while, as noted above, our model displays an interesting ambiguity in this respect. See also Velasco (1992), where dynamics in an Eaton-type model are studied, assuming adjustment costs to capital accumulation, and that the government cannot borrow or lend in international capital markets.

2. Equilibrium indeterminacy is an old theoretical issue (see, for example, Calvo (1978) where indeterminacy is discussed in terms of a growth model). Recently, there has been renewed interest in the context of 'new' growth theory (see, for example, Matsuyama, 1991; De Gregorio, 1993; and Rodrik, 1993). The latter, however, emphasise the role of production externalities and increasing returns to scale, in contrast with the present one in which the key element is distortionary taxation.

3. This definition is quite different from the usual one in the capital-flight literature that emphasises the legal status of those flows. See, for example, Dooley (1988).

4. Extensions to variable τ are discussed in Section IV.

5. Alternatively, we could assume that output is produced by physical and human capital, and that net output is a declining function of human–capital growth (as in Uzawa (1965)). This device sets a natural upper bound to growth. Otherwise, the central insights are the same.

6. This may also help to elucidate the puzzlingly high apparent marginal productivity of the Marshall Plan (see Eichengreen and Uzan, 1992), and the economic miracles discussed in Lucas (1993).

7. This is consistent with a situation in which the firm is the only source of income for the individual and, at $t = 0$, all the firm's physical capital is owned by domestic residents (that is, the representative individual).

8. *CA* measures (minus) the initial *private sector's* short-run need for foreign capital.

9. Notice, however, that nothing prevents the equilibrium from being at a corner.

10. The welfare gain is measured by the constant percentage by which LGE consumption should be increased so that utility is the same as in the capital-controls equilibrium.

11. The associated values for α are approximately equal to 0.10, which are unrealistically low. Realistic values for α, maintaining the same qualitative results, could be obtained by assuming 'adjustment costs' that are proportional to investment. For example, if the factor of proportionality is 2, one can show that α is around 0.30.

12. The domestic interest rate, θ, in these examples is always less than the international one. The differences between r and ρ are less than $7*10^{-4}$ in the foreign-capital-dependence region (that is, $CA < 0$). Such differences are larger (in absolute value) for the region where $CA > 0$, but they never exceed 1 per cent.

13. Interestingly, in all the welfare-loss cases reported in Table 10.1, actual

growth under no-capital mobility attains its maximum value, $\bar{z}$!

14. This conclusion may need to be qualified strongly in the presence of other realistic distortions. For a recent discussion of the 'capital-inflows' problem, see Calvo *et al.* (1993).

15. This section greatly benefited from discussions with Andrés Velasco.

16. For a related discussion, see Dooley and Svensson (1990).

17. This point has recently been emphasised by Tanzi (1993).

18. Interestingly, by Equations (10.13a and 10.13b), if the increased perceived rate of return is equivalent to a rise in parameter α, both δ^1 and δ^2 shift up, and the size of the indeterminacy region, $D^2 - D^1 = \alpha(\delta^2 - \delta^1)$, increases!

References

Calvo, Guillermo A. (1978) 'On the Indeterminacy of Interest Rates and Wages with Perfect Foresight', *Journal of Economic Theory* (December).

Calvo, Guillermo A. and Fabrizio Coricelli (1993) 'Output Collapse in Eastern Europe: The Role of Credit', *International Monetary Fund Staff Papers* (March).

Calvo, Guillermo A., Leonardo Leiderman and Carmen Reinhart (1993) 'Capital Inflows and Real Exchange Rate Appreciation in Latin America: The Role of External Factors', *International Monetary Fund Staff Papers* (March), pp. 108–51.

De Gregorio, José (1993) 'Liquidity Constraints, Human Capital Accumulation and Growth', Unpublished MS (April).

Dooley, Michael (1988) 'Capital Flight: A Response to Differences in Financial Risks', *International Monetary Fund Staff Papers* (September).

Dooley, Michael and Lars Svensson (1990) 'Policy Consistencyand External Debt Service', IMF Working Paper 90/103 (April).

Eaton, Jonathan (1987) 'Public Debt Guarantees and Private Capital Flight', *World Bank Economic Review* (January), pp. 337–95.

Eichengreen, Barry and Marc Uzan (1992) 'The Marshall Plan: Economic Effects and Implications for Eastern Europe and the Former USSR', *Economic Policy*, vol. 14 (April) pp. 14–75.

Kornai, János (1993) 'Transformational Recession', Discussion Papers, Collegium Budapest, Institute for Advanced Studies, June. Forthcoming in *Économie Appliquée*.

Lucas, Robert E., Jr (1993) 'Making a Miracle', *Econometrica*, vol. 61 (March), pp. 251–72.

Matsuyama, Kiminori (1991) 'Increasing Returns, Industrialization, and Indeterminacy of Equilibrium', *Quarterly Journal of Economics* (May) pp. 617–50.

Rodrik, Dani (1993) 'Do Low-Income Countries Have a High-Wage Option?,' Unpublished MS, Columbia University, May.

Tanzi, Vito (1993) 'Fiscal Policy and Economic Restructuring of Economies in Transition', IMF Working Paper WP/93/22 (March).

Uzawa, Hirofumi (1965) 'Optimum Technical Change in an Aggregate Model of Economic Growth', *International Economic Review*, vol. 6, pp. 18–31.

Velasco, Andrés (1992) 'Animal Spirits, Capital Repatriation and Investment', C. V. Starr Center for Applied Economics, New York University, RR No. 92–43, September.

11 Economic Growth under Alternative Development Strategies: Latin America from the 1940s to the 1990s

Andrés Solimano

State dirigisme and import substitution provided the engine for growth in Latin America from the 1940s to the late 1970s. Although the growth performance of the region was respectable in that period, with annual growth of around 5 per cent, the development model started to run out of steam in the 1970s and definitely collapsed in the 1980s under the pressure of the debt crisis and growing macroeconomic instability. Under these circumstances, governments altered their development strategies in the direction of opening up their economies, reducing the role of the state; and deregulating activities previously precluded for the private sector.

This chapter examines three propositions regarding Latin-American growth and its links with policy transformation: (i) The postwar growth performance of Latin America, from the 1940s to the onset of the debt crisis in the early 1980s, say, relied strongly on factor accumulation, with a declining contribution of total factor productivity growth over time (a sort of 'extensive' growth pattern); (ii) The accumulated experience of market-based reform shows that reform can be followed by either recessionary or expansionist output responses in the short term. The magnitude of initial disequilibria, external factors, and the response of exports and investment to the reform policies, are the basic determinants of those growth outcomes; (iii) The long-run growth impact of market reform is still an unsettled issue, and evidence suggests that a sustained acceleration of growth after reform may come with a long lag (a decade or so). The dominant view stresses an increase in total factor productivity growth as a main channel for an acceleration of growth after reforms that improve the quality of resource allocation and the productivity of investment.

The critique of the traditional development model followed in Latin America – based on import substitution and state dirigisme – focuses not so much on a failure of that model in delivering acceptable rates of output growth, but on the fact that this was an 'extensive' pattern of growth relying mainly on factor accumulation (capital and labour) with a reduced contribution of total factor productivity growth associated with a policy regime based on import substitution and state dirigisme that brought a distorting structure of incentives in the economy. The empirical evidence reviewed here tends to support this view on the sources of growth and traditional development model. It also shows that, macroeconomically, the growth process in several countries of the region was often accompanied by recurrent balance of payments crises and inflationary pressures.

The contention that the short-term growth impact of reform is influenced by, besides other factors, the phase of the business cycle and the external conditions faced by the reforming economy, is examined in a sample of countries starting reform from a variety of initial conditions in the 1970s, 1980s and 1990s. In that perspective, Chile adopted market-based reforms in the second half of the 1970s in a context of increasingly abundant capital flows, existing spare capacity, and unemployed labour. As a result, growth rapidly accelerated after major reforms were undertaken. In contrast, reform programmes adopted in the 1980s in Mexico and Bolivia did so under the hardship posed by the external debt crisis and the sharp cut-off of foreign financing to the region. These programmes were followed either by stagnation or by modest growth. More recently, in the early 1990s, reform programmes have taken place in severely distressed economies such as Argentina and Peru, as well as in the more economically stable Colombia. Under a more favourable international environment than that of the 1980s, particularly regarding capital inflows, these programmes have been followed almost immediately by renewed growth.

In evaluating the impact of reform on long-run growth, we face the problem of too few observations. Chile is the economy in the region with the longest experience – nearly two decades – with comprehensive market-based reform. Mexico and Bolivia have also adopted comprehensive reform measures, but only since the mid-1980s. Empirical evidence for Chile points up a positive effect of reform on long-term GDP and productivity growth, but also shows a substantial lag in the impact of reform on capital formation: a key ingredient for sustainable, capacity-based output expansion.

This chapter is organised into four sections plus the introduction.

The first section discusses conceptual issues surrounding the relationships between stabilisation, reform and growth. The second section looks at the historical and more recent growth record of seven Latin-American economies that have adopted, to differing degrees, programmes of market-based reform since the 1960s. The third section presents econometric evidence of sources of growth from the 1940s to the 1980s for these reforming economies, and then provides additional evidence about the long-run impact of reform on the rate of economic growth in Chile and Mexico. The last section contains concluding remarks.

I GROWTH UNDER ALTERNATIVE POLICY REGIMES: CONCEPTUAL ISSUES

This section reviews the main features of growth under two main policy regimes: state dirigisme-cum-import substitution (the development model of Latin America between the 1940s and 1980s); and market-based development.

1.1 State Dirigisme and Import Substitution

Growth under state dirigisme and import substitution was driven mainly by capital-intensive investment. On the one hand, public investment was envisaged as a key policy device for mobilising domestic savings, boosting growth and avoiding the potential co-ordination failures of decentralised markets. Public investment focused on sectors such as energy, public utilities, telecommunications, and infrastructure activities that tend to be capital-intensive. On the one hand, private investment was stimulated through subsidised credit, tax rebates and preferential exchange rates. The import tariffs structure favoured the import of machinery, equipment and inputs; this apparatus of investment promotion tended also to make growth rely on the expansion of capital-intensive activities and the imports of capital goods.

At the macro level, the growth pattern often came along with two main disequilibria: chronic inflation and recurrent balance of payments crises. The inflationary pressure came from two sources: first, the tendency for the state sector to expand led to increasing pressures on public spending which, by causing rigidities in the tax system, was reflected in the appearance of fiscal deficits, financed in many cases by money creation. A second source of inflationary pressure was associated with distributive conflicts among different groups (for example, powerful urban labour unions, the industrialist-capitalist class, capital and landowners) over their relative shares in national income. This gave rise to the traditional wage–price–devaluation spiral that, under accommodative monetary policies, produces inflation.

The recurrent balance of payments crisis in Latin America under import substitution is related to two main factors: one factor, endemic to the region, is linked in particular to external vulnerability, international commodity price shocks that hit hard the economies whose export earning are concentrated on a few primary commodities. The second factor behind recurrent balance of payments crises was a tendency for real currency overvaluation associated with a protected tariff structure, which, in the end, increased the import content of output growth. Very often the balance of payments became a binding constraint to sustained growth, as expansionary cycles threatened balance of payment equilibrium, thus inviting stop-and-go macro policies.

1.2 Market-Based Development

The debt crises and macroeconomic turbulence of the 1980s made the underlying problems of the postwar development model of Latin America emerge in full force. Disappointment with the traditional development model led to the adoption of a new policy regime that sought to couple macroeconomic stability with a smaller state, open foreign trade regimes and liberalise markets. Mapping and measuring the impact of these reforms on the rate of economic growth is a complex task. In fact, there are several methodological problems. Among these are: (a) The sample of actual country cases with a long experience with market reform is small. This is in contrast with the large sample of country experiences with import substitution and state dirigisme, a development strategy that lasted for several decades; (b) At the analytical level, there is ambiguity as to whether the reforms affect the level and/or the rate of growth of output; (c) There is an implicit identification problem in determining the relative contribution of the different components of reform: macro stabilisation, and microeconomic and institutional reforms in terms of their effects on the rate of economic growth; (d) We know little about how the time phasing and interaction between these main components of overall reform affect economic growth; (e) Individual reform policies do not always produce a growth effect that goes in the same direction; (f) Identifying the relevant transmission mechanisms – consumption, investment, exports on the demand side, and capital formation and productivity growth on the supply side – on how reform policies affect the rate of economic growth; and (g) There are considerable lags in the effects of policies measures on capital formation, productivity and GDP growth. With these caveats in mind, we shall review briefly the expected growth effects of the different components of a reform package.

1.3   Macro Stabilisation

Many reform programmes in Latin America started from deteriorated macroeconomic conditions characterised by high and/or erratic inflation, large fiscal deficits and unsustainable current account disequilibria. This has been an important force propelling reform.[1]

Macroeconomic instability reflected in inflation, exchange rate volatility, stop–go policies, hampers economic growth for several reasons:[2] (a) it discourages irreversible investment outlays; (b) it introduces noise and unpredictability reducing the informational content of price signals, worsening the quality of resource allocation and, possibly, productivity growth; (c) under inflationary conditions, entrepreneurs and firms devote an increasing portion of their time and effort to avoiding inflationary losses (or making inflationary gains) from assets management rather than actual production and innovation.[3] Therefore the restoration of macroeconomic stability is a basic precondition for fostering growth. Moreover, the type of stabilisation programme adopted to restoring macro stability matters for determining the short-term growth impact of reform.[4]

Orthodox or money-based programmes such as those applied in Chile in 1975, Bolivia in 1985, Peru in 1990 and other examples centred on a permanent reduction in the rate of growth of the money supply and the fiscal deficit to reduce inflation. These programmes tend to be recessionary in the short run because restrictive monetary policies push real interest rates up, depressing aggregate demand, output and employment. The extent of output, contraction depends on several factors, chiefly, the credibility of the programme and the degree of wage and price rigidity and the existence of institutional mechanisms of indexation that 'filter' the impact of slower money growth on the rate of inflation.

Exchange-rate-based stabilisation (Southern Cone in the late 1970s, Argentina Convertibility plan in 1991) rely on the exchange rate as the key nominal anchor for disinflation. These programmes tend to be expansionary in the short term. Domestic absorption (consumption and investment) increases after slowing down the rate of devaluation (or fixing it altogether), for two reasons: first, the rise in real wages that often takes place at the beginning of the programme stimulates current consumption; second, the initial drop in real interest rates associated with a slower pace of devaluation encourages investment and the consumption of durable goods. All these effects are expansionary.[5] However, this is not the full story. The real exchange rate overvaluation that often develops during these programmes squeezes export- and import-competing industries, over time, on the supply side. Moreover, the real appreciation invites substitution of demand away from domestic goods and toward (transitorily) cheaper foreign goods. Clearly, the initial expansion of economic activity gives way to a downturn later. More dramatically, if the currency appreciation leads to a balance of payments crisis (as happened in the Southern Cone in the early 1980s and Mexico in late 1994), then the downturn can turn into a full-blown recession to reduce imports quickly.

The effects of *multiple anchor programmes or heterodox plans* (Israel in 1985, and the Mexican stabilisation plans after 1988) on growth are more ambiguous. The main rationale for these programmes is the co-ordinated use of several nominal anchors to avoid, or dampen, the often large recession that comes with orthodox stabilisation and the undesired changes in key relative prices, associated with exchange-rate-based stabilisation. In general, one can expect these (multiple anchor) programmes to be moderately restrictive, as monetary and fiscal restraint is needed to support the anchors. In practice, the Mexican programme of 1981–9 and the Israeli one of 1985 were moderately recessive in the early phases of implementation.

To summarise, in the long run, the shift from inflationary conditions to more stable macro conditions have positive effects on long-term growth; however, the transition is more complex and depends largely on the type of stabilisation programme adopted: that is, the choice of nominal anchor(s), and the stance of the accompanying fiscal and monetary policies – all conditioned by the external environment under which stabilisation takes place. In general, no stabilisation programme can avoid some recession; the real difference across programmes is between recession now or recession later, during the course of disinflation.

1.4 Structural Reforms

The structural reforms of a programme of market-based transformation have a longer-run horizon. The chief transmission mechanisms to growth are capital formation and the rate of total factor productivity growth. These reforms cover several areas. Let us start with *trade liberalisation*. In general, the effect of trade reform on output growth (measured as the degree of external openness – for example, the share of exports plus imports over GDP or as an index of import tariffs and other trade restrictions), capital formation and productivity growth are subject to dispute. One argument for a positive correlation between the degree of external openness and the rate of total factor productivity growth is that the more open the economy, the more the country can adopt (or import) technical innovations developed in foreign countries.[6] Nevertheless, it is still an open question as to whether this is a level effect (once and for all) or a rate of change effect (more permanent).[7] The impact of trade reform on aggregate capital formation is also potentially ambiguous and depends on factors such as the credibility of the foreign trade reform and the differences in capital intensity between export- and import-competing industries.[8]

Financial deepening is expected to generate a positive effect on capital formation and productivity growth by easing credit constraints, mobilising savings, and enabling a better evaluation and screening of good investment and innovation projects. These effects, however, are of a long-run nature. In the short term, financial liberalisation undertaken when macroeconomic stabilisation is still incomplete, and full regulation, tends possibly to be accompanied by high real interest rates and financial fragility.[9] Empirical evidence such as Easterly (1993) and King and Levine (1993) suggests an adverse effect on growth of moderate-to-large negative real interest rates and of low coefficients of monetisation (a proxy of financial repression) for a cross-section of developing economies. Two main arguments are used to rationalise these findings showing a negative effect of financial repression on growth: a depressing effect on the average rate of return on capital (Easterly) or a lower rate of technical innovation (King and Levine).

The effects of privatisation on growth are more likely to operate in the long run, provided that total factor productivity growth is accelerated and private investment responds positively to the new business opportunities made available by privatisation. In the short run, however, the effects are more ambiguous, as privatisation tends to be accompanied by cuts in public investment that can be contractionary, and by an often timid initial response of private investment.[10]

Summing up, the growth effects of structural reforms (trade liberalisation, financial reform and privatisation) are perhaps ambiguous in the short run. The positive growth effects of market reform are more likely to come in the medium to long run as the new policy reform is consolidated and the private sector reacts more fully to the new opportunities opened up by the reform.

Table 11.1   Rates of growth of GDP eight Latin-American economies, 1950–94 (annual averages, percentages)

	1950–80	*1980–90*	*1990–4*
Argentina	3.2	−1.1	6.2
Bolivia	3.4	−0.1	3.9
Brazil	6.9	1.5	1.0
Chile	3.4	2.8	6.1
Colombia	5.0	3.4	4.0
Mexico	6.4	1.6	3.0
Peru	4.5	−0.3	2.9
Venezuela	5.9	1.0	3.8
Average	**4.8**	**1.1**	**3.9**

Sources: Hofman (1991); Elias (1992); ECLA (various issues).

II   COUNTRY EXPERIENCES: SHORT- AND MEDIUM-RUN GROWTH EFFECTS OF POLICY REFORM

The Latin American economies grew at an annual average rate close to 5.0 per cent (eight countries, Table 11.1) or 5.5 per cent (nineteen countries) between 1950 and 1980.[11,12] The best growth performers in that period were the two largest economies of the region, Mexico and Brazil, with annual rates of GDP growth between 6.5 and 7 per cent. That dynamism exhibited by the region as a whole came to an abrupt end in the early 1980s, after the onset of the debt crisis that forced debtor countries to adopt stiff austerity measures. As a consequence of these shocks, average GDP growth for the group of eight economies declined to 1.1 per cent between 1980 and 1990 (Table 11.1), nearly a fifth of the average rate of growth of the period 1950–1980. In 1990–4 the picture started to change (Table 11.1) and GDP growth recovered to an annual average rate close to 4 per cent. Interestingly, the fastest-growing economies in the 1950–80 period, Brazil and Mexico, have been among the slowest growers during most of the 1980s and early 1990s.

Table 11.2 presents GDP growth rates for countries that have undertaken programmes of market-based reform in the 1970s, 1980s and 1990s. It presents for each country the historical growth record (1950–80) and averages of growth rates for several years before the after the starting of market-based reforms.

In the 1970s, Chile launched the probably most comprehensive programme of stabilisation and reform in the region. On the stabilisation front, the programme comprised money-based stabilisation in 1975,

Table 11.2 Rate of GDP growth, historical averages, before and after reform

Country	Historical period	Year(s) starting reform	Historical period	3 years before	GDP growth rates years(2) starting reform	3 years after	5 years after	10 years after
Progs. of the 1970s								
Chile	1950–70	1974–5	3.9	0.7	-6.7	7.2	7.5	3.7/4.6[a]
Progs. of the 1980s								
Mexico	1950–80	1983	6.4	5.2	-5.3	1.0	1.2	2.0
Bolivia	1950–80	1985	3.4	-3.7	-0.1	0.7	1.7	2.3[b]
Venezuela	1950–80	1989	5.9	6.0	-7.8	8.0	5.7[d]	–
Progs. of the 1990s								
Colombia	1950–80	1990	5.0	4.4	4.0	3.3	–	–
Argentina	1950–80	1991	3.2	-2.8	8.9	7.3[c]	–	–
Peru	1950–80	1991	4.5	-8.5	2.1	1.9[b]	–	–

Notes:
a 18 years after.
b 8 years after.
c 2 years after.
d 4 years after.

followed by an exchange-rate-based stabilisation plan in 1978–9.[13] On the structural front, during the second half of the 1970s tariffs to trade were drastically reduced, the financial market liberalised, and public enterprises privatised. The average rate of growth during the three years before 1974–5 was very sluggish, and in 1975 the Chilean economy contracted sharply. Afterwards growth resumed forcefully, helped by the existence of excess capacity and unemployed labour. Moreover, there were large productivity gains following the reforms. However, it is interesting to note that steady GDP growth in Chile – at annual rates of around 7 per cent – has been achieved only since the mid-1980s (and running through the 1990s), nearly a decade after reforms were launched. During the transition period towards high and sustained growth, the process was affected by policy failures, external shocks and large economic fluctuations.

Comprehensive market-based reform in the 1980s comprised, in the main, Mexico and Bolivia. In Mexico, reforms followed two stages: initial fiscal and external adjustment (1983–5) with trade liberalisation, deregulation and privatisation, and further stabilisation taking place after 1985.[14] Surprisingly enough, the post-reform growth rate of Mexico has been less than a third of its average rate for the period 1950–80. Bolivia suffered mounting and explosive inflation and negative growth in the first half of the 1980s before adopting the stabilisation plan of 1985 and other liberalisation policies. These policies contributed to stopping and reversing the output collapse of the high inflation period. Since then, per capita growth has been positive but modes.[15] The general lesson of the reform programme initiated in the 1980s is that policy reform was not followed by any spectacular upsurge in the rate of economic growth. Beyond country-specific factors, the unsupportive common external environment of most of the 1980s – particularly in terms of a negative external transfer to Latin America – stands as an important common explanation for the sluggish post-reform growth performance in Mexico and Bolivia.[16]

In the early 1990s, Argentina and Peru joined the group of comprehensive reformers after being hit by hyperinflation and dramatic economic decline. Both countries succeeded in stopping hyperinflation and initiated programmes of trade liberalisation, financial reform, deregulation and privatisation. The growth response to these policies in the two countries has been quite sizeable, denoting a considerable enthusiasm of the private sector (both national and foreign) for the new policies. Moreover, the recoveries took place from initially depressed output levels after the period of stagnation that characterised the high-inflation years. In a way, the initial growth response in Argentina and Peru is similar to the strong Chilean recovery of the second half of the 1970s. Like the late 1970s, the early 1990s is a period of large capital inflows to Latin America.[17] Clearly the size and direction of capital inflows are important determining factors of the different growth response to the reform programs of the 1980s and 1990s.

Finally, it is interesting to mention the case of Colombia, a country with a long tradition of prudence in macro policies and gradualism in the adoption of structural reforms. In contrast to Argentina and Peru, macro conditions were relatively stable in Colombia before reform. The economy was growing at a rate of around 4 per cent per year (see Table 7.2) certainly a respectable record for the stagnated 1980s. This of course made it more difficult to achieve a rapid acceleration of growth after the reforms.

III   LONG-RUN GROWTH UNDER STATE DIRIGISME AND MARKET REFORM: ECONOMETRIC EVIDENCE

We have observed that the overall growth record of the main Latin-American economies in the pre-reform period, 1950–80, was quite respectable. As we document in this section, however, this growth pattern relied strongly on factor accumulation (labour and capital), with a declining contribution of total factor productivity growth to overall GDP expansion. Table 11.3 provides Elias (1992) decomposition of sources of growth between factor accumulation and total factor productivity (TFP) growth for Argentina, Brazil, Chile, Bolivia, Mexico, Peru and Venezuela for each decade from the 1940s to the 1980s.

From this growth decomposition we find that the average – across countries and decades – contribution of TFP growth to GDP growth was 20 per cent. This is a relatively low number when compared to a larger sample of developing countries and developed economies. In fact, Chenery *et al.* (1986) report, for a similar period, a share of TFP growth in total value-added growth of 31 per cent for developing countries and 50 per cent for developed economies. Nevertheless, it is worth noting that in the first two decades of import substitution and state dirigisme, the 1940s and 1950s, the contribution of total factor productivity growth was sizeable, particularly in the three largest economies of Latin American: Argentina, Brazil and Mexico. However, as Table 11.3 and Figure 11.1 show, a declining rate of TFP growth takes place since the 1960s in most of these economies, a trend that further deepened in the 1970s.

Table 11.3   Sources of growth, 1940–80 selected Latin-American economies (average rate of change per year)

	GDP growth (%)	Contribution factor accumulation (%)	Total factor productivity growth (%)
Argentina			
1940–50	5.1	2.0	3.1
1950–60	3.3	2.5	0.8
1960–70	3.8	3.6	0.2
1970–80	2.7	3.0	−0.3
Average (1940–80)	3.7	2.7	1.0
Brazil			
1940–50	5.5	N/A	N/A
1950–60	6.8	3.2	3.6
1960–70	5.9	4.5	1.4
1970–80	8.2	7.1	1.1
Average (1940–80)	6.6	4.9	2.0
Chile			
1940–50	3.3	1.4	1.9
1950–60	3.5	2.8	0.7
1960–70	5.0	3.7	1.3
1970–80	3.1	2.1	1.0
Average (1940–80)	3.7	2.5	1.2
Colombia			
1940–50	4.1	3.0	1.1
1950–60	4.6	3.7	0.9
1960–70	5.2	4.4	0.8
1970–80	5.8	5.2	0.6
Average (1940–80)	4.9	4.1	0.8
Mexico			
1940–50	6.0	1.6	4.4
1950–60	5.6	4.6	1.0
1960–70	7.1	5.9	1.2
1970–80	6.2	6.1	0.1
Average (1940–80)	6.2	4.6	1.6
Peru			
1940–50	4.4	3.9	0.5
1950–60	3.9	6.5	−2.6
1960–70	5.3	4.3	1.0
1970–80	3.7	4.2	−0.5
Average (1940–80)	4.3	4.7	−0.4
Venezuela			
1940–50	N/A	N/A	N/A
1950–60	7.9	5.7	2.2
1960–70	5.4	4.0	1.4
1970–80	3.9	5.6	−1.7
Average (1940–80)	5.7	5.1	0.6

Source: elaborated from Elias (1992).

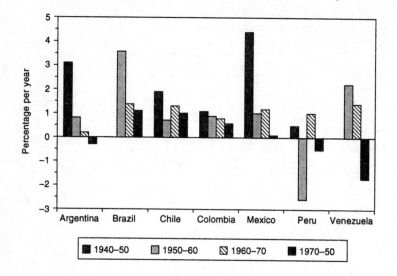

Figure 11.1   Total factor productivity growth

Importantly, this evidence shows that the traditional development
model in Latin America was showing clear signs of exhaustion and
dynamic inefficiency (in terms of declining productivity growth) well
before the debt crisis of the 1980s, when growth rates fell sharply or
became negative.[18]

3.1   Evidence for Chile

Let us look in more detail at the econometric evidence on the impact
of the reforms on long-run growth in Chile. A sources of growth regression for the period 1951–89 (see Lefort and Solimano, 1993) with
a dummy for post-1974 reform shows:

$$GY = 0.002 + 0.593 \ (GKNR) + 0.407 \ (GL) - 0.0698 \ (DREC) +$$
$$\quad (0.358) \quad\quad (7.927) \quad\quad\quad\quad\quad\quad\quad\quad (-3.92)$$

$$0.016 \ (DREF)$$
$$\quad (1.96)$$

$$Rsq \ (adj.) = 0.82$$

$$DW = 1.81$$

Where *GY* stands for the rate of growth of real GDP; *GKNR* is the rate of growth of the stock of non-residential capital; *GL* is the rate of growth of employment; *DREC* is a recession dummy taking values 1 for 1975 and 1982–83 and zero for the other years; and *DREF* is a reform dummy activated after 1974. The *t* -statistics are in parenthesis. It is interesting to note that the reform dummy shows a statistically significant increase in the rate of growth of total factor productivity after the adoption of the reforms.[19]

A similar result is obtained when running separate regressions for before and after reform samples:

Before reform, period 1951–73:

$$GY = \quad -0.001 \quad + 0.703 \ GKNR + 0.297 \ GL$$
$$(-0.136) \qquad (6.65)$$

$$Rsq \ (adj.) = 0.734$$

$$DW = 1.93$$

After reform, period 1974–89:

$$GY = 0.016 + 0.52 \ GKNR + 0.479 \ GL \ - \ 0.065 \ DREC$$
$$(2.27) \qquad (4.731) \qquad\qquad\qquad (-3.22)$$

$$Rsq \ (adj.) = 0.874$$

$$DW = 1.26$$

It is interesting to note that the constant of the regression in the period 1951–73 is slightly negative and statistically insignificant, suggesting almost nil average TFP growth. In contrast, the constant goes up to a rate of 1.6 per cent per year in the period 1974–89 and is statistically significant. Again, this provides evidence of an acceleration in the rate of growth of total factor productivity after the reforms.

This trend is shown also in Table 11.4, which portrays a change in the relative contribution of factor accumulation and TFP growth to the observed rates of growth of GDP after 1974. Of the 3.5 percentage points of average GDP growth in the period 1951–73 (pre-reform period), 0.2 percentage points are explained by total factor productivity growth, with the rest being explained by capital accumulation and labour growth.

Table 11.4 Decomposition analysis of sources of growth, supply and demand factors, Chile 1951–92 (percentage average annual change)

	GDP growth	Rate of growth of labour	Total labour contribution	Rate of growth of N-R cap.	Rate of growth of cap. util.	Total capital contribution	TFP growth	Demand factors[a]		
								Rate of growth, consumption	Rate of growth, investment	Rate of growth, exports
1951–92	3.64	2.48	1.01	3.46	0.05	2.08	0.54	3.05	4.38	8.94
1951–73 Pre-reforms	3.49	2.00	0.81	4.57	-0.36	2.49	0.18	3.91	1.11	6.06
1974–92 Reform period	3.82	3.06	1.25	2.12	0.55	1.59	0.98	2.45	6.62	10.92
1974 Normalization	0.97	-0.14	-0.06	1.54	4.92	3.83	-2.80	-18.27	19.11	45.95
1975 Stabilisation and recession	-12.91	-7.98	-3.25	1.22	-9.87	-5.13	-4.53	-11.42	-22.77	2.35
1976–81 Implementation of major economic reforms	7.20	3.77	1.54	2.10	1.74	2.28	3.39	7.96	12.25	11.16
1982–3 Recession and financial crisis	-7.40	-7.55	-3.07	1.48	-2.24	-0.45	-3.87	-7.76	-24.41	-2.67
1984–8 Recovery and re-consolidation of reforms	5.51	9.29	3.78	-0.08	1.66	0.94	0.79	3.89	11.55	7.68
1989–92 Sustained growth	7.12	3.07	1.25	5.60	0.30	3.50	2.38	6.16	11.73	12.13

Notes: (a) The rates of growth of the demand components for the whole sample and the pre-reform period correspond to 1961–92 and 1961–73.

Source: Lefort and Solimano (1993).

In contrast, in the period 1974–92 (post-reform), of the average annual rate of GDP growth of 3.8 per cent, the contribution of TFP growth is roughly 1 per cent. That represents a substantial increase in the relative contribution of TFP growth in the later period.

Table 11.4 also provides a supply and demand decomposition of GDP growth in the post-1974 period. Interestingly, the results show that TFP growth accelerated more both in 1976–81, straight after the implementation of the main structural reforms, and in 1989–92, a period of sustained growth. Table 11.4 also shows that exports have almost doubled their contribution to GDP growth in the period 1974–92 in comparison with 1951–73. Clearly, Chilean growth after the reforms has been driven mainly by exports.

An important question posed at the outset of this chapter is the relative contribution of macro stabilisation *vis-à-vis* structural reforms to GDP growth and the transmission mechanisms at work. Lefort and Solimano (1993) run partial regressions for explaining capital formation, productivity growth and GDP expansion as a function of a set of macro structural reforms and external sector variables. The macroeconomic variables (inflation, the variability of the real exchange rate, the growth rate of public spending) had the highest explanatory value for the rate of GDP growth; in addition, the regressions show that these macro variables were also the most important group of determinants of capital accumulation. This confirms the presumption that investment is very sensitive to instability and this is probably the chief mechanism of transmission of macroeconomic disturbances into output growth. Another interesting result obtained is that the two structural reform variables – an index of import tariffs and a variable of financial deepening – have a positive and significant impact on GDP growth, acting primarily through the rate of growth of total factor productivity.

3.2 Mexico

In Mexico, the effect of the reforms on GDP growth was tested with the dummy variables method. The results of a sources of growth equation for the period 1951–89 is the following (see Lefort and Solimano, 1993):

$$GY = 0.011 + 0.474 \ GKNR + 0.526 \ GL - 0.046 \ DREC -$$
$$ (2.14) \qquad (4.27) \qquad\qquad\qquad (-2.99)$$

$$ 0.003 \ (DREF)$$
$$ (-0.265)$$

$$Rsq \ (adj.) \ = \ 0.651$$

$$DW \ = \ 2.04$$

This regression shows a negative but insignificant coefficient for the reform dummy variable (*DREF*) that is activated after 1985 in the GDP growth equation. This result is partly surprising, though it may reflect a small post-reform sample that fails to capture the full impact of the reform on GDP growth.

Several interesting findings stand out from the growth decomposition displayed in Table 11.5. First, as noted in previous sections, the implementation of reforms in Mexico was not followed by a strong growth performance, although GDP growth started to accelerate moderately from 1988 to 1994. This moderate upswing contrasts with the stagnation observed in the first phase of the reforms, in the period 1982–7. Second, in the pre-reform period, average annual TFP growth was around 1.2 per cent, out of 6.5 percentage points of GDP growth.[20] Clearly, its contribution to average growth was rather modest in comparison with the contribution of capital accumulation. Third, in the period after 1988 there was an increase in TFP growth (to 0.5 per cent per year), still a low figure. Fourth, on the demand side, growth was driven mainly by investment and only partly by export expansion.

IV FINAL REMARKS

This chapter points in the direction of a wide variety of short-term growth responses to the adoption of stabilisation and liberalisation policies. Growth responded quickly to the reforms in Chile in the second half of the 1970s, and in Argentina and Peru in the early 1990s. In contrast, sluggish growth followed comprehensive stabilisation and restructuring policies in Mexico and Bolivia in the 1980s, the decade of the debt crisis and the drying-up of foreign financing to Latin-American countries.

In a long-term perspective, existing econometric evidence on growth patterns for seven Latin-American economies from the 1940s to the 1980s shows that GDP growth was mainly explained by factor accumulation, with a relatively small contribution of total factor productivity growth to GDP expansion. In addition, TFP growth exhibited a declining trend, starting in the 1960s. This suggests the exhaustion (and dynamic inefficiency) of the growth pattern followed by Latin America under

Table 11.5 Decomposition analysis of sources of growth, supply and demand factors, Mexico 1951–91 (percentage average annual change)

	GDP growth	Rate of growth of labour	Total labour contribution	Rate of growth of Capital[b]	Total capital contribution	TFP growth	Demand factors[a]		
							Rate of growth consumption	Rate of growth, investment	Rate of growth, exports
1951–91	5.26	2.92	1.54	6.12	2.90	0.82	4.99	7.08	5.43
1951–81 Pre-reform period (developmentalist model)	6.58	3.78	1.99	7.12	3.37	1.21	5.84	9.98	5.44
1951–77 Inward-orientated growth	6.27	3.07	1.61	6.87	3.26	1.40	5.57	8.80	4.94
1978–81 Oil boom	8.63	8.57	4.51	8.76	4.15	-0.03	7.63	17.97	8.78
1982–91 Adjustment and reform period	1.16	0.25	0.13	3.02	1.43	-0.40	2.37	-1.93	5.40
1982–5 Debt crisis and first adjustment period	0.34	-0.79	-0.42	4.16	1.97	-1.21	0.53	-8.06	12.73
1986–7 Oil shock and trade opening	-1.04	-0.52	-0.27	-0.30	-0.14	-0.62	0.04	-2.66	-11.40
1988–91 Stabilisation and intensification structural reforms	3.08	1.69	0.89	3.55	1.68	0.52	5.38	4.57	-4.93

Notes:
a The rates of growth of the demand components for the whole sample and the pre-reform period correspond to 1961–92 and
b Non-residential capital adjusted by the change of capital utilisation.

Source: Lefort and Solimano (1993).

import substitution and state dirigisme, well before the onset of the debt crisis and the overall collapse of growth in the 1980s.

However, the restoration of growth after market reform is also complicated. The empirical evidence at the individual country level shows a long and bumpy road to *sustained* growth after market reform in Chile. Beyond the initial cycle of expansion (mid- to late 1970s) and bust (1982–3), the reforms initiated in the 1970s started to pay off in terms of steady supply-driven growth in the mid- to late 1980s and throughout the 1990s. Econometric evidence for Chile indicates a statistically significant acceleration in TFP growth after 1974 (when the reforms started), after controlling for short-term macro fluctuations and factor accumulation. In addition, Mexico and Bolivia are still in the slow-to-moderate growth phase, ample reform notwithstanding.

Summing up, growth in the 'golden age' of state dirigisme in Latin America, the 1940s and 1950s, say, was relatively high, but was followed by dynamic inefficiency (low contribution of productive growth since the 1960s). In contrast, growth in a mature and consolidated liberalised market economy is more driven by productivity growth and thus potentially more efficient. The costly period is clearly in the transition phase, when stagnation and/or instability precedes the road to prosperity.

Notes

1. For a fuller discussion of different factors encouraging reform in Latin America and othe regions, see Solimano *et al.*, 1994, chs 1 and 12.
2. See Fischer, 1993; Pindyck and Solimano, 1993; and Bruno, 1993.
3. See Patinkin, 1993.
4. See Calvo and Vegh, 1994; Kiguel and Liviatan, 1992; Solimano, 1990; and Corbo and Solimano, 1991.
5. This is the mirror effect of the contractionary devaluation case pointed out by Díaz-Alejandro, 1964, because of a redistributive effect between wage earners and profit recipients.
6. See Edwards, 1993.
7. See Rodrik, 1992.
8. See Solimano, 1992.
9. See Dornbusch and Reynoso, 1989; and Akyuz, 1993.
10. See Servén *et al.*, 1994 for an analysis of the growth effects of privatisation in developing countries.
11. The rate of GDP growth of 5.5 per cent in that period corresponds to an average of twenty economies; see Cardoso and Fishlow, 1993.
12. See De Gregorio, 1992; Corbo and Rojas, 1993; and Lefort and Solimano,

1993 for empirical analysis of growth in Latin America.
13. See Corbo and Solimano, 1991.
14. See Aspe, 1993; and Lustig, 1992 for analysis of Mexico.
15. See Morales, 1991 for an analysis of the Bolivian case.
16. It is interesting that the 'stagnationist' result holds both for the orthodox stabilisation plan of Bolivia and the heterodox one of Mexico.
17. There are some important differences between the two periods, however. In the 1990s, most capital inflows are portfolio capital and foreign direct investment. In contrast in the late 1970s and early 1980s, capital inflows mainly took the form of external borrowing from commercial banks. See Calvo *et al.*, 1993.
18. In the early 1970s a socialist and/or 'populist' response to the trend of stagnation (or modest growth) evident in the 1960s was tried in Chile under President Allende, in Peru under President Velasco-Alvarado, and in Mexico under President Echeverría. These programmes stressed the need for an expansion of the state sector through nationalisation, coupled with more aggressive aggregate demand policies, as ways to accelerate economic growth and redistribute income. See Dornbusch and Edwards, 1991, and other references contained there, for analysis of this 'left-wing policy response' to the exhaustion of the import-substitution model in the region.
19. In fact, the dummy amounts to a shift in the constant of the regression, say an increase in the rate of growth of Hicks-neutral total factor productivity growth.
20. See Young, 1994 for evidence of TFP growth rates for a large cross-section of developing and OECD economies.

References

Akyuz, Y. (1993) 'Financial Liberalization: The Key Issues', in Y. Akyuz and G. Held (eds) *Finance and the Real Economy* (UNU/WIDER)

Aspe, P. (1993) *Economic Transformation. The Mexican Way* (Cambridge, Mass.: MIT Press).

Bruno, M. (1993) 'Inflation and Growth in An Integrated Approach', NBER Working Paper No. 4422 (August).

Calvo, G. and C. Vegh (1994) 'Inflation Stabilization and Nominal Anchors', *Contemporary Economic Policy* (April).

Calvo G., L. Leiderman and C. Reinhart (1993) 'Capital Flows and Real Exchange Rate Appreciation in Latin America: The Role of External Factors', IMF *Staff Papers*, vol. 40, no. 1.

Cardoso, E. (1993) 'Macroeconomic Environment and Capital Formation in Latin America', ch. 7 in L. Serven and A. Solimano (eds), *Striving for Growth After Adjustment: The Role of Capital Formation* (World Bank).

Cardoso, E. and A. Fishlow (1992) 'Latin American Economic Development: 1950–1980', *Journal of Latin American Studies*, vol. 24.

Chenery, H., S. Robinson and M. Syrquin (1986) *Industrialization and Growth* (Oxford University Press).

Corbo, V. and P. Rojas (1993) 'Investment, Macroeconomic Stability and Growth:

The Latin American Experience' *Anàlisis Económico*, vol. 8, no. 1 (June).

Corbo, V. and A. Solimano (1991) 'Chile's Experience with Stabilization Revisited', in M. Bruno, S. Fischer, E. Helpmann and N. Liviatan (eds), *Lessons of Economic Stabilization and its Aftermath* (Cambridge, Mass.: MIT Press).

Díaz-Alejandro, C. (1964) 'A Note on the Impact of Devaluation and the Distributive Effect', *Journal of Political Economy*, vol. 71.

De Gregorio, J. (1992) 'Economic Growth in Latin America', *Journal of Development Economics*, vol. 39.

Dornbusch, R. and S. Edwards (eds) (1991) *The Macroeconomics of Populism in Latin America* (London and Chicago: University of Chicago Press).

Dornbusch, R. and A. Reynoso (1989) 'Financial Factors in Economic Development', *American Economic Review, Papers and Proceedings*, vol. 7.

Easterly, W. (1993) 'How Much do Distortions Affect Growth', *Journal of Monetary Economics* (December).

ECLAC (various issues) *Preliminary Economic Report on Latin America and the Caribbean.*

Edwards, S. (1993) 'Trade Policy, Exchange Rates and Growth', Paper presented at the Conference 'Stabilization, Adjustment and Growth', IDB, 17–18 December.

Elias, V. (1992) *Sources of Growth, A Study of Seven Latin American Economies* (San Francisco: International Center for Economic Growth).

Fischer, S. (1993) 'Macroeconomic Factors in Growth', *Journal of Monetary Economics*, vol. 32, no. 3 (December).

Hofman, A. (1991) 'The Role of Capital in Latin America: A Comparative Perspective of Six Countries for 1950–1989', ECLA-UN Working Paper no. 4, Santiago, Chile.

International Monetary Fund, (various issues) *International Financial Statistics – Data Base.* Washington D.C.

Kiguel, M. and N. Liviatan (1992) 'When do Heterodox Stabilization Programs Work? Lessons from Experience', *The World Bank Research Observer*, vol. 7, no. 1, (January).

King, R. and R. Levine (1993) 'Finance, Entrepreneurship and Growth: Theory and Evidence', *Journal of Monetary Economics*, vol. 32, no. 3.

Lefort F. and A. Solimano (1993) 'Economic Growth after Market-Based Reform in Latin America: The Cases of Chile and Mexico' Mimeo, World Bank.

Lustig, N. (1992) *Mexico. The Remaking of An Economy* (Washington DC: Brookings Institution).

Morales, J.A. (1991) 'The Transition from Stabilization to Sustained Growth in Bolivia', in M. Bruno *et al. Lessons of Economic Stabilization and Its Aftermath* (Cambridge, Mass.: MIT Press).

Patinkin, D. (1993) 'Israel's Stabilization Program of 1985 or Some Basic Truths of Monetary Theory', *Journal of Economic Perspectives*, vol. 7, no. 2 (Spring).

Pindyck, R. and A. Solimano (1993) 'Economic Instability and Aggregate Investment', NBER Working Paper no. 4380; also in O. Blanchard and S. Fischer (eds) *Macroeconomic Annual 1993* (Cambridge, Mass.: NBER MIT Press).

Rodrik, D. (1992) 'Closing the Productivity Gap: Does Trade Liberalization

Really Help?', in G. K. Helleiner (ed.), *Trade Policy, Industrialization and Development* (Oxford: Clarendon Press).

Serven, L. and A. Solimano (eds) (1993) *Striving for Growth After Adjustment: the Role of Capital Formation*, ch. 2, World Bank.

Serven, L., A. Solimano and R. Soto (1994) 'The Macroeconomics of Public Enterprise Reform and Privatization. Theory and Evidence from Developing Countries', World Bank (March).

Solimano, A. (1990) 'Inflation and the Costs of Stabilization: Historical and Recent Experiences and Policy Lessons?', *The World Bank Research Observer*, vol. 5, no. 2 (July).

Solimano, A. (1992) 'Understanding the Investment Cycle in Adjustment Programs. Evidence from Reforming Economies', Policy Research Department PRD Working Paper 921 (May) World Bank.

Solimano, A. (1993) 'How Private Investment Reacts to Changing Macroeconomic Conditions. The Case of Chile in the Eighties', in A. Chihibber *et al.* (eds), *Reviving Private Investment in Developing Countries,* (Amsterdam: North-Holland).

Solimano, A. (1994) 'State Dirigisme, Market Reform and Economic Growth: A Look at the Evidence for Latin America' Mimeo, World Bank.

Solimano, A., O. Sunkel and M. Blejer (eds) (1994) *Rebuilding Capitalism. Alternative Roads after Socialism and Diriqisme* (Ann-Arbor, Mich.: University of Michigan Press).

Young, A. (1994) 'Lessons from East-Asian NICs: A Contrarian View', *European Economic Review, Papers and Proceedings* (May).

Index